Empowerment Training for Your Power Dog

Unleash the Positive Potential in Bully and Mastiff Breeds, Pit Bulls, and Other Strong Dogs

Dawn Antoniak-Mitchell, CPDT-KSA, CBCC-KA

Dogwise™ Publishing

Wenatchee, Washington U.S.A.

Empowerment Training For Your Power Dog
Unleash the Positive Potential in Bully and Mastiff Breeds, Pit Bulls, and Other Strong Dogs
Dawn Antoniak-Mitchell, CPDT-KSA, CBCC-KA

Dogwise Publishing
A Division of Direct Book Service, Inc.
403 South Mission Street, Wenatchee, Washington 98801
1-509-663-9115, 1-800-776-2665
www.dogwisepublishing.com / info@dogwisepublishing.com

Graphic design: Lindsay Peternell
Cover design: Lindsay Peternell

Library of Congress Cataloging-in-Publication Data

Names: Antoniak-Mitchell, Dawn, 1966- author.
Title: Empowerment training for your power dog : unleash the positive
   potential in bully and mastiff breeds, pit bulls, and other strong dogs /
   Dawn Antoniak-Mitchell, CPDT-KSA, CBCC-KA.
Description: Wenatchee, Washington : Dogwise Publishing, [2019] | Includes
   bibliographical references and index.
Identifiers: LCCN 2018061075 | ISBN 9781617812323
Subjects: LCSH: Mastiff breeds--Training.
Classification: LCC SF429.M36 A58 2019 | DDC 636.73--dc23 LC record available at
https://lccn.loc.gov/2018061075

Photography and graphics: Dawn Antoniak-Mitchell; Dianne Dowden and Sasha (Australian Shepherd); Laurie Erickson (photographer); Jim Johnson and Trixie (French Bulldog/ Beagle cross); Kristi Jones and Jack (Rottweiler mix) and Jill (Pug); Charlie Leavitt and Stanley (Boston Terrier); Jeff Mitchell and Ember (Dalmatian); Sharon Sysel and Rock von Diesel II (Rottweiler); Stephanie Tornquist and Amira (Boxer) and Mowgli (American Bulldog mix); Marabeth White and Carly (Dalmatian) and Panda (Dalmatian); Freepix Common Use License, WikiMedia Common Use License, and Library of Congress Common Use License (images in the public domain).

ISBN: 978-1-61781-232-3

Printed in the U.S.A.

To Grandma

Acknowledgements

I owe many thanks to many people who helped me bring this book from a vague vision to a published reality. Once again, to all the wonderful people at Dogwise— thank you for your patience, support, and expert guidance throughout this project. I am thankful to you all in more ways than you know. To my BonaFide instructor family, the deepest gratitude for your support and for keeping me on track. You all rock! To my friends, colleagues, and clients in the canine community who provided input, experience, photographs, and an opportunity to share your power dogs in a small way through this book, my sincere thanks. Without you, there would be no book. To Jeff, for the freedom, opportunity, and support to do crazy things like this. And for the astute resolution of my grammatical panic attacks. I love you.

And, most importantly, to my grandmother, Dorothy Favors, who passed away while I was working on this project. She was my fiercest ally my entire life, and the staunchest supporter of my obsession with all things canine. Thank you for everything, Grandma. The years I was blessed to have you in my life were not nearly enough.

Table of Contents

Preface

Unlike my previous training books, this book was a surprisingly difficult one for me to write. The training portion of the book was relatively easy to put on paper; I use these types of exercises on a regular basis with my training students who own bully breeds, mastiffs, and other physically strong dogs. It was the breed histories that I struggled with—I was definitely not prepared for the emotional rollercoaster I would be on while researching the power breeds. The past always informs the present, so it's foolish to ignore it, no matter how unpleasant that past may have been. Every type or breed of dog we have today was developed for some specific purpose. Humans were pragmatists throughout most of our history with dogs; dogs were kept primarily to serve mankind in one capacity or another. Owning a dog strictly for companionship was a luxury only the wealthiest people could afford until well into the late 1800s; most people could only afford to keep a dog if the dog could work to earn his keep. The type of work dogs historically did still influences behavior in today's dogs, even though we rarely ask our dogs to perform their ancestral jobs anymore. I believe that understanding a breed's history is essential to helping that breed adapt to the present and move positively into the future, so we don't lose the wonderful diversity we have in our dogs.

So, off I went, headlong down the rabbit hole, chasing after historical information about the power breeds. I approach my canine research in the same manner I approach my legal research. I collect as many facts as I can and investigate all sides of an issue as thoroughly as possible. But I simply wasn't prepared for how emotionally difficult much of the information I gathered was going to be for me to process. I read books that I would never otherwise have any reason or desire to read. I read about the ferocious war dogs the ancients used against one another, the savage use of power breeds against native cultures and enslaved peoples throughout the world, and the use of power breeds in the "bait" sports (historical gambling and social activities pitting dogs against nearly every imaginable form of life, including bears, bulls, monkeys, tigers, badgers, donkeys, horses, and even humans) and dog-fight pits. I read historical and contemporary accounts of dog attacks on people and other dogs (outside the fighting pit context), and the disturbing issues surrounding present-day illegal dog fighting. I waded through websites extolling the aggressive "virtues" of certain lines of power dogs, which all but explicitly state these dogs are still being bred for use in the pit, and read disturbing arguments for allowing these breeds to do what they are being bred and trained to do—fight. I examined statutes and ordinances related to "vicious" dogs and "dangerous" dog breeds, as well as the social and legislative history behind their enactments. This is all an unpleasant, but important, part of modern power dog history that can't be ignored or whitewashed. It is what it is and needs to be understood by every power dog owner and anyone who works with power dogs in training or rescue, if the power dogs we know and love today are to be respected and protected for the future.

Thankfully, in contrast to the depravity and cruelty that riddles the history of the power breeds, I also found just as much information related to the bravery and intelligence of these dogs. They have served as family guardians, police and military dogs, therapy dogs, service dogs, and faithful companions to countless people over the centuries. Beautiful power dogs have graced the rings of dog shows, instead of the rings of fight pits. There are many educational websites that share the numerous positive virtues of the power breeds that are often overlooked because of the negative reputations many of these breeds have acquired over the years. I read through websites discussing the efforts conscientious breeders are making to develop lines of dogs with less "fire" in them than previous generations had, so they can fit better into modern society. These positives certainly didn't diminish the negatives I learned about power dogs, but they did serve as bright counterpoints to what I learned about the dark brutality that fueled the creation and development of most power breeds we have today.

Power dogs continue to capture the minds, hearts, and homes of people, just as they did in previous generations. The vast majority of power dog owners and their dogs go about their lives uneventfully, just like owners of so many other types of dogs do, each and every day. Power dogs are neither angels nor demons; they are *dogs*, developed for specific historic purposes, altered somewhat over time to better fit into our current society. They are influenced by instincts but capable of learning how to control them (if properly taught). They are capable of neither malice nor idol worship, but can certainly experience joy, fear, pain, and loss. They are dogs and, as such, can only react in canine ways to our human world. It is our job to help them adapt to, and behave in, our world, for their sake as well as ours. Power dog success stories almost always come from those dogs and owners who live their lives together somewhere in the middle—a balance of nature *and* nurture, genetics *and* environment, love *and* training, combined in a way that meets the needs of the individual dog and his human family.

Living successfully with a power dog requires you to understand both the bad and the good in your dog's past, assess and acknowledge the unique dog you have today, and manage and train him so you two can have a quality future together. I hope that by writing this book I can help you and your power dog find that middle ground and start writing your own power dog success story.

1

An Introduction to Power Dogs

Empower (v.) – to encourage and support the ability to do something.

Cambridge Dictionary, online edition

The power dogs, as I define them, are an eclectic group of breeds. The work these breeds did ranged from serving as animals of war and big-game catch dogs to ferocious fighters and personal and property guardians. They are physically and mentally strong dogs, regardless of their size, originally bred to perform physically demanding and often dangerous work for the benefit (or amusement) of humans. For the purposes of my book, I've defined a power dog as any dog who possesses one or more of the following traits:

- Extreme power due to his physical strength or simply his massive size

- An ancestry rooted in hunting big game, fighting other animals, or guarding people or property against other people

- Exceptional devotion to his family, which may express itself in extreme wariness and aggressive behavior toward anyone outside his immediate family

- Extreme tenacity, coupled with high pain tolerance, intelligence, and independence

- Aggressiveness toward other dogs and animals that is not due to fear or defensive behavior, that would likely result in injury to the other animal without human intervention

These traits allowed power dog ancestors to do their work successfully, but most are not as desirable (or necessary) in our modern world as they once were. Some power breeds have been selectively bred to be less aggressive, and more social, but these ancestral instincts still exist to some degree in every power dog alive today, evidenced by the fact that purebred dog registries and breed clubs worldwide still acknowledge these traits in the breed standards of many of the power breeds. These traits can be challenging to live with. And even if your power dog doesn't openly exhibit any of these traits, it is important that you recognize the potential that still exists in your dog, based on his ancestry. Owning a power breed is definitely *not* for the lazy or uneducated, but the work it takes to live successfully with one of these dogs is rewarded many times over with the funny, playful, family-oriented personalities these dogs share with us. Many of these dogs are loyal, energetic, playful, and able to learn many useful behaviors; they can make fabulous pets and well-behaved canine citizens if you use the power dog–centric management and training techniques we will explore throughout the rest of this book.

Which breeds are power dogs?

The largest genomic map of dog breeds developed to date was unveiled in 2017 by Heidi Parker and her colleagues in the journal *Cell Reports*. This enormous canine family tree shows that all dog breeds fall into one of 23 different **clades** (groups of dogs who evolved from a common ancestor). Nearly all the breeds I chose to include in this book belong to the European mastiff clade (dogs with Mastiff breeds origins) or the Asian spitz clade. A few other breeds were selected based on their original primary ancestral work or their physical attributes alone. For example, I chose to include Dalmatians in my power dog group because of their historic development as property guards (i.e., horses and coaches), even though Parker's genetic analysis reveals they are most closely related to pointers and setters. I also included Rottweilers; although originally used to drive cattle and pull butchers' wagons, the breed was also used to protect the livestock and wagons against thieves, and Rottweilers are exceptionally powerful for their size. I don't, however, include most livestock guardian dogs such as the Great Pyrenees, nor certain herding and working dogs like the German Shepherd, in my grouping of power dog breeds, simply because their original uses were primarily in herding or protecting livestock from other animals (rather than humans). Emphasis on other types of ancestral work gives these dogs a different set of breed traits than the power breeds typically exhibit, even though several of these excluded breeds were later used to protect property against humans. Clearly there is a great deal of subjectivity in the breeds I chose to include in this book. But if the behavioral or physical characteristics of your dog fit with any of those I described above or later in this book, please consider your dog a power dog, whether or not I included his breed in my group! Power dogs are simply those dogs who fit a set of criteria I created for the purposes of this training book, regardless of the breed. (See Appendix A for a complete listing of power dogs.)

Looking at power dogs objectively

While writing this book, I tried to avoid the emotional and political baggage currently associated with many of the power breeds, particularly the American Pit Bull Terrier (and any other type of dog that politicians or the public choose to include under the generic label "pit bull"), as well as the social pressure that often comes to bear to be on the "correct" side of the "pit bull issue." I don't think any other breeds have such a divisive effect on the public as the power breeds. Ask people if they have an opinion about any of the power breeds (particularly "pit bulls"), dog fighting, or breed-specific legislation, and many are more than happy to weigh in on the subject, regardless of the factual basis for their hard-held beliefs. It seems that everyone knows someone who heard about somebody who once had a relative who had either a magically wonderful or horrifically awful experience with one of these types of dogs. Opinions are often quite extreme—people seem to either curse the power breeds or worship them, regardless of whether they ever actually owned, met, or worked with one. Many people blindly agree with the imposition of breed-specific legislation as the only way to keep humanity safe from these vicious dogs, or equally blindly oppose the imposition of any ownership requirements to hold owners accountable for their dogs' behavior, labeling such legislation as an overreaching restriction of property rights. Some people absolve humans completely and blame a dog's pedigree alone for any violent behavior the dog engages in, while others believe that humans are 100% exclusively responsible for their dogs' behavior, completely ignoring the role instincts and organic factors play in all canine behavior. Some people see absolutely no need for any of these breeds to exist in modern society, while others will do anything possible to preserve these dogs and help them adapt to the modern world. Some people I've met consider their power dogs as living weapons to use against all comers, while others see them as literal child substitutes. These extreme viewpoints polarize power dog owners and non-owners alike and can make finding common ground or having a meaningful conversation about these dogs very difficult.

I believe these extreme viewpoints arise, in large part, from the all-or-nothing beliefs many people have about how an individual dog's behavior is developed and expressed. At one end of this belief system spectrum is the notion that any dog, if simply "loved enough" and raised in the correct environment, will be perfectly stable and predictable in any situation he will ever encounter. People who believe this way think a dog's environment is entirely responsible for his behavior; with appropriate environmental comfort and enough compassion, any dog's instincts or personal history of abuse, training, etc. can be completely overridden, or, conversely, developed to extreme forms of expression. This is the "Disney" view of dog behavior; a dog "knows" what is expected of him and how to behave appropriately (based on human values, morals, and expectations), just like dogs do in the Disney movies. A dog's genetic makeup, past history, and breed instincts are completely ignored in this view of dog behavior. His owners are absolved of all responsibility for managing and training the dog; all they need to do is provide the dog love and a safe environment to live in and the dog will take care of the rest. People with this view of canine behavior may say things like:

- "My dog would *never* harm a child—he knows better!"

- "My dog ripped up that pillow just to get even with me for not giving him a treat last night!"

- "My dog was rescued from a fight ring, but he knows he's safe now, so he'll be fine at the dog park."

This is a very dangerous belief system for *any* dog owner to have.

At the other end of this belief spectrum is the idea that a dog's breed sets his behavior in stone from the moment he's born. People who believe this way think that power breeds (and mixes involving those breeds) are inherently aggressive, unstable, and unpredictable due entirely to their ancestry (or, conversely, are unfailingly stable, loyal, and willing to tolerate any type of treatment from their families without responding, simply by virtue of their pedigrees). These people view genetics and instincts as immutable, and believe no amount of training, management, or motivation will ever change the expression of those genes and instincts. This is the "hell hound" view of dog behavior, which condemns or sanctifies a dog simply because of his parentage, regardless of the individual dog's behavior and training. This view plays a big role in the imposition of breed-specific legislation in many jurisdictions; in some cases, it can even cost a dog his life for no reason other than he *looks* like a dog who *might* be dangerous. This view completely disregards the impact proper basic care, consistent management, and humane training can make on the expression of instinctual and previously learned behaviors. People with this view of dog behavior may say things like:

- "My dog will let my kids do anything to him—after all, he's a_____!"

- "My _____ can't walk around the block with me because he's too big."

- "We need to ban all _____; everyone knows they are simply too dangerous to allow in our community!"

These are all statements that represent this viewpoint; simply fill in the blank with your power breed. This view also absolves the owner from all responsibility for his dog's behavior, but for different reasons than the Disney view.

Unfortunately, there is no direct, simple way to change someone's core beliefs, including those about dog behavior, if that person doesn't want them changed. (This is why discussing politics or religion can be very difficult with some people.) Emotions often run high during these types of discussions and sometimes they degrade to meaningless personal attacks completely unrelated to the topic at hand. There is a psychological phenomenon known as the **backfire effect** that explains why this happens. The **amygdala** is a part of the brain that helps protect a person from any real threat in the environment, but it also sometimes tries to protect against imagined threats, as well. It plays a role in emotions, and in research studies it becomes very active when a person's core beliefs are challenged. Most core beliefs develop over a lifetime, as a result of personal experiences and the information a person collects from various sources, like books, other people, the news, and the internet. Because the human brain really likes to keep its world consistent and the body safe, it resists any idea that is in direct conflict with a core belief. The amygdala treats that idea as if it were an actual physical threat, resulting in emotional, and sometimes very irrational, responses to the new information. Adding more information, no matter how factual or persuasive, only causes the brain to continue to ignore or attack the new, "dangerous" ideas. Trying even harder to convince someone a core belief is incorrect will continue to backfire and cause the brain to further protect the belief if that person isn't prepared to consider changing it. If you've ever had a conversation with someone who constantly responds to anything you say with "Yeah, but…," you were probably touching on one or more core beliefs that the brain was trying to protect. Core beliefs can only be changed if a person *wants* them to change; even for people who *want* to learn and possibly change their core beliefs, it takes time for the initial emotional brain response to the imaginary threat to subside and the logical part of the brain to take over, listen, and process the new information. Put simply, you can lead people to information, but you can never force them to accept it, regardless of how factually correct or persuasive you are. Trying to change a person's long-held beliefs about how dog behavior develops can be a challenge and will only work if that person wants them to change.

Finding the balance between nature and nurture

I believe strongly in the importance of objectively working with both nature (a dog's genetics and instincts) *and* nurture (a dog's environmental experiences and training) in order to live a successful, middle-of-the-road life with any dog. My reason for writing this book is not to change anyone's core beliefs about power breeds per se. I am simply presenting information for you to consider that will enable you to find your own balance between nature and nurture with your power dog, and to learn how to work with his breed instincts, instead of against them, to effectively teach him how to live successfully in today's world. I hope this information will help anyone who owns, trains, or rescues power breeds expand their appreciation and understanding of these incredible dogs and the instincts that drive their behavior. The training exercises I've included will help power dogs cope with life in the modern, often urban or suburban, world they must live in. Of course, every dog is a unique individual, so not every trait described will apply to every power dog and not every exercise described will be necessary to teach each dog. But even if you don't believe your dog fits within the power breed group as I define it here, the training and management exercises I've included will still benefit both of you and will help you learn to work together. And the joy and satisfaction of a journey well-traveled together is what dog ownership is really all about. I hope this book will help you along your way.

How the rest of this book is organized

Understanding power dog history in a broad sense and working with your power dog's instincts as they are expressed in his unique personality are the best ways to empower him to become an exceptional companion for many years to come. This book provides you the keys to unleash that potential in your power dog using **empowerment training**.

Chapters 2 and 3 will explore the first key to power dog empowerment—understanding the good, the bad, the ugly, and the beautiful of power breed history. Chapter 2 will examine a selection of breeds that represent the wide range of historical uses for these types of dogs, as well as the common instincts and behavioral traits in these breeds and some of the differences between them. Chapter 3 will then help you decide if a power dog is the best choice for you and your family if you don't already own one or are considering adding another one to your family.

Chapters 4 and 5 explain the second key to power dog empowerment—understanding how nature and nurture play roles in dog behavior and how dogs learn. The Humane Hierarchy is also defined here; the remainder of the book is organized according to this approach to changing behavior. How to select and use motivators to train your power dog is covered in Chapter 6.

Chapter 7 deals with the third key to power dog empowerment—activities to help your power dog remain physically and mentally healthy. Without appropriate exercise and mental enrichment, it will be difficult for your dog to be an exceptional companion.

Chapter 8 is devoted to the fourth key to power dog empowerment—socialization. This is *the* most important activity you must do with your power dog to minimize the chances he will be aggressive with people or other dogs. If you purchase a puppy, your socialization work starts as soon as you take him from the breeder's house; if you adopt an older puppy or adult dog, the process is slightly different, but nonetheless critical for you to go through, right from the start.

Chapters 9 focuses on the fifth key to power dog empowerment—management. Proper training equipment and management will produce quick behavioral results for many common problems power dog owners face. These techniques don't teach your dog what to do, but set him up so he won't (or can't) do certain undesirable behaviors in the first place. Making changes in your dog's environment and eliminating things that previously triggered undesirable behaviors are key steps to take before trying to permanently change your dog's behaviors through training.

Chapter 10 provides the sixth, and final, key to power dog empowerment—training. Training and behavioral modification exercises may take longer than simple management techniques to effect changes in your dog's behavior, but this is how new learned behaviors, and permanent changes in your dog's previously learned behaviors, are acquired. Training is how you specifically show your dog what behavior you want him to do. Combined with management, training will help your power dog become a wonderful family companion and a positive ambassador for his breed.

Chapter 11 addresses legal and insurance issues you need to be aware of when you own a power dog. Even if you don't live in an area that has a breed-specific ordinance in place, if you travel with your dog, it is possible you might find yourself in a place where there is an ordinance you must comply with, depending on your dog's breed or predominant breed mix.

Finally, selected resources are listed at the end of the book to help you research your breed in more detail and obtain equipment that will make your training easier. Unlike my previous training books, I purposely excluded many of the references I found that contain exceptionally graphic historical descriptions and suggestions for using power dogs to injure or kill other animals (and in one book, how to track and maim humans!), glorify the use of power dogs in this way in contemporary society, or promote raising dogs for dog fighting. Some of the books I did include in the reading list do have a few disturbing descriptions, but I don't believe they glorify these types of activities. Rather they provide historical context (regardless of what some of the book titles alone might suggest). I also included the primary research papers that I cite for anyone who has a scientific interest, as well as sources for training equipment mentioned throughout the book.

Power dogs have been valued family companions for generations, and are some of the best-known dog breeds that exist today. They are also some of the most misunderstood and emotion-evoking breeds. By learning all you can about your power dog, applying the management and training techniques in the following chapters, and complying with any applicable ordinances that affect your dog, you can help your dog become an exceptional companion, a positive breed ambassador, and a means to help change people's attitudes toward these dogs for the better, one interaction at a time.

Understanding Rocky's instincts will help his owner
teach him to be the best Rottweiler he can be.

2

Power Dog History

Power (n.) – great or marked ability to do or act; strength; might; force.

Merriam-Webster's Collegiate Dictionary, online edition

More than any other group of dogs, the power dogs (specifically those of molosser, mastiff, bully-mastiff, bull-and-terrier, and bull dog origins) have the most shocking and spectacular breed histories. These breeds have been used for some of the most gruesome purposes man ever set dogs to do, and also some of the most noble. The power dogs are an awesome, awe-inspiring group of dogs who have the capacity to be the best companions anyone could want, or the most feared living weapons a person could possess. This chapter will explore the first key to power dog empowerment—understanding your power dog's ancestry so that you can work with your dog's instincts, rather than against them, and set appropriate goals and expectations for his behavior.

A brief history of the power breeds

Power breeds can be split into three broad groups, based on their original/ancestral work:

- Breeds originally developed to protect people and homes, land, and personal property from other people

- Breeds created to fight dogs and other animals

- Breeds created to serve as general hunters or "catch" dogs (dogs who grab and hold prey until the hunter can kill it) against large, fierce game animals like wild boar and big cats

Over the centuries, the work many of these breeds did began to overlap; some of the power breeds originally developed as guardian and hunting breeds were also used for fighting, many of the fighting breeds started being used as guardians of people and property, and several of the fighting breeds became strictly companion dogs. Some breeds have changed considerably over the years, while others have changed very little. But the potential (no matter how weak it may be) remains within every power dog alive today to do the work his ancestors once did. Understanding your power dog's ancestry will help you fully appreciate the potential contained within your dog and effectively build a trusting, positive relationship with him as a well-mannered, well-loved canine family member.

Personal and property guardians

Long before cell phones, security systems, and 9-1-1, there were dogs to help protect people and property from harm. Power breeds such as the Mastiff, Bullmastiff, Doberman Pinscher, Cane Corso, and even the Dalmatian, were all originally developed to serve as property guardians or personal guardians. Most of these breeds are very large dogs, and all are strong and can be rather independent when it comes to deciding who is a threat and who is a friend. Their loyalty to *their family* makes them tremendous family companions, but they aren't always so accommodating to anyone outside that group without considerable socialization and training. The following breeds represent the diversity found in this group of power dogs.

The Mastiff is an ancient breed created to serve as a powerful guard, war, and fighting dog. Early mastiff-type dogs were particularly ferocious and made formidable opponents on the ancient battlefields. The Romans helped spread these early mastiff-type dogs throughout Europe, eventually bringing them as far as the British Isles. Because of their ferocity, the Forest Laws of Henry III (1207 – 1272) required all mastiff-type dogs to be expeditated (three toes chopped off each front foot) to prevent the dogs from chasing and killing the royal deer. It has been speculated by some authors that in 1601, Shakespeare was playing on a reference to Mastiffs when he penned in *Julius Caesar*, Act III, Scene 1: "Cry havoc, and let slip the dogs of war." Mastiffs were used over the centuries in the baiting ring, on opponents such as bear and bull, merely for entertainment; some canine historians claim these dogs also enjoyed the dubious distinction of being the only tame animals ever used to fight humans in the Roman Colosseum. Many of the guardian and fighting power breeds we have today are descended from the Mastiff, including the Bullmastiff, Bulldog, Boston Terrier, Boerboel, Bull Terrier, and Boxer.

As human living conditions changed over the centuries, so did the Mastiff. Through the careful breeding efforts of English breeders over the last two centuries, the modern Mastiff is typically far more mellow than his ancestors were. But his huge size, weight, and power can still be very difficult to handle if he isn't well trained, and guarding instincts still remain fairly strong in this breed. The Fédération Cynologique Internationale (FCI), the largest dog registry in the world, states in its breed standard that the ideal Mastiff temperament is "[a] combination of grandeur and courage. Calm, affectionate to owners, but capable of guarding. Usually indifferent with strangers; timidity is unacceptable." The United Kennel Club (UKC) notes, "In America, the breed is now noted as a devoted family pet and may still serve as a protector mainly by its imposing size." Standing at a minimum of 27 inches tall at the shoulder, and weighing well over 100 pounds, this "imposing size" alone makes socialization and training critical for all Mastiffs.

This image of Mastiffs being used in bear baiting is from Richard Pynson's Antibossicon, written in 1521, and reflects one of the original uses of the breed.

The Bullmastiff was developed in the mid-1800s to help gamekeepers on English estates protect their masters' property from poachers; it is one of the very few dog breeds ever developed specifically as man stoppers (i.e., dogs created specifically to locate and hold humans). Originally referred to as the Gamekeeper's dog or the Gamekeeper's mastiff, Bullmastiffs were used to locate and hold poachers until the authorities arrived to take them away. Because poaching could be punishable by death at that time, the Bullmastiff needed to be strong and determined enough to hold down a terrified, struggling man who was fighting to save his very life from the gallows. The breed was created from two of the oldest guarding and fighting dogs in England (the Bulldog and the Mastiff), and they were kept as working dogs well into the 1900s.

Bullmastiffs are now primarily companions, but the breed's size, power, and willingness to protect family and property if need be still exist in today's dogs. The FCI notes, "The Bullmastiff is intelligent and observant.... His bravery and courage in defending against intruders is legendary." The American Kennel Club (AKC) describes the

Bullmastiff's temperament as "[f]earless and confident, yet docile. The dog combines the reliability, intelligence, and willingness to please required in a dependable family companion and protector." Although breeders have "softened" the breed's temperament to help the dogs fit better into modern life as a pet, the Bullmastiff's guarding instincts are still alive and well even in the most pampered individuals, and socialization is critical for these dogs to live peaceably in today's world.

This Richard Ansdell painting, Poacher at Bay, shows a poacher and his illegal catch being held by the Gamekeeper's mastiff. Painted in 1865, it shows an early type of Bullmastiff at work.

The Cane Corso is one of the power breeds who very recently achieved full breed recognition from the AKC. This Italian breed was brought back from the brink of extinction in the 1970s by a group of dedicated breeders and is slowly gaining a following in the United States with people who want a companion who also serves as a willing and able guard dog. According to the AKC breed standard, Cane Corsi "have been employed in the hunting of large wild animals and also as an 'auxiliary warrior' in battles [and as a] property, cattle and personal guard…. [The breed's] name derives from the Latin 'Cohors' which means 'Guardian' or 'Protector'." The AKC highlights the traits that allow this breed to successfully protect their families and homes: "… their imposing appearance is their first line of defense against intruders… [a]n understated air of cool competence, the kind of demeanor you'd expect from a professional bodyguard, is the breed's 'trademark' and completes the picture of a dog not to be trifled with. Corsi are peerless protectors… Corsi are smart, trainable, eager to please… docile and intensely loyal with *their* humans." (Emphasis added.) Notice the choice of words here; the breed is specifically described as being docile and loyal toward *their* family. This does not mean they are docile toward people in general. First-time power dog owners often make the mistake of assuming if their dogs are good with their own families, they will automatically be equally good with their families' friends, relatives, delivery people, repair workers, or anyone else who comes into their home as a welcomed guest. But a Corso can't naturally be both a peerless family and property protector and at the same time a friend to anyone and everyone who comes into his home. Early and ongoing training, extensive socialization, and commonsense management are required to help a Corso fit into any family successfully.

The Cane Corso was a valued working companion in rural Italy, but the breed was nearly lost by the 1970s. Dedicated fans of the breed brought it back to life as a guardian and protector.

The Doberman Pinscher is one example of a well-known companion dog that many people might not consider a power dog. However, this breed was originally developed by Karl Dobermann around 1890 specifically to work as a fierce personal guardian. As a tax collector, Dobermann often carried large sums of money with him (and he probably wasn't the most popular person in Apolda, Germany, at the time, thanks to his occupation); he needed a dog who was large, strong, and able to protect him as he went about his duties. So he set about to create a protection dog by crossing several breeds, including the Rottweiler, to create the Doberman. Long known as a loyal and dependable war and police dog, the breed has also become popular as a companion. The AKC breed standard calls for a Doberman to be "…watchful, determined, alert, fearless, loyal, and obedient," but not vicious. However, the standard also states: "An aggressive or belligerent attitude toward other dogs shall *not* be deemed viciousness." (Emphasis added.) This breed has only existed for slightly over 100 years, and many Dobes still demonstrate their ancestors' strong guarding instincts and reactivity toward other dogs.

Another example of a breed most people probably wouldn't think about when they hear the term "power dog" is the Dalmatian. Many people are attracted to this very high-energy breed due to its beautiful spotted coat, without realizing that this breed was originally developed to serve primarily as a guard dog. Although the latest genetic analyses place the breed in the pointer/setter clade, their behavior and historical uses identify them as a power dog for the purposes of this book. Dalmatians were historically used primarily as coach dogs, protecting coaches and passengers on the road and overnight at roadside accommodations. Dals later guarded firehouse horses and equipment in the days when rival private firefighting companies often sabotaged each other's equipment to eliminate competition for fire suppression services. They also served as sentinel dogs on the Dalmatia-Croatia border and served in many capacities as war dogs for the American and British military. The breed is still known to be a good guard dog, although modern breeders have worked to create a dog who is more adaptable to living in urban environments. As the AKC notes in *The Complete Dog Book*: "…his protective instinct is highly developed and he has the courage to defend." Their strength, guarding heritage, and independence make Dalmatians challenging to live with if they aren't properly socialized, exercised, and trained.

Dalmatians like these are often associated with horses because of their history of guarding horse-drawn transportation and affinity for interacting with horses.

Fighting and baiting breeds

This group of power breeds reflects the truly dark side of the human/canine relationship. By perfecting the physical and temperamental characteristics of these breeds to fight other animals, and cultivating an intense loyalty toward their human masters that can be easily exploited to encourage these dogs to fight to the death, the fighting breeds have been abused beyond imagination over the centuries, all in the name of "entertainment" and ego-gratification. People who bred and owned these dogs had everything to lose if they didn't produce dog-aggressive dogs who could succeed in the pit. The weaker individuals were killed in the ring or not allowed to breed, so only the gamest of the fighting dogs originally passed on their genes. But those dogs who were overly aggressive toward their owners were also weeded out of the gene pool; if a pit man couldn't live with his dog or handle his dog in the pit, the dog was as useless to him as one who wouldn't fight in the first place. Accepting humans didn't necessarily extend to strangers though, and that fierce loyalty to family also made many of these breeds excellent guard dogs.

Most fighting breeds make incredible family companions today, but centuries of fighting still leave a distinct legacy of aggression toward other dogs in many individuals. There are always exceptions within every breed, but in general, the fighting breeds are a dog-aggressive group that require thoughtful socialization, consistent training, and patience to help them overcome their fighting ancestry or, in the case of far too many rescued dogs, their own personal fighting experiences. There are many dogs still subjected to dog fighting today and in some places, the baiting sports also still survive and thrive. (A television ad shown in 2017 for stopanimalsuffering.org World Animal Protection Organization features Lela the bear being used in a contemporary bear baiting event and shows two power dogs attacking the chained bear.) These activities may not be as prevalent as they once were, but they still exist in many parts of the world, including the United States. Historical fighting breeds include those as diverse as the Bulldog, American Pit Bull Terrier, Akita, American Staffordshire Terrier, Boxer, Boston Terrier, and Perro de Presa Canario.

[Author's note: The term "pit bull" refers to a loose collection of dogs typically similar in build to the American Pit Bull Terrier and American Staffordshire Terrier, regardless of their actual breed ancestry (i.e., any type of dog suited to the fight pit, rather than any particular dog breed). The American Pit Bull Terrier is a specific breed of dog, with well-defined physical and temperamental traits. The public tends to use these terms interchangeably; in this book, I use APBT to refer to the specific breed, and "pit bull" to refer to any dog physically resembling a dog traditionally used for fighting or baiting sports.]

The Bulldog is one of the original baiting and fighting breeds and is an ancestor to many other power breeds. Originally much taller, longer-legged, and athletic than the modern version of the breed often referred to as the English Bulldog, the early Bulldog was developed to participate in bullbaiting matches and, later, dog-fighting matches. The shortened muzzle, broad chest, and sheer power of these dogs helped them grab on to the nose of a bull or other large animal they were pitted against and hold on, eventually bringing the quarry to its knees in exhaustion. The exceptional grip strength, power, tenacity, and viciousness of the original Bulldog were used to develop many other fighting breeds, as well as breeds used for hunting and manstopping. Crosses of these dogs with early terrier breeds resulted in slightly smaller, even more tenacious pit breeds, including the American Pit Bull Terrier and the Boston Terrier. The exaggerated physical features of the modern Bulldog started being refined after baiting sports became illegal in the U.K. and conformation dog shows and kennel clubs came into being in the late 1800s. Although the modern Bulldog may not be as physically robust as his ancestors, the fire of the old baiting dogs can still occasionally appear in today's dogs, particularly around other dogs and animals, without appropriate socialization and training.

This Bulldog was typical of the breed in the early 1900s—very different physically and temperamentally from the modern version.

The American Pit Bull Terrier (APBT) was originally developed in the United States in the 19th century as a fighting dog; from their powerful physiques to their short coats and small ears, APBTs were carefully developed to be formidable adversaries in the dog pits of the time. Because of the breed's tenacity, fearlessness, and strength, the United States was often represented by a pit bull–type dog in propaganda campaigns during World War I (Great Britain was often depicted as another fighting power breed, the Bulldog). Many real APBTs and other power breeds served in the canine units of Allied militaries during both World Wars. When the AKC refused to recognize the APBT in its breed registry in large part because of the breed's contemporary use as a fighting dog, C. Z. Bennett founded the United Kennel Club in 1898 to recognize the breed. He wrote the first APBT breed standard and assigned UKC registration number 1 to his own APBT, Bennett's Ring. The UKC has since become the second largest all-breed dog registry in the United States.

At the same time the breed was being refined by some people for use in the dog pit, they also started becoming a very popular companion dog for people with absolutely no interest in dog fighting. American breeders who were interested in APBTs strictly as companions began working with the breed, eventually creating the closely related American Staffordshire Terrier, which gained AKC recognition in 1936. Presidents Theodore Roosevelt and Franklin Delano Roosevelt both brought APBTs to the White House during their terms in office. The APBT continues to be a very popular companion dog today, in spite of the rise of breed-specific legislation in many locations.

The dog-fighting heritage of this breed is reflected in its UKC breed standard: "The essential characteristics of the breed are strength, confidence, and zest for life…. Because most APBTs exhibit some level of dog aggression and because of its powerful physique, the APBT requires an owner who will carefully socialize and obedience train the dog…. Aggressive behavior toward humans is uncharacteristic of the breed and highly undesirable." Breeds that for centuries were used to fight other dogs are, not surprisingly, breeds that still may not be friendly toward other dogs. Because of the breed's history of dog fighting, sensational media coverage of attacks on humans by "pit bulls," and the attraction many less-than-ideal owners have for these types of dogs as status symbols and money makers in the fight pits, this breed (along with other dogs lumped under the generic label "pit bull") is almost always included in breed-specific ordinances and bans throughout the United States and the world. It is often the breed cited as the primary reason for instituting this type of legislation. Although APBTs can be aggressive toward other dogs, they are usually quite tolerant and affectionate toward their own families and most other people if they are properly socialized and trained. The vast majority live their entire lives as uneventfully as any other breed of dog.

During World War I, England was often represented as a Bulldog, France as a French Bulldog, and the United States as an American Pit Bull Terrier in propaganda materials.

The Akita is one of the better known examples of the spitz-derived group of power dogs and is the largest of the six native Japanese spitz-type dogs. According to the Japan Kennel Club, the breed descended from dogs used to hunt deer and bear. When local Japanese rulers began promoting dog fighting as a morale booster for their soldiers, the breed was refined and used as a fighting dog from the early 1600s until the early 1900s, when dog fighting was finally outlawed. In the last half of the 19th century, Tosa Inu and Mastiffs were crossed with Akitas to make heavier, fiercer fighting dogs. The end of legal dog fighting and two World Wars nearly caused the Akita's extinction; efforts by breeders in Japan and the United States after World War II to save the breed resulted in two different strains of Akitas, varying slightly in size and appearance. Some breed registries, such as the FCI, now recognize these as two distinct breeds; the Akita (or American Akita) is the American breed, while the Akita

Inu is the Japanese breed. However, they all retain their fighting heritage to some extent. Although the American parent club of the Akita makes no direct mention of the breed's dog-fighting history, the AKC breed standard describes the breed's temperament as "[a]lert and responsive, dignified and courageous. *Akitas may be intolerant of other dogs, particularly of the same sex.*" (Emphasis added.)

The dapper little Boston Terrier is one example of a small power dog (the French Bulldog and Pug are two other examples). Although it might be hard to imagine the average outgoing Boston ever engaging in a dog pit fight, the breed was originally developed as a fighting dog for the smaller, urban fighting pits of the northeastern United States in the late 1800s. The breed was originally called the American Bull Terrier, but the name was changed to Boston Terrier in 1891. Genetic analyses published by Parker in 2017 show that the Bulldog, French Bulldog, and American Staffordshire Terrier figure in the Boston Terrier's ancestry. Bostons are a relatively recent breed (compared to some of the other power breeds) and, although they have been bred to have temperaments more suitable to being companions than fighters today, they still retain the tenacity, strength, and courage of their larger Bulldog and other pit-fighting bull-and-terrier breed ancestors. The AKC breed standard describes these dogs as "friendly and lively" and, like most other power breeds, they do best when they are treated as part of the family. The UKC breed standard further says, "The dog conveys an impression of determination, strength and activity; with style of a high order." Although these dogs are small and engaging, they are still good examples of power dogs and should be respected as such.

This handsome Boston Terrier is larger than most present day Bostons, reflecting the original American Bull Terrier type of fighting dog.

The Boxer is one of the most well-known companion breeds we have today. This breed originally served humans as both property guards and as fighters, set primarily against bulls and bears, depending on the size of the dog. Although these dogs are usually affectionate and very patient with their families, they can become quite focused and determined if they believe their people or homes are being threatened in any way. This breed is typical of many of the medium-sized modern power dogs in temperament and personality; "fun-loving, bright, active, and loyal" is how the AKC describes the typical Boxer temperament. However, the AKC also suggests that Boxers should be supervised with other dogs, which is a tip of the hat to the breed's fighting heritage. The FCI breed standard describes the Boxer temperament as "fearless, self-confident, calm, and equable. Temperament is of the utmost importance and requires careful attention. Devotion and loyalty towards his master and his entire household, his watchfulness and self-assured courage as a defender are famous. He is harmless with his family but distrustful of strangers. Happy and friendly in play, yet fearless in a serious situation." These two registries, both interested in the preservation and promotion of purebred dogs, paint quite different pictures of the ideal temperament in the same breed. A Boxer from AKC-registered ancestors might not inherit quite the same temperament as one from FCI-registered ancestors. Knowing as much as possible about your dog's pedigree and the individual dogs in it, particularly the sire and dam, can help you anticipate your dog's inherited traits and address them proactively.

Boxers like this one have been family companions for generations.

The Perro de Presa Canario (Canary Dog) was developed in the Canary Islands as a fighting dog. Dog fighting was legal there until the 1940s, and after it was outlawed, the breed found another use as a guard dog for people, property, and livestock. The AKC has admitted the Presa into the Foundation Stock Service, which is the first step toward full AKC breed recognition. According to the UKC, Presas were also used to exterminate wild and stray dogs that once populated the islands. The UKC breed description specifically mentions that the Presa is "extremely affectionate, docile, and well behaved with its owner and family, but is wary of strangers and aggressive with other dogs." The FCI breed standard describes the ideal breed temperament as "[o]bedient and docile with family members, very devoted to its master, but can be suspicious of strangers." This is an example of a breed that may be fantastic as a companion dog for you and your immediate family, but difficult to live with in an urban or suburban setting because the breed isn't particularly good with strangers and other dogs. A Presa weighing in between 85 and 135 pounds might not be a good choice to add to a typical multi-dog household, either. These dogs require a considerable commitment to consistent management, effective training, and patience to bring them effectively into everyday life because their fighting and guarding instincts are still quite strong. There are many localities and even some countries that ban ownership of Canary Dogs.

This vintage image of a Canary Dog shows the massive size these dogs often attain.

General hunting breeds

Several different power breeds were originally used to hunt, hold, or kill large, fierce game animals. The Great Dane, Dogo Argentino, and Fila Brasiliero are three of these breeds who exemplify this group of power dogs. While the Great Dane is already a popular companion, the Dogo isn't (although it will likely increase in popularity in the United States now that the breed is going through the process of AKC recognition). The Fila, however, is not very common outside its home country, in part due to its ferocity. The Dogo and Fila are subject to breed-specific bans in many nations, as well as falling under breed-specific ordinances in many locations throughout the United States.

It may be difficult to believe today, but the Great Dane was once used to hunt ferocious wild boar in Europe.

Great Danes are one of many power breeds whose use evolved over the generations to meet their owners' changing needs. This well-known power dog breed was originally developed by the German aristocracy for hunting wild boar in the 15th and 16th centuries. These dogs were quite heavy and coarse in build, unlike the refined, dignified dogs we have today. As the wild boar populations declined, the dogs were put to work as fierce guardians. More recently, breeders have selectively bred for more tolerance of strangers as the work of the Great Dane assumed mostly a companion role, although acting in a protective manner is still typical of many of these giant dogs. Regardless of an individual dog's protective instincts, the sheer size of these dogs makes living with one a challenge; not only are Great Danes tall (28 – 34 inches tall at the shoulder), they are also heavy (100 – 200 pounds). Like most of the other power breeds, the AKC mentions that this breed does better with supervision around children or other dogs, reflecting both their guardian history as well as their large size. The AKC breed standard describes the ideal Great Dane temperament as "spirited, courageous, always friendly and dependable, and never timid or aggressive."

The Dogo Argentino, an Argentinian breed, was originally developed to help hunters bring down dangerous game, including wild boar, pumas, and jaguars. The breed also has a reputation as a courageous guard dog. Its development began in the 1920s, spearheaded by an Argentinian physician who carefully bred several different power breeds together to arrive at the Dogo. A recent addition to the breeds working toward breed recognition by the AKC, the ideal Dogo personality is described as "loyal, trust-worthy, and, above all else, courageous." As with most of the other power breeds, the AKC suggests Dogos are better with supervision around children, as well as other dogs, and notes these large dogs require vigorous exercise to stay at their physical and temperamental best.

Dr. Antonio Martinez began developing the Dogo Argentino in 1925. His aim was to create a dog capable of catching and holding a wild boar weighing up to 400 pounds until the hunter could kill the quarry.

The Fila Brasiliero is an old Brazilian breed used to track, attack, and hold game animals until the hunter arrives to kill them. These dogs were also occasionally used against runaway slaves to stop and hold them until they could be recaptured by their owners. This breed is known to be deeply suspicious of strangers, and some breeders who seek to retain the original characteristics of the breed believe that puppies must show aggression toward strangers by the time they reach 6 months of age if they have the correct Fila temperament. Some breed purists believe that selectively breeding and training Filas so they are more acceptable to keep in urban areas is destroying the breed; according to these fanciers, the aggressive nature of a Fila is what the breed was originally developed for and if it is removed, the dog is no longer truly a Fila. The Portuguese word for their temperament is *ojeriza*, which directly translated into English means "dislike and distrust." Because of their aggressive nature, the breed is not allowed to be imported into many countries throughout the world, including the United Kingdom and Denmark. The liabilities of owning this type of dog in a modern urban or suburban setting make it unlikely the breed will ever become very popular, and the Fila serves as a good reminder of the type of temperament many of the power breeds once possessed.

This vintage image of a Fila Brasiliero emphasizes the sheer size of this breed; an aggressive dog this big can be extremely difficult to live with in an urban setting.

The power of instinct-centric training

The power of **instinct-centric training** comes from understanding the very essence of the power dog you have brought into your home and appreciating your power dog for what he is, rather than trying to make him into something he isn't. Embrace your dog—*all* of your dog, including his ancestry, because that ancestry influences his instincts. The harsh history of the power breeds in no way means *your* dog is "vicious," "bad," or otherwise unfit for existence simply because of his pedigree and appearance. It simply means he is what he is—an individual dog of a particular breed or mix of breeds, capable of hearing the voices of his ancestors calling him to perform certain tasks. Sometimes, in just the perfect set of circumstances, those ancestral voices are heard. Denying their existence leaves you helpless to manage or prevent the consequences if that ever happens to your dog. If you accept responsibility for *all* of your dog, you will be able to proactively keep most, or all, of those voices silent and enjoy many years of a wonderful relationship with your power dog.

Appreciating your power dog for what he is does *not* mean you should use the fact that he is a power dog to excuse, justify, or accept unsafe or unacceptable behaviors. Good manners are good manners, regardless of the dog's breed. Every dog owner has a responsibility to teach his dog to behave in an acceptable manner in the environment he lives in, both inside your home and out in the real world. Even a dog who lives in a rural area with little human contact, or one who isn't taken out in public often, still requires veterinary care, and he may need to be boarded if you travel or become ill and must depend on someone else to care for him, or if you need to travel with him unexpectedly. A strong, independent, and/or protective power dog with little or no training will be difficult to manage in these situations. Understanding your power dog's ancestry will help you appreciate and learn to work *with* your dog's instincts, rather than against them. This is the first key to empowering your power dog to become the most exceptional companion he can be!

3

Is a Power Dog Right for You?

Understanding your dog and knowing how to control him, develop his potentials, and resolve behavior problems, emotional conflicts and frustrations are no less essential than love and respect.

Michael W. Fox, DVM, author, animal rights activist

The decision to bring a dog into your family is a big one, regardless of the type of dog you get. Life with a power dog can be challenging in several unique ways; it is important that you honestly assess your ability and willingness to live with these challenges before you actually bring a power dog into your home and heart. The time, effort, and training consistency required to successfully live with any power dog are considerable. Additionally, there are social pressures and legal obligations that go along with owning certain power breeds that you will have to deal with if you bring one into your family. This chapter provides you some food for thought and will help you make the best decision possible about whether a power dog is the right choice for you!

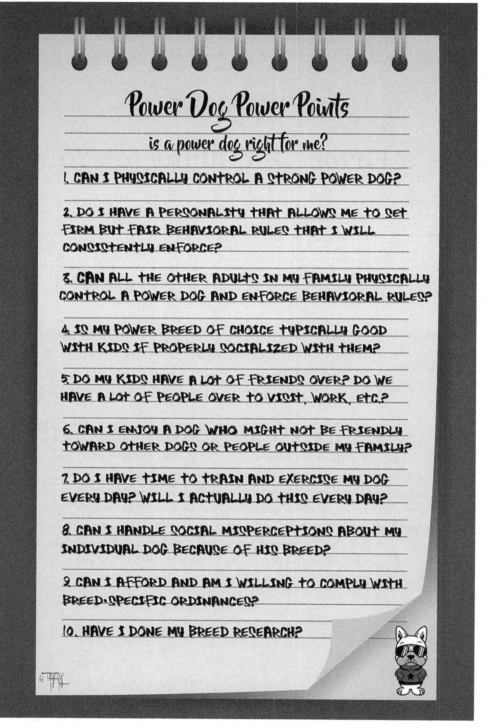

Power Dog Power Points

is a power dog right for me?

1. CAN I PHYSICALLY CONTROL A STRONG POWER DOG?

2. DO I HAVE A PERSONALITY THAT ALLOWS ME TO SET FIRM BUT FAIR BEHAVIORAL RULES THAT I WILL CONSISTENTLY ENFORCE?

3. CAN ALL THE OTHER ADULTS IN MY FAMILY PHYSICALLY CONTROL A POWER DOG AND ENFORCE BEHAVIORAL RULES?

4. IS MY POWER BREED OF CHOICE TYPICALLY GOOD WITH KIDS IF PROPERLY SOCIALIZED WITH THEM?

5. DO MY KIDS HAVE A LOT OF FRIENDS OVER? DO WE HAVE A LOT OF PEOPLE OVER TO VISIT, WORK, ETC.?

6. CAN I ENJOY A DOG WHO MIGHT NOT BE FRIENDLY TOWARD OTHER DOGS OR PEOPLE OUTSIDE MY FAMILY?

7. DO I HAVE TIME TO TRAIN AND EXERCISE MY DOG EVERY DAY? WILL I ACTUALLY DO THIS EVERY DAY?

8. CAN I HANDLE SOCIAL MISPERCEPTIONS ABOUT MY INDIVIDUAL DOG BECAUSE OF HIS BREED?

9. CAN I AFFORD AND AM I WILLING TO COMPLY WITH BREED-SPECIFIC ORDINANCES?

10. HAVE I DONE MY BREED RESEARCH?

Carefully consider if a power dog is the right choice for you before you bring one into your family.

Personal considerations

Carl Semencic, an outspoken advocate of bully breeds, manstoppers, and large guardian breeds, posed a question in his book *Pit Bulls and Tenacious Guard Dogs* that merits careful thought:

> *In addition to the temperamental suitability of the owner, the practical question of physical suitability should also be taken into consideration [when deciding to get a powerful dog as a family companion]. Remember that even a well-trained dog that respects its owner is still an animal, after all. All of the breeds are relatively large and strong dogs. Some of these breeds are huge and tremendously powerful. A small person, owning a huge, untrained [power] dog in a heavily populated environment is trouble waiting to happen. A large person who is elderly or for some other reason not a powerful person should also avoid selecting a powerful dog for companionship.*

There is no way to rely on physical control or coercion with these types of dogs; leashes, collars, and harnesses won't stop a giant dog who hasn't been taught how to behave, or one whose protective instincts overwhelm him because he hasn't been properly socialized. Realistically assessing your ability to live with a strong and possibly quite large dog is important if you want an enjoyable relationship with any dog you bring into your family.

Family considerations

Another consideration is whether *everyone* in the family can live with a dog who possesses exceptional strength, size, or the instincts to protect his family at all costs. This is not to say that power dogs can't make superb family pets, but if you have an adult in the family who can't physically control a powerful dog, is a power breed a good choice with so many other breeds to explore? Also, is the dog suitable for a family with children? Some power dogs are better suited to live in a family with children than others, although most are very devoted companions to all their family members, regardless of age. Another consideration when there are children in the family is the coming and going of your children's friends. While your dog may very well love and respect *your* children, he may feel the need to protect your children from their friends, or simply try to push those outsiders around, which can have serious consequences. Even if your large power dog is loving toward all strangers, his sheer size alone may scare some guests, especially young children, who come into your home.

Prevalence of dog-directed aggression

In their research study "Breed Differences in Canine Aggression," Deborah Duffy and her colleagues found that there was higher-than-average dog-directed aggression in most of the power breeds they surveyed. Although they caution that it would be "inappropriate to make predictions about a given dog's propensity for aggressive behavior based solely on its breed," their findings, as well as studies by Roll and Unshelm and others, rated pit bulls, Boxers, Akitas, Rottweilers, and Doberman Pinschers high on the scale for dog-directed aggression. (The other breeds that rated high on this scale were mostly working terrier breeds.) Interestingly, this study also found that "pit bull" aggression toward strange humans was about the same as the average rate for all the breeds in the study, even though these types of dogs are often considered "dangerous" dogs and are the target of many breed-specific ordinances. As Duffy points out, this finding is consistent with the view that "this breed has been selectively bred for aggression toward other dogs rather than humans." If it is important to you that your dog is dog-friendly, consider choosing a breed known for that trait in the first place, then socializing and training him around other dogs to improve the odds that you will end up with a dog who enjoys the company of other dogs. The odds are far less in your favor when you start with a breed known to have dog-aggressive traits and then try to suppress those instincts.

Societal perceptions

Some power dogs are owned by people who aim to keep the dog-fighting culture alive or who use power dogs for intimidation and status symbols. This, rather than instincts inherent in the breeds themselves, has resulted in the dogs having a particular reputation in the popular media, as well as legislative chambers around the globe. There are definitely some dogs in every breed who have such strong protective instincts and are so naturally aggressive that they are not suitable for living in urban areas; however, these individual dogs are the exception to the rule, and not limited to just the power breeds. If a person wants a power dog for something other than companionship, the guarding and fighting instincts that exist somewhere in every power dog can be brought to the surface through training, abuse, or neglect. These are the dogs who receive the most media attention, after they become involved in extreme acts of violence on other dogs or people. The power dogs who go about their daily lives as wonderful family companions and working animals are rarely covered on the news. The average person, whose concept of the power breeds arises solely from this media coverage, is apt to have a very skewed idea about how many individual dogs are actually truly dangerous animals. As a result of this bias, you might experience overt bullying, prejudice, fear, or other negative social experiences simply because you own a power dog, regardless of how sweet and well-trained your dog actually is. Is your skin thick enough to handle this?

The history of your breed is what it is; there is no way to erase the fact that some power breeds were developed to chase humans, some to fight dogs or other animals, and still others to protect hearth and home to the death, if need be. If this history didn't exist, you wouldn't have the wonderful power dog companion you have today. To deny that the news and social media have presented enough examples of power dogs severely injuring or killing people to scare some people you meet while out walking your dog is simply setting yourself up for anger and defensiveness every time you take your power dog out in public. These horrific incidents have happened, regardless of the reasons they did. Disfigured and dead people (especially children) make news and will stick in people's minds more strongly than all the positive stories about power dogs as therapy dogs, service dogs, and wonderful companions combined will ever do. If this type of unfair treatment will keep you from enjoying a power dog, then it might be a better choice for you to pick a more "socially acceptable" breed. If you do decide to own a power dog (particularly those who resemble an APBT to one degree or another), or you already own one, you will need to make up your mind to enjoy him, no matter what. Don't give anyone else permission to take the joy of owning a power breed away from you! Be responsible for teaching your dog how to be a good canine citizen, be proud of your beautiful, intelligent canine companion, and enjoy the fact that you two are out representing power breeds with class and style. Let the haters hate because, deep down, they wish they had an awesome dog like yours, rather than because your dog's behavior reinforces the stereotypes they already hold about the breed. Don't feed into the stereotypes by allowing your dog to behave inappropriately or getting into unpleasant verbal exchanges with anyone who doesn't approve of your choice of dogs. Be a power dog ambassador at all times and you will do far more to educate the public about these dogs than any amount of negative internet rhetoric or dog park shouting matches will ever do.

With your power dog sitting politely at your side modeling the good behavior these dogs can and do exhibit on a daily basis, you can have an informative, calm, productive conversation with anyone who cares to learn more about your dog. But to do that, you must first acknowledge where the *other* person is coming from. Have they had personal negative experiences with a power breed? Have they read negative information on social media or heard it on the news? Do they like *any* dog? (Hard for some dog lovers to believe, but there are plenty of people in this world who are either afraid of dogs in general or simply don't like them.) No matter how wonderful, sweet, funny, loving, obedient, loyal, and socially appropriate you know your power dog is, no one else, besides the few people who have actually interacted with your dog, knows that! Very, very, *very* few people have any clue at all about your power breed of choice, and absolutely no one outside your circle of family and friends knows your dog as an individual. It is very easy to forget this. Acknowledge the other person's viewpoint, then provide factual information, but only *if* that person appears to be open to hearing what you have to say. All the facts in the world won't change someone's mind if the backfire effect occurs, so don't expect everyone you meet to accept what you tell them about your dog. But hopefully, through setting a good example of dog ownership and opening up to people truly interested in learning about your dog, you will be able to change a few people's minds about these dogs!

Legal obligations

Appreciating the complete adult package contained in the little puppy you choose to bring home is critical with the power breeds, particularly the larger ones. These dogs can be challenging to own; even the most docile, well-trained power dog may still produce legal, insurance, and societal obligations that other breeds don't create. Unfair? Absolutely! The truth? You bet! That's an ugly part of life with many power breeds in today's urban society. Are you ready, willing, and able to take responsibility for a powerful dog who has protection or fighting instincts in his genes? Any dog you bring into your home is a companion first; any ego-gratifying effects from owning a power dog and any protection benefits you receive from him should be of secondary importance. If you live in a place where breed-specific ordinances are in effect and the thought of muzzling your sweet, well-mannered power dog every time you go out in public really bothers you, you have three legal choices: (1) find a way to make peace with these legal requirements and comply with them, (2) choose a different breed of dog that isn't affected by breed-specific legislation, or (3) move somewhere that doesn't already have any restrictions in place and isn't likely to have any in the future. Ignoring breed-specific legislation only perpetuates the stereotype of power dog owners as irresponsible people and certainly doesn't help change people's attitudes toward power dogs. Also, consider whether you can afford other requirements such as additional fencing and extra insurance coverage you may have to provide. And, speaking of insurance, many insurance companies have lists of dog breeds that they won't insure, and most are power breeds. Are you prepared to have some difficulty finding insurance coverage or paying higher premiums if necessary?

Do your research

When it comes to doing breed research, many first-time dog owners never go beyond looking at a few pictures on the internet and talking to a few breeders who may have pups readily available for new homes. While it is definitely a good start, this limited effort probably won't give you a very realistic picture of what it takes to live successfully with a power dog. Talking only with breeders or people who really love their dogs will probably provide you with only the good points about their preferred breeds. Carl Semencic brings up another interesting observation in his book *Pit Bulls and Tenacious Guard Dogs*:

> I don't think I have ever spoken to any breeder or enthusiast of any breed who has freely admitted that his breed is a terrible choice as a family dog or even a children's dog. Breeders of fine dogs are usually people who love their dogs and, as such, they view their dogs as being very lovable. Fully believing that theirs is a lovable breed, it is not easy for most breeders to recognize their breed's limitations; therefore, a breeder's praise for his or her dogs is usually an honest, if sometimes misleading, appraisal rather than in intentional act of deception. The result, however, can be the same, so a word of caution is in order here....

All dog breeds have negative attributes as well as positive ones; if you talk with a breeder or read information that only speaks of a breed as a shining example of canine virtue, intelligence, undying loyalty, and uncanny discriminatory skills, you have come across an example of what Semencic was talking about. If all the research you've done makes a breed sound too good to be true, keep digging. You want the full picture *before* you get your power dog, not after you bring him home.

When you do your internet research, be sure to look at information provided by breed clubs. These are groups of people dedicated to their breeds, and a wealth of information can be found on these websites, including the breed standard. This is the description of the "ideal" breed representative, and is what responsible breeders strive to produce. Check out the standards and information provided by several breed registries, such as the AKC, UKC, and FCI. Each organization has a slightly different "ideal" standard for the same breed. Some registries emphasize preservation of original breed temperaments and traits, while others emphasize breeding temperaments more suitable for modern living. Read books written by fanciers about the breeds that interest you. Contact local kennel clubs and obedience clubs to see if any members own the breed you are interested in, or go to shows to chat with owners there and see dogs in person. Do as much background research as possible before you contact specific breeders so you know what questions you'd like to ask them about their dogs.

After you have some basic knowledge about the power breed that interests you, move on to actually talking with breeders and seeing as many examples of that type of dog as possible before you buy your power puppy. Breeders can have a significant impact on your puppy's health and temperament; be sure to interview breeders as carefully as they should interview you so you end up with a healthy power puppy who has already had considerable socialization experiences before you even bring him home. See the next page for a list of questions to ask a breeder. Even if you want to adopt a rescue, it is still useful to see as many breed examples as possible, so you can better assess the rescues you later consider.

Power Dog Power Points

questions to ask breeders

1. HOW LONG HAVE YOU BEEN INVOLVED IN THE BREED?

2. HOW MANY LITTERS HAVE YOU BRED?

3. DO YOU OWN THE SIRE AND DAM? CAN I SEE THEM?

4. HOW OFTEN DO YOU BREED LITTERS?

5. HAVE THE PARENTS HAD ALL THEIR HEALTH TESTS?

6. WHAT IS THE PEDIGREE BEHIND THIS LITTER?

7. WHAT ARE THE GOOD TRAITS OF THIS BREED?

8. WHAT ARE THE BAD TRAITS OF THIS BREED?

9. DESCRIBE THE TEMPERAMENTS OF THE PARENTS.

10. WHAT HEALTH GUARANTEES DO YOU OFFER ON PUPS?

11. WHAT SOCIAL EXPERIENCES HAVE YOU GIVEN THE PUPPIES? (PEOPLE, NOISES, SIGHTS, CAR, CRATE, ETC)

12. ARE THE PUPPIES CRATE TRAINED AND HOUSEBROKEN?

13. DESCRIBE THE IDEAL OWNER FOR YOUR PUPPIES. DO I FIT YOUR REQUIREMENTS?

Breeders range from very experienced, educated, and honest fanciers striving to perfect their chosen breed to inexperienced, uneducated, and/or unethical producers raising dogs strictly for monetary gain or even illegal purposes. If this is your first power dog, be prepared for some ethical breeders to be hesitant, or even refuse, to sell you one of their power puppies for any number of legitimate reasons. These are the people who know the breed best; they understand and will share both the positives *and* the negatives of life with these dogs, and understand what it really takes to live with one. Breeders who only give you a picture of the breed as a dog who can be trusted with every person and in every possible situation are looking to make a sale, not to protect the puppies they produced. If it sounds too good to be true, it is! There is no such thing as the perfect dog, and certainly no such thing as the perfect power breed. These are all dogs, being asked to survive and function in a human world. Responsible breeders will tell you both sides of the story. They want the best matches possible for their puppies. They have also likely been approached by people who want one of their dogs for irresponsible, if not outright illegal, reasons, so it is understandable that they may be extra cautious when it comes to placing puppies, especially to first-time dog owners. Don't be discouraged; ask breeders what you can do to create a home that they would be willing to place one of their puppies in. Win them over with your commitment to being a responsible owner if this is the breed you really want. If a breeder is willing to hand you a puppy upon receipt of payment, without interviewing you extensively, you probably won't be happy with the puppy you end up with. The internet can make even the most horrendous puppy mill look like a boutique breeder, so be sure to do your homework and don't fall victim to cute puppy eyes or assurances that you don't need to see the parents or where the puppy was raised. Remember, you are bringing a very strong, possibly very large, protective dog into your family—be patient and persistent in your search for your dream power puppy to avoid ending up with an adult power dog nightmare.

The down side to getting a puppy from the very best breeder possible is that if the breeder is dedicated to preserving the breed in its original form, that may very well include a temperament that is not well-suited to most modern family situations or inexperienced power dog owners. Some breed purists argue that a guard dog without natural guarding tendencies, or a fighting dog who isn't dog-aggressive, isn't a true representative of a guard breed or fighting breed, regardless of what role the dog will fulfill in his family. Talking with as many breeders as possible will help you find a breeder who balances physical and temperament characteristics in a way that will help the puppy you get fit well into your family. Some power breed advocates, like Carl Semencic, take a very dim view of making the temperament of the power breeds more suitable to the average family situation:

> To require [a dog who shows aggression] to leave the [show] ring for this reason may well be detrimental to the preservation of true breed type. A representative of a fighting breed that displays aggression toward other dogs at a show is the only dog eligible for judging in the mind of anyone who understands breed standards; all others should be considered lacking in this respect. It is the ultimate in hypocrisy to

either make a champion of any of the fighting dogs that do not display aggression toward other dogs or to call for aggression in the breed standard and then not judge that characteristic at a show. The AKC is unfortunately guilty of both.

Whether you agree with this view or not, you need to ask breeders what their views are on the topic of temperament. They are the ones producing the puppies you are considering taking home.

If you are interested in one of the rare power breeds, you definitely need to do your homework. In 2017, there were 75 breeds listed in the AKC's Foundation Stock Service, all relatively rare in the United States and working toward full AKC breed recognition. Fifteen of these breeds (20%) have fighting or guarding origins, and eight of those power breeds are already either outright banned or have ownership restrictions placed on them at the city or county level in various states throughout the United States and/or at the national level in countries throughout the world. For example, the Dogo Argentino is banned completely or banned from importation in 13 different countries. To avoid being blindsided by this type of information, do your homework using as many sources as possible. The AKC makes no mention of these bans anywhere on their website because the dogs are legal to own in most jurisdictions in the United States, but there are many places in this country where Dogos are already banned. The rarer the breed, the greater the chances that there are health, temperament, and legal surprises lurking somewhere in the shadows, so be sure to thoroughly check for them. This is one reason it is so very important to do extensive homework *before* deciding to bring any dog into your home, but in particular if you are interested in getting a power dog or a rare breed.

Is a rescue power dog right for you?

Instead of purchasing a power puppy from a breeder, some people choose to adopt a dog from a shelter or rescue group. There is certainly no shortage of power dogs in need of responsible, loving homes. Sue Sternberg, in her book *Assessing Aggression Thresholds in Dogs*, suggests that the percentage of large, muscular "guarding and fighting" type dogs in urban shelters has increased substantially in recent years. But not every responsible, loving home is a good fit for a rescue power dog. If, after doing your basic breed research, you are considering getting a rescue, here are a few other things to think about before actually bringing one home.

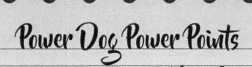

Power Dog Power Points

is a rescue power dog right for me?

1. AM I COMFORTABLE NOT KNOWING FOR SURE WHAT POWER BREED OR BREED MIX I ADOPT?

2. CAN I ACCEPT IF MY RESCUE POWER DOG'S TRUE PERSONALITY ENDS UP BEING DIFFERENT THAN WHAT IT WAS WHEN I FIRST ADOPTED HIM?

3. AM I ABLE AND WILLING TO PUT IN THE TIME AND EFFORT IT TAKES TO KEEP MY FAMILY AND MY NEW DOG SAFE WHILE HE ADJUSTS TO HIS NEW HOME?

4. DO I HAVE THE TIME AND DISCIPLINE TO TRAIN AND EXERCISE MY RESCUE DOG TO HELP HIM ADJUST AND BE THE BEST COMPANION HE CAN BECOME?

5. IS EVERYONE IN MY FAMILY ABLE AND WILLING TO HAVE PATIENCE WHILE OUR RESCUE POWER DOG SETTLES IN WITH HIS NEW FAMILY?

6. CAN I STILL LOVE AND ENJOY MY RESCUE POWER DOG IF HE DOESN'T END UP BEING THE TYPE OF COMPANION I HAD HOPED HE WOULD BECOME?

7. CAN I ACCEPT NOT KNOWING THE COMPLETE PERSONAL HISTORY OF MY RESCUE POWER DOG?

8. CAN I ACCEPT THAT SOME SERIOUS BEHAVIORAL ISSUES CAN'T EVER BE "FIXED" NO MATTER HOW MUCH I LOVE MY NEW DOG?

Rescue dogs of any breed often present unique challenges due to their past experiences; are you up to the challenge?

What is he?

Dogs who perform the same types of work often have similar physical and mental traits. Bulldog-type dogs were developed centuries ago in places as diverse and, at the time, isolated from one another as Europe, South America, and Asia. Form usually follows function, and the dogs were all used for similar purposes, so they all had similar physical appearances. This type of breeding still exists today, particularly within illegal dog-fighting circles. Far too many power dogs are still being bred to fight; their pedigrees and the fine points of their physical appearances are far less important than their ability to fight and win money for their owners. New power breeds are continually being developed by crossing two or more existing fighting breeds (e.g., the Larson Lakeview Bulldogge was developed from a mixture of American Bulldog, American Pit Bull Terrier, English Bulldog, Bull Terrier, Bullmastiff, and English Mastiff). Many of the new breeds resemble more well-established breeds in appearance, but not necessarily in temperament. It can be difficult for the average shelter intake worker to identify many of the relatively "new" fighting and protection breeds, like the Detroit Rock Dog, also known as the American Panja Mastiff. This breed arose from the drug, gang, and dog-fighting culture in Detroit and is a fearsome personal protection dog. These dogs sometimes show up in shelters and can easily be misidentified as American Bulldogs, Mastiffs, or other more benign power breeds or power breed crosses. The average person coming into a shelter to adopt a power dog is simply not equipped to own this type of dog, so correctly identifying power dogs as best as can be done and paying close attention to the behavior and temperaments of individual dogs brought into the shelter is critical to safely and permanently adopting them out. When you adopt a rescue dog of unknown origin, there is always a possibility that you might end up adopting a type of dog completely different than you were looking for.

It's also important to keep in mind that some dogs who may look "bully" or "pitty" don't have a drop of power dog in them, while others who don't look at all like a typical power breed may still have the temperament and traits of those types of dogs. Many breeds look similar, and what is identified as a Bulldog may, in fact, be a misidentified Abraxas Bulldogge (a breed known to be extremely aggressive, intolerant of strangers, and confrontational around other dogs). DNA testing can help better identify your dog's ancestry, but few shelters or rescue groups have the funds to test their dogs. And many of the newer fighting breeds would simply show up as crosses of various power dogs, but that provides no information about the temperament of the individual dog. If you choose to rescue a power dog, are you comfortable with the thought that you might not ever know what your dog's breed really is? And are you prepared to deal with physical problems, regardless of the cost, that may result from previous abuse, neglect, or poor breeding practices?

What you see isn't always what you get

Further complicating matters is the fact that when a dog comes into a rescue or a shelter, he may well be sick, injured, or simply overwhelmed by his circumstances. Like any other animal taken into rescue, it can be difficult to ascertain, beyond any reasonable doubt, what a dog's true breed heritage is or what his temperament will be once he is in his forever home, based strictly on what he looks like and how he behaved while he was in the shelter or being fostered. Dogs can suffer from something simplistically comparable to PTSD in humans. Certain trigger stimuli can elicit a completely unexpected response from the dog; that trigger might not be present while the dog is in the shelter, so no one knows about it before you adopt the dog. Or the dog might be one of those individuals who, because of genetics and/or training, has unsafe and undesirable traits that come out as the dog becomes more comfortable in his new home. Being confined in noisy kennel areas with other dogs can make some dogs appear to be more dog-aggressive than they are in more typical home environments or, conversely, more passive than they actually are. The less time a dog spends in a shelter or foster home, the less information is available to potential adopters about the dog's temperament and behavior. And any information provided is only as useful as the person providing it is knowledgeable about canine behavior and experienced working with rescues or any particular breed. Rescue dogs, especially those rescued from known fighting situations, need to be evaluated by professionals who are as objective as dog-loving people can be, and placed carefully with new owners who have the time and knowledge to help them safely and successfully adapt to their new environments. Are you prepared to accept that your rescue dog's personality will evolve as he becomes more comfortable in his new family and might not resemble the personality he had when you first brought him home?

How patient are you?

Rescue dogs may take several months or longer to settle into their new homes. When you first bring a rescue home, you are a complete stranger to that dog, and probably just one in a long line of strangers who have been in and out of his life since he was brought into rescue. Some dogs shut down under the stress of living in a shelter or being moved through foster homes, while others become overly excited or even aggressive because of the changes. Not only must you deal with whatever behaviors your dog exhibits when you first bring him home, you must expect that his personality will change as he becomes more comfortable with his permanent home. That mellow, sweet power dog who stole your heart may become pushy and demanding as time goes by, without proper training and management on your part. Conversely, the nervous dog who barks at your children or spouse whenever they enter his space may eventually calm down and come to accept them as family with time, and proper management and counter-conditioning. Are you ready, willing, and able to deal with all these unknowns when you rescue a dog, and are you able to accomplish this safely with any power breed you choose to adopt?

Additionally, it may take longer to change an inappropriate behavior in an adult dog who has had months or years practicing it than it would to teach a puppy an appropriate behavior in the first place. For example, a dog who has spent years pulling his owner down the street on their walks together will probably need more time to learn to walk consistently and reliably on a loose leash than a puppy who has never been allowed to pull his owner around in the first place. You have no idea about the environmental influences your dog experienced before he came into rescue. Even those dogs who are given up from non-fighting situations were given up for a reason, and often that is a lack of fit with his original family (e.g., the dog simply became too large and/or too expensive for his original owner to keep), expression of normal instinctual behaviors (particularly dog aggression), and/or inappropriate behavior due to lack of socialization and basic obedience training. Are you prepared for the training challenges that may present themselves with a rescue? Is the rest of your family prepared? Can you accept that your dog may never be the type of companion you had hoped he would be due to his history, and still live with and love him? Are you prepared to keep everyone (including your family) safe while your dog adapts to his new family, new environment, and new behavioral expectations? Many owners are fully prepared and committed to meet these challenges and are rewarded with incredible companions, but others aren't prepared, and either end up surrendering the dog again or isolating him away from the family for the rest of his life. Do you really have the time and patience it might take to teach a rescue dog how to behave acceptably in your home?

It is a big commitment to bring any dog home, but there is an extra element of challenge with adopting a rescue dog. It is important to that dog that you honestly assess your willingness and ability to do whatever it takes to help him adapt to his new life. Many people are quite able to successfully live with a rescue dog, even one from an abusive background, but others aren't.

If you decide owning a rescue dog is not a realistic option for you and your family but you still want to help these dogs, consider donating your time, items the organization needs to care for the dogs they take in, money, or professional services toward their care. Many breed-specific rescues need this type of assistance as much as they need foster and adoptive homes for the dogs in their care.

So, is a power dog right for you?

Power dogs are marvelous animals; in the proper homes, they make some of the best canine companions any person could ever want. If you haven't brought a power dog home yet, do your research so you are confident that a power dog will truly fit into your home and lifestyle. If a power dog doesn't seem like a good fit, find another breed that will work better. If a power dog is a good choice for you, then enjoy the process of finding that special individual puppy or dog to add to your family! The time you take to really think through getting a dog before you do will help you and your new canine family member get off to a great start together. And if you already have a power dog in your home, doing more research to learn about your dog's breed ancestry will help deepen your understanding and appreciation of him; that's a win for both of you!

4

Canine Behavior Basics

… all breeds of dog descended from the old Bulldog [i.e., many power dog breeds] place more demands on their owner than do other dogs. An expert on this problem rightly claims that these dogs tolerate no fool as their master. Moreover, there are two sorts of fools! The one – the more dangerous – wakens the ferocity slumbering in this breed, turns it into a real danger to himself, his family, and the people around him. The other, more harmless fool, accepts too little responsibility and has too little insight to turn the dog into a respectable citizen through proper training. In each case we must say that any complications that arise are not the dog's fault, but its master's.

Carl Fleig, author, Fighting Dog Breeds

Once you've done your breed research and thoroughly explored the first key to power dog empowerment, you are ready to explore the second key—understanding the mix of influences that shape your dog's unique personality and behavior, including instincts, environment, and training. Once you understand this, you will be able to manage and train your dog effectively, so he can become a fantastic family companion and a positive power dog ambassador!

Inescapable instincts

Genetics are one of the very first influences on any dog's behavior, so it is important to understand what your power dog has inherited from his ancestors that might impact his behavior. Just like coat color, skull shape, and other physical characteristics, expression of instinctual behaviors can be selectively bred for in dogs. The genes that control these instincts and their associated behavioral traits exist in your dog from conception, and you will have to live with them for your dog's entire life.

Instincts are behaviors that don't require any initial learning for the dog to perform them when the proper set of circumstances is encountered; a dog is "hard-wired" with them at birth. These behaviors are related to the survival of the individual dog, as well as the survival of the species as a whole. Some of these behaviors become less pronounced over time, while others become stronger as a dog matures. Over the centuries, humans have altered the expression of canine instincts through selective breeding to create breeds suited for specific purposes. For example, to create a guard dog breed, only the dogs who instinctually defended their territories aggressively were allowed to reproduce; as a result, future generations of these dogs showed increasingly stronger instincts to protect their territories. These dogs, with their enhanced territorial protection instincts, eventually become quite useful to man as property guardians. From among those dogs, similar selection for all the other physical traits necessary to be an effective property guardian eventually led to the creation of distinct types or breeds of guard dogs. Whether an individual dog today is ever expected to protect his owner's property or not, he will still possess, to some degree, the enhanced instinctual territorial behaviors that were selected for when his breed was first created.

The instincts your dog is born with form the basic outline of your dog's behavior, like the outline of a picture in a coloring book. You may be able to slightly enlarge or shrink the behavioral outline, but no matter what you do, the picture will remain basically the same. Experiences, training, health, and individual genetic inheritance are the color and texture placed inside that breed outline to create your one-of-a-kind dog. Every dog breed has its own outline, determined by the type of work the breed was developed to perform and the way instinctual behaviors have been manipulated over generations of selective breeding. With thoughtful training, many instinct-based behaviors can be controlled to varying degrees, but none of them can ever be completely eliminated. If you are patient, consistent, persistent, and realistic with your training expectations and accept that instincts can be controlled, but never completely eliminated, you are well on your way to having a positive, productive training journey with your power dog!

Although you can fill your dog's behavioral outline in many different ways to influence the development of his unique personality, you can never completely eliminate the impact his breed instincts will have on his behavior.

British canine behaviorist John Rogerson, in *The Dog Vinci Code*, offers an interesting example that emphasizes the futility of trying to completely eliminate instinctual behaviors in your dog. He asks you to imagine taking your Doberman Pinscher to a trainer and asking the trainer to change your dog's short, black coat, long muzzle, and height into a long, light-colored coat, short muzzle, and shorter height. Obviously, this is impossible! You'd probably think someone who would make a request like this couldn't possibly be serious. All of these traits have been hard-wired into your Doberman genetically; they are part of what makes a Doberman a Doberman.

Rogerson then goes on to the second part of his scenario: You take the same Doberman to a trainer and ask the trainer to stop your adolescent dog from barking at strangers as they approach your property, and to teach him to be friendly and welcoming toward them. Sounds completely reasonable, right? But is it really any more reasonable than trying to change your dog's physical appearance? What you are actually asking the trainer to do in this case is reverse what your dog is genetically programmed to do—guard you and your property! Dobermans were developed to do this type of work. The trainer can certainly show you how to teach your Doberman to be quiet on cue, and how to increase your dog's tolerance of strangers through socialization, but you can never erase his instinctive urge to guard you and your property. That instinct to protect is also part of what makes a Doberman a Doberman! If that type of instinctual behavior and the effort it takes to manage it doesn't fit with your expectations or your lifestyle, then a Doberman might not be the right dog for you to bring into your family. Genetic traits will always exist. The potential to do the work his ancestors were bred to do will always exist in your dog, simply because he is the breed (or mix of breeds) he is. Your dog can be trained to perform tasks or behave in a way similar to other breeds, but he will never be fundamentally transformed into something he can't be—another type of dog. As Rogerson sums up: "…Genetics, then, give the dog the [instinctual] possibility, the environment gives opportunities for the instinct to develop, and training puts the instinct under the influence of the trainer." Understanding the influence of your dog's genetics is critical to understanding and living successfully with your power dog.

Normal isn't necessarily acceptable

Although understanding breed instincts allows you to better understand what "normal," instinct-based behavior is for your power dog, normal behavior is *not* necessarily *acceptable* behavior. When a dog becomes overly stimulated or stressed, his behaviors often reflect his breed instincts, and, more often than not, those behaviors are unacceptable in modern urban life. For example, when a power dog sees a stranger approaching the house for the first time, his normal instinct-based response may be to protect his territory. Depending on his specific breed, he might simply watch the stranger for any threatening behaviors, he might growl and bark menacingly, or he may immediately rush toward the stranger to physically stop the approach. This is all perfectly normal behavior for breeds historically used as property guardians. Nevertheless, such uncontrolled instinctual behavior is not acceptable in most everyday situations; you don't want a dog who tries to scare off the postal carrier or your child's friends. Training is needed to refine and control those instincts and develop an acceptable companion dog. These dogs must be taught to tolerate the presence of other people and animals from time to time, particularly if you live in an urban or suburban area where the presence of strangers and other animals is an everyday occurrence. No amount of training will ever completely extinguish his instincts, but you can definitely teach your dog to control his urges most of the time. It is absolutely mandatory that owners always accept responsibility and intervene in situations where their power dogs may be acting in a manner that is perfectly normal from a canine perspective, yet completely inappropriate by human standards. Not only is this important for everyone's safety, but dog-related ordinances typically punish owners if their dogs menace people or other animals, or bark excessively.

Sometimes, in spite of appropriate training and management, instincts are still expressed in inappropriate ways. The behavioral phenomenon known as "predatory drift" is an example of instincts unexpectedly being acted upon when just the right environmental circumstances occur. The instinct to chase and kill any potential food source exists in every dog, regardless of ancestry. Dogs can be taught not to chase after small animals, but that instinct to find food can never be completely extinguished. Every once in a while, when just the right set of events falls into place, even a well-trained dog's predatory instincts can come to the surface, resulting in harm or death to another animal, including other dogs and young children. We will look at this subject in more detail in Chapter 8.

Biological factors

Canine behavior is influenced by many different developmental and physical factors, in addition to breed-specific genetic history. Before a puppy is even born, his uterine environment can impact his development; the dam's overall health and hormonal influences from the rest of the litter in utero influence early development. As a puppy matures, normal physical, mental, and hormonal changes will cause predictable changes in his behavior. Most dog owners have heard of the "fear period" normal puppies pass through between 8 and 12 weeks old. During this time, your puppy is starting to understand that there are things in the environment that are potentially dangerous. An outgoing 7-week-old puppy may suddenly become fearful during this phase, and then completely regain his confidence by the time he's 16 weeks old. This change in his behavior is a completely normal part of canine development and can't be prevented, only managed. Likewise, when your puppy goes through puberty, his reproductive urges and territoriality will naturally increase, even if he's already altered (although sexual urges are usually weaker in altered dogs). Other biological factors, such as illness, injury, and his age when he is altered can also affect his development and impact his behavior. And, of course, as a dog ages, physical changes will normally occur. Arthritis, vision and hearing loss, and even dementia can influence an older dog's behavior.

Environmental influences

Environmental influences on your puppy start the moment your puppy is born. Puppy brains grow just like all the other parts of their bodies; without proper environmental stimulation during the brain's growth period, the brain won't develop to its full potential, and instinctual behaviors may be expressed in abnormal or unacceptable ways for a family pet.

You have considerable control over your puppy's environment after you bring him home, but if a significant amount of inappropriate learning has already taken place before you get him, then your ability to change his behavior may be limited. Puppies are learning about the world, and how to interact with it, from the moment they are born. A puppy's mother is the first influence on his behavior; she starts to teach him what is acceptable and unacceptable puppy behavior. If the dam is shy or aggressive toward humans, her puppies may very well initially mirror her behavior. A puppy's littermates also influence development. For example, if a puppy is the runt of the litter, chances are he will be bullied and will learn certain coping skills to help him survive that may influence his behavior as an adult. The experiences the breeder provides the puppy continue to build on that foundation; new people, new sights and sounds, and other experiences will start to shape how your puppy interacts with his world. If he has little or no interaction with the world beyond his whelping box and the person who feeds him, your puppy will come to you deprived of critical learning experiences. You will need to work extra hard at socialization to try to make up for this if you want a confident, calm companion.

The experiences you give your puppy once you bring him home should continue to either enhance the genetic instincts and behaviors you want to increase in your puppy, or diminish the unwanted ones. For example, some power dogs are born with a strong predisposition to be protective of their human family. You can exert some influence on how strongly your dog expresses those instincts by the environment you raise him in. If your puppy is kept at home where he rarely sees anyone outside of his family, he won't have the opportunity to learn about other people in the world, and his instinctive wariness of strangers will be enhanced by his isolation. But if your puppy is properly exposed to new people on a regular basis, he will learn that strangers aren't always threats, and his instinctive wariness will be decreased. Add in management and training, and you will end up with a confident, well-mannered adult dog who may never really *like* strangers, but will behave in an acceptable manner around them.

The same concept applies to canine social skills. Dogs have the instinctive ability to express themselves in ways that other dogs understand. However, if a dog is not given the opportunity to practice and refine these communication skills (particularly during the first 16 weeks of his life), his fluency may be greatly diminished and he may have problems throughout his life being socially appropriate with other dogs. Your puppy needs to interact with dogs of various sizes and shapes, intact and altered, male and female, and of various ages so he learns to communicate appropriately with all types of dogs, which will help lessen any dog-aggressive tendencies he may have. Some dogs, simply due to their enormous adult size, need to learn early on that nearly every other dog they will ever encounter will be smaller than themselves, so they need to adjust their play styles accordingly to avoid scaring (and smashing!) canine buddies. It is also the best time for *you* to learn how to intervene and keep your puppy from getting too aroused during play; if you can't control and redirect your power puppy when he is only 25 pounds, how will you do it when he is 50, 100, or 150 pounds? If your puppy only interacts with the dogs he lives with, his communication skills will be limited by the degree of fluency his housemates have in canine communication. The odds of him acting inappropriately with dogs he later meets outside the family are greatly increased.

Training is also a form of environmental influence on your dog's behavior. What you intentionally teach your dog, as well as the methods you use to teach him, impact his behavior and influence the expression of his instincts. If you teach your dog to act aggressively toward strangers, his protective instincts will be enhanced; if you teach him to be tolerant toward them, the expression of his protective instincts will be decreased.

If you understand the basic influences that shape a dog's behavior, you can effectively help your power dog behave in a way that is acceptable to you, your family, and society, without placing unrealistic expectations on him to be anything other than what he is at heart—a power dog.

5

Learning Theory in a Nutshell

Nature abhors a vacuum.

Aristotle, philosopher

Your power dog is always learning. Every time you interact with him, he is learning something about his relationship with you. What he learns is, in large part, under your control. If you don't teach him how you want him to behave, his instincts will fill in the blanks and he will start to treat you like a dog—literally! This chapter will explain a few basic learning theory concepts to help you learn how to teach your dog in a way that makes sense to *him*, so he will be able to learn what you want him to learn more quickly and easily.

Classical conditioning

There are several ways dogs learn how to react to, and interact with, the world around them. **Classical conditioning** is one common way dogs learn. This is the type of learning Ivan Pavlov saw in action in his drooling research dogs and is sometimes referred to as "Pavlovian learning." Classical conditioning involves learning by association; a previously meaningless stimulus in your dog's environment (e.g., the sound of a dog food bag being opened) becomes associated with a stimulus (e.g., food) that naturally produces a behavior (e.g., drooling). Your dog doesn't have to be taught how to drool when he sees and smells food. His body automatically starts salivating to prepare to eat at mealtime. But he isn't born automatically drooling when he hears the sound of a crinkly food bag. He learns, by association, that the sound of you opening the food bag is always followed by his meal; by continuing to pair the sound of the food bag opening with his meal, your dog will eventually begin to drool when he hears the sound of the dog food bag being opened (even if there is no food around) because he anticipates the arrival of his food, and his body automatically drools when food is near. This is classical conditioning at work, and is one method that you can use when you are teaching your dog certain types of behaviors.

Operant conditioning

Operant conditioning is another mode of learning, and the one most commonly used in dog training. This type of learning happens when a dog's behavior is influenced by the consequences that immediately follow his behavior. If the consequence that immediately follows a behavior is something the dog wants, needs, or simply enjoys, that behavior is more likely to happen again. If the consequence that immediately follows the behavior is something he doesn't like, that behavior is not as likely to happen again. By controlling the consequences that follow a dog's behavior, you can affect the likelihood the behavior will happen again. If you've heard the term "positive reinforcement training," you've heard of one variation of operant conditioning.

Operant conditioning is typically divided into four quadrants:

- Positive reinforcement

- Negative reinforcement

- Positive punishment

- Negative punishment

In operant conditioning, the terms **positive** and **negative** mean *adding* (positive) or *subtracting* (negative) something from your dog's environment to influence the likelihood your dog will perform a particular behavior again. **Reinforcement** is anything that *increases* the likelihood a behavior will occur again, while **punishment** is anything that *decreases* the likelihood a behavior will occur again. Training sometimes involves crossing quadrants, so it is useful to have a basic understanding of what all four quadrants are and how they work.

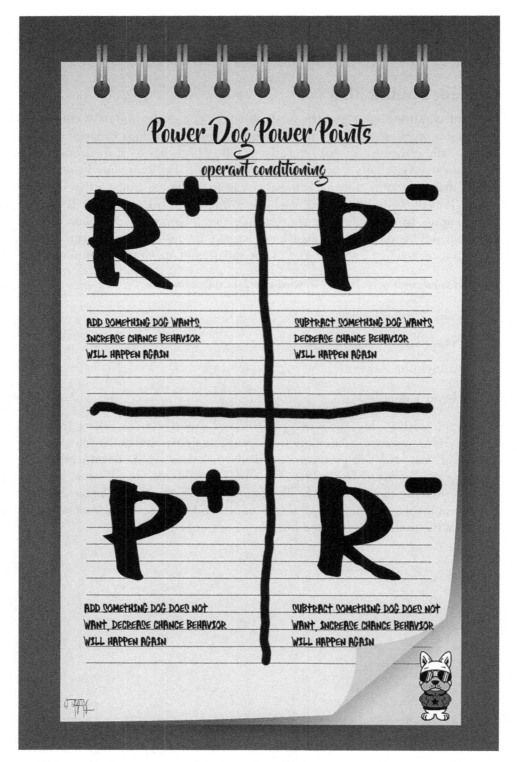

Understanding how operant conditioning works will help your training become more effective.

Positive reinforcement

Positive reinforcement involves *adding* something your dog *wants* to *gain* to his environment after he performs a desired behavior. This quadrant *increases* the likelihood that behavior will occur in the future. For example, if you say "Sit" and your dog sits, you might give him a treat he likes as a reinforcer for that behavior. The dog performed a desired behavior and you "added" a treat as a consequence of that behavior—you used positive reinforcement to increase the likelihood that the next time you say "Sit," your dog will sit, in anticipation of receiving another treat. Most people are familiar with this quadrant of operant conditioning (you may already use this with your children or dogs), even if they aren't aware of the scientific definition.

Positive punishment

Positive punishment involves *adding* something your dog *wants* to *avoid* to his environment when the dog performs an undesired behavior. This quadrant *decreases* the likelihood the behavior will occur in the future. The dog will change his behavior to avoid the unpleasant addition to his environment. For example, suppose you cue your dog to "Sit" and he just stands there and stares at you instead of sitting. You then give him a sharp slap on the rump because he didn't sit. By adding a punisher to your dog's environment when he performs an incorrect behavior (slap on the rump for standing instead of sitting), you decrease the chances that your dog will remain standing the next time you say "Sit." When you train using positive punishment, your dog performs the correct (or at least a different) behavior to avoid an unpleasant consequence. (Unfortunately, while he may sit the next time to avoid another slap, he might also lie down, walk away, shake with fear, or act aggressively, depending on his response to the punisher.)

Negative punishment

Negative punishment involves *subtracting* something the dog *wants* to *gain* from his environment when the dog performs an undesired behavior. This quadrant also *decreases* the likelihood the behavior will occur again in the future. Suppose you cue your dog to sit when a person approaches to pet him, but instead of sitting, he starts jumping excitedly in anticipation of being petted. You ask the person to immediately turn and walk away from your dog because he didn't sit. You are using negative punishment because you took what the dog wanted (attention from the approaching person) away when the dog performed an undesired behavior (jumping up). By taking away the chance to be petted, you decrease the likelihood your dog will jump up the next time someone approaches him. Most of us tend to think of punishment as some type of unpleasant physical contact, but punishers also involve the loss of opportunity to gain something the dog wants. Losing the chance to be petted can be an effective punishment for a dog who really enjoys interacting with people.

Negative reinforcement

Negative reinforcement involves *subtracting* something the dog *wants* to *avoid* from his environment when the dog performs a correct behavior. This quadrant *increases* the likelihood the behavior will occur in the future. In this quadrant, when you say "Sit," you also immediately give a sharp collar correction upward, putting unpleasant pressure on your dog's neck. As soon as your dog's rear hits the floor, you release the pressure. You removed something the dog wanted to avoid (pressure on his neck) when the dog performed the desired behavior (sit), thereby increasing the likelihood that your dog will sit the next time you say "Sit." This quadrant is prevalent in some traditional training methods, such as the pinched-ear method of teaching a dog to retrieve an object.

Which quadrants work best with a power dog?

If you understand the basics of operant conditioning, you understand why various training techniques work and how to fairly and effectively train your dog. Although all four quadrants of learning theory do work to increase desired behaviors and decrease undesired behaviors, the vast majority of the time using positive reinforcement and its natural corollary, negative punishment, is what works best. By giving your dog something he wants in exchange for performing a behavior you want, and removing something he wants when he doesn't, you will establish a fair, respectful working relationship that you can readily manipulate to bring out the best in your dog. In addition to being more learner-friendly and humane quadrants to work in, these two quadrants are far less likely to trigger adverse behavioral responses from dogs than the other two.

The negatives of positive punishment

Owners of large, exceptionally strong power dogs may be tempted to rely on promises of quick behavioral fixes offered by trainers who promote the use of shock collars (aka e-collars, tingle collars, static collars, and other less painful-sounding names), prong collars, physical punishment, and other forms of positive punishment in the mistaken belief that since power dogs generally have a high tolerance for physical pain, no harm can come from using these tools and techniques. Or they might not be able to physically manage a large, powerful dog and believe that the only way to "control" a massive dog is through brute force and intimidation. But in reality, you can safely and effectively train any dog, regardless of breed, size, or strength, with good management and positive reinforcement/negative punishment training techniques, without risking the negative fallout that can come from using positive punishment techniques.

Just because a dog may *tolerate* discomfort or pain, that doesn't mean he doesn't still feel the pain; it simply means he is motivated to continue his behavior in spite of the pain. Many trainers who advocate the use of any type of collar that utilizes electric stimulation claim that a dog experiences no pain with the collar, that the "tingle," "sensation," or "static shock" simply provides the dog information about right and wrong behaviors. But think about this claim for a moment. E-collars are used as a punisher—something a dog will work to avoid. So it makes no sense to say that such collars cause no discomfort to a dog; if that were the case, the collar wouldn't work to change behavior. This training tool relies on unpleasant physical sensations to stop undesired behaviors and isn't as benign as some trainers would have you believe. While it is true that a punisher doesn't *have* to involve pain (some dogs are punished by an angry scowl or harsh word), most positive punishment techniques used to train large, strong dogs involve some type of physical pain, and this is a very dangerous punisher to use.

Once you introduce pain into training, you open the door to many undesirable, and potentially dangerous, consequences. First, when you train a dog using any training method, you can never completely control the association your dog makes between the reinforcer or punisher you are using and what you are trying to teach him. When you use positive punishment, your dog hopefully associates his discomfort with the behavior he is engaging in at the moment he is punished, and stops that particular behavior to avoid the punisher in the future. But he could also associate the pain with something else in his environment, particularly if your timing is off during the delivery of the punisher; another dog, a person, a moving vehicle, or anything else he is paying attention to at the moment he is corrected could be erroneously associated in your dog's mind with the pain he is experiencing. This can lead to strengthening the very behavior you were trying to eliminate in the first place, or creating new, even more dangerous behaviors, particularly when you are working with a breed originally developed to fight or aggress toward humans.

Second, when you use pain or discomfort during training, you increase the stress the dog experiences. As stress increases, the ability to learn decreases and instinctual behaviors start to appear. Since most power dogs were used to fight or hunt other animals, increasing the stress during training increases the chances that dangerous instinctual behaviors may surface, even if the dog has never exhibited these behaviors before. We will look at this aspect of training in more detail later in this chapter.

Third, using positive punishment focuses on what you *don't* want your dog to do, instead of showing him how to do what you actually *want* him to do. Using positive punishment might stop an unwanted behavior, but will do absolutely nothing to guarantee you replace that one with a wanted behavior.

Fourth, the equipment you need to use consistently to train using positive punishment can readily fail. Batteries can go dead and prong collar links can come undone, leaving you no control over your dog. These are also very obvious pieces of equipment to the dog; the collar is either on the dog or off. It is hard to gradually fade the shock collar away so the dog behaves when it isn't there. With positive reinforcement, it is easy to fade the reinforcement away so eventually the dog will respond to you, with or without the reinforcer. It is also very easy to replace one type of reinforcer with another; we will look at how to do this in more detail in Chapter 6.

Finally, using pain to train is not a humane method when other options are available that are just as scientifically valid and don't risk the negative consequences. Just because it may (or may not!) take longer to see results with positive reinforcement–based methods, that doesn't mean they are less effective or useless. You always have alternatives available to you, even if those alternatives aren't "convenient" or you don't believe you have the time to put into using them. If you can't physically control your dog on walks, find ways to exercise your dog at home until you teach him how to walk properly on leash. If your dog is reactive toward other dogs, work through a counter-conditioning program with a behaviorist; if that isn't possible, you may have to give up taking him to the dog park and stop leaving him unsupervised in the yard where he can run the fence trying to attack other dogs who pass by. If you truly can't make the time to train your dog or are physically unable to manage your dog, get help. There are many trainers, behaviorists, and dog walkers who can assist you with your dog. If you are afraid of your dog or losing control of him, you might need to reconsider whether he is truly the right dog for your family. Using painful training methods to compensate for your fear will only make matters worse; your dog won't understand why you are worried. He will only know you are constantly anxious around him, and sometimes that anxiety leads to pain for him. There are always options other than inflicting pain on your dog; the question is whether you choose to explore and utilize them.

[Author's note: The terms "reward" and "correction" are usually used in everyday dog training discussions, instead of the scientifically correct terms "reinforcer" and "punisher." Because this isn't a book on learning theory, the more common terms "reward" and "correction" will be used for the remainder of the book.]

The four stages of learning

Regardless of which quadrant of operant conditioning you use, learning a new behavior is rarely an instantaneous event. Most learning occurs in stages, and never as a series of precisely predictable improvements. Training classes may get your dog through the first stage of learning, but you will need to keep working with him long after the class ends to get through the rest of the learning stages for every behavior you teach him.

The first stage in learning any new behavior involves acquiring new knowledge. This is the step most people think of when they think about "learning." The second stage involves using that new knowledge until the learner is fluent, or automatic, in its use. The third stage involves applying this new knowledge to other situations where it is relevant. The fourth stage involves maintaining the knowledge for the learner's lifetime so that the knowledge becomes part of the behavioral repertoire of the learner. Understanding these four stages of learning will help you move your dog forward in his training quickly and easily, and will help you maintain his learned skills for the rest of his life.

Let's look at the steps involved in teaching your dog to sit and how the four stages of learning apply to the process.

Acquisition

When you first start teaching your dog to sit, he has no idea what you expect him to do when you say "Sit." He must learn how to lift his head up and back, shift his weight back, lower his rump all the way to the floor, tuck his feet underneath himself, and move his tail into a comfortable position, all just to perform the simple behavior you call "Sit." Initially, you will have to help him figure out how to accomplish all this. It takes a lot of mental concentration for your dog to focus on what you want and move all his body parts correctly. He is acquiring new knowledge and is in the first stage of the learning process.

Fluency

Eventually, with enough repetitions and experience, your dog starts sitting on his own when you say the word "Sit." His actions become automatic when you say that word and he can begin to perform this behavior reliably, but only in familiar places with few distractions around. You don't have to help him into a sit now; he knows how to move his body into position. He is in the second stage of learning, where he becomes fluent in performing a sit behavior. He no longer has to concentrate as much physically to sit on cue and doesn't need quite so much help from you to perform the behavior.

Generalization

As your dog obtains even more experience with "Sit," you start cueing him to perform that behavior in different places or around different distractions. You ask for the behavior in the yard, in the park, or while someone comes through your front door. You are broadening your dog's experience with "Sit" and asking him to perform that behavior in many different situations. This is the third stage in the learning process. Dogs do not generalize new learned behaviors to different situations very well on their own (which is why so many dogs will do beautiful sits at home but can't do a single sit when they come to class); you have to show your dog that "Sit" means "Sit," no matter where he is or what is going on around him. This third stage is often the one that dog owners skip over during their training, yet it really should be the one that is given the most time and effort. Bob Bailey, a world-renowned animal trainer with decades of experience training many different species, points out that when you teach an animal a new behavior, you spend approximately 10% of your time actually teaching the behavior, and 90% of your time developing the animal's environmental confidence so he learns to perform the behavior any time, any place. In competitive obedience training, this is referred to as "proofing" the behavior.

Integration

Integrating the sit behavior into your dog's everyday life so he maintains that behavior is the fourth stage of learning. If you cue your dog to sit as a regular part of his lifestyle, your dog will continue to perform that behavior for the rest of his life. If, however, you quit asking for the behavior, it will start to weaken, and your dog will eventually begin to perform it less reliably. It isn't enough to spend a few weeks out of your dog's life attending a training class to teach him to sit. You have to incorporate this behavior into his everyday life to keep it strong. The more difficult the behavior is for your dog to perform, the more quickly it will deteriorate if you quit asking him to perform it on a regular basis.

Embrace the mistakes

Learning never happens in a perfectly straight progression of improvements. When you first start teaching your dog a new behavior, you will probably see him perform that behavior with flashes of brilliance, along with significant periods of averageness, and occasional moments of total disaster. As your dog gains a better understanding of the new behavior, his brilliant performances become more frequent and the mistakes become less frequent. His general learning trend is moving toward "perfection," even though there have been some highs and lows along the way. Ideally, your training plan will keep disasters to a bare minimum so your dog's learning happens as smoothly and quickly as possible, but no matter how careful you are in setting up your training sessions, your dog *will* make a mistake now and then. There is no such thing as 100% consistent, perfect performance for dogs (or people!). If your dog never appears to make a mistake, you are not actually teaching him anything new. You are merely practicing something he already knows well. Mistakes are a normal part of learning.

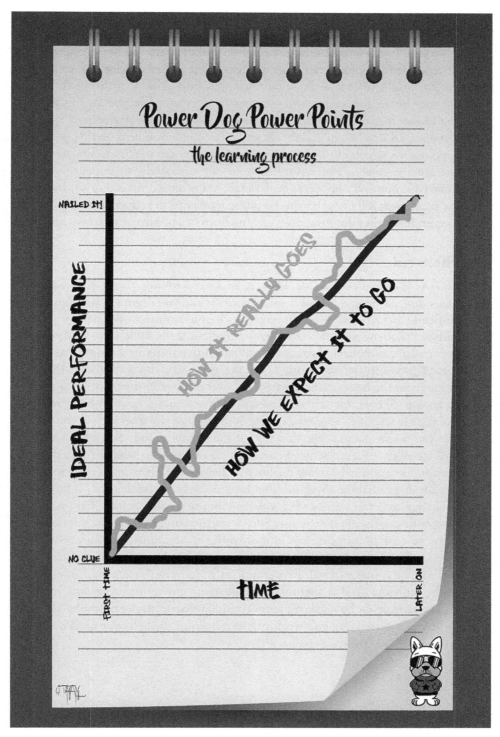

Learning isn't a predictable process; mistakes will happen along the way, so make the most of them!

The peaks and valleys of learning are nothing more than pieces of information that will allow you to assess what your dog does or doesn't understand at any particular point in the training process. If you look at mistakes as information to help you refine your training, you will continue to improve your dog's understanding of the behavior you are teaching him. For example, if you are working on teaching your dog to sit and he performs brilliantly in your home, but seems to forget what "Sit" means when you are in your front yard, you can look at this "mistake" as your dog's way of telling you either: (1) that he doesn't understand that he can and should sit on cue even when he is outside, or (2) that he isn't motivated enough to sit when he is out there. You can use this information to set up future training sessions where you help your dog successfully sit in your front yard. Eventually, your dog will only occasionally make mistakes when cued to sit, no matter where he is, and you will know how to keep him motivated to perform in many different situations. Embrace your dog's mistakes, and use them in a positive way to help him learn.

The 80% rule

Sometimes it is difficult to decide when to make the training more challenging for your power dog, particularly as his fluency increases and you begin to train him around more difficult distractions. One handy yardstick you can use to decide when to add more difficult challenges to the training environment is the **80% rule**. Cue your dog to perform whatever behavior you are working on five times in a training session. If your dog can perform the behavior: (1) the *first* time, (2) with a *single* cue, (3) in the *manner you want* the behavior performed, (4) four out of five times (*80%*) in a single training session, 5) over *three or four separate training* sessions, he is probably ready for you to make the training more challenging so his behavioral fluency will continue to improve. You might increase the duration of the behavior, the value of the environmental distractions, or the distance between you and your dog while he is performing the behavior, to continue building his fluency. Be honest! There is no prize for trying to force your dog to handle situations that he isn't ready for yet. It's okay if he can't do a behavior four out of five times when you test him; that's simply information that lets you know your dog needs more experience with the conditions he is training under now before you ask him to perform in more difficult situations. Just keep working at that same level of difficulty until he can be successful at least 80% of the time. If he can't perform even one successful repetition in a training session, that information tells you he probably needs a slightly less challenging environment to work in at this point in his learning, or he needs more motivation to perform the behavior. Make the environment less distracting and work awhile longer on the behavior until he is truly ready to handle more difficult challenges.

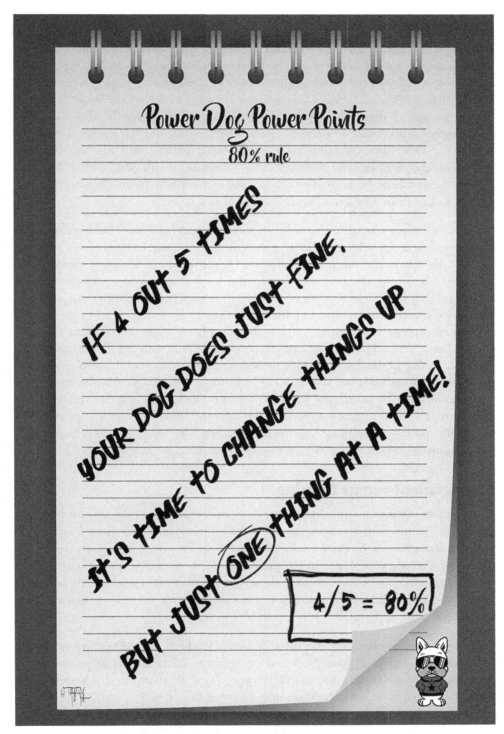

Keeping the 80% rule in mind will help you keep your dog's training moving forward at an appropriate pace.

Knowing versus doing

Training a dog always involves a certain amount of guesswork, especially when you expect a dog to behave one way and he behaves another way instead. You must rely on the imperfect method of observing his outward behavior to guess whether or not learning has actually occurred, since you have no way to peek inside his skull and see the microscopic changes that occur in the brain as learning physically takes place. The 80% rule helps you make an educated guess whether your dog has learned a behavior or not. But even when your dog has learned a behavior, he is still a living, thinking, feeling, independent animal, and there is no guarantee he will perform that behavior each and every time he is cued to do so. You aren't 100% perfect performing any learned behavior, so why would you expect your dog to be?

Many things affect whether a dog will perform a learned behavior. The dog might not be feeling well, or something in the environment might be interfering with his ability to perform the behavior. Stress may be affecting his performance. You may not be giving your dog clear, consistent cues, causing confusion. A dog also might not perform a learned behavior simply because he isn't motivated enough to perform at that particular moment. Motivation reflects what is most important to a dog at any given point in time and the amount of effort he is willing to put into gaining what is important to him. Your dog doesn't choose to avoid performing a behavior just to get even with you for something that happened earlier in the day or because he wants to make you mad. Lack of motivation simply means that from your *dog's* point of view, there isn't enough value in earning the reward or avoiding the correction for him to perform the learned behavior you cued him to perform. He may know how to perform the behavior, but still not do it because he isn't sufficiently motivated. Learning how to effectively motivate your dog will help you train more effectively and efficiently. We will consider motivators in more detail in Chapter 6.

Management versus training

Management involves manipulating your dog's environment to influence his behavior and is a key component of empowerment training. It can provide a quick fix for many problem behaviors so you can retain your sanity while working through the slower process of teaching your dog new, acceptable behaviors. Your dog doesn't learn how to behave appropriately by management alone, but you can often get immediate behavioral results that will help the learning process along if you incorporate management techniques along with training.

Let's say you have a power dog who, for several years, has been allowed to jump on anyone who walks through your door. Now you are trying to teach him to sit politely when guests come into your home. You must teach your dog to sit, to stay in that position until released, and to ignore people coming into your home to achieve this training goal. That's a lot to learn! To speed up the learning process and minimize confusion, you should teach the new door-greeting behaviors while simultaneously using environmental management to prevent him from continuing to jump on guests while he's learning. There are many different ways to manage your dog's behavior so he can't jump on people. Putting him on a leash so you can physically control him *before* your guests come in or putting him in another room when guests arrive, so he doesn't even have access to those people until he has calmed down, are just two options to manage his door-greeting behavior. You are using management to remove the opportunity for him to jump. If you allow him to continuing jumping on people at the door while simultaneously trying to teach him to sit when guests arrive, you will confuse him. If you want your dog to eventually learn a new behavior that is reliable, but you don't have time to teach, be sure to manage the environment so the old behaviors can't be practiced. Training takes time, particularly when you are trying to change a behavior your dog has engaged in for a long time. If you prevent your dog from doing the unacceptable behavior at the same time you are teaching him a new, acceptable one, you will change his behavior more quickly and minimize frustration for both of you.

Environmental management is also an easy way to keep dogs from learning bad habits in the first place. If shoes are put away where your dog can't get to them, he can never learn that chewing on them is fun. If he is never allowed to jump on company, he's not as likely to do that to get attention. Managing your dog's environment so that he is only able to do what you want him to do is a relatively easy way to develop good behaviors in your dog. But, of course, reality prevents us from managing our dog's environment that closely. You might forget to put your shoes in the closet, and guests might encourage your dog to jump up on them. In spite of your best intentions, your dog may develop bad habits. But if you develop a good training plan and combine that with the most consistent environmental management possible in your home, you can nip bad habits in the bud and help your power dog behave in ways that make him a true joy to have as part of the family.

What they learn first, they learn best

Think about how you want to interact with your power dog after he has learned what you expect of him. Do you want to be forced to raise your voice and move like a bad break dancer to get your dog's attention and response? Or do you want to be able to give your dog instructions in a normal, conversational tone of voice and use calm, clear, and simple physical cues when necessary? There is a huge difference between being genuine and being crazy when you train and reward your dog. There certainly are times when whooping and hollering in excitement might be appropriate to let your dog know just how awesome he is, but most of the time, a simple, sincere show of affection, verbal praise, and other appropriate rewards are the best fit with the businesslike attitude of the typical power dog. If you start off working with your dog in the manner you would like to work with him for his lifetime, he will never know any other way to interact with you. If you raise your voice and jump around when you are first teaching him a behavior, he will eventually expect that type of behavior from you every time the two of you interact.

In moments of stress, behavior deteriorates. Stress can by created by things the dog wants to obtain or things the dog wants to avoid. Excitement and fear are both forms of stress and can interfere with your dog's performance. Under sufficient stress, learned behaviors can deteriorate to the way they were performed when they were first learned. What does this mean for dog training? If you had to yell, jump around, and wave cookies to get your dog's attention when you were first teaching him to pay attention to you, then you may have to resort to those behaviors to get his attention when he is under extreme stress, because his attention behavior deteriorated to its earlier state. This is true even if you eventually showed your dog that you could quietly and calmly cue him to give you attention later in the training process. Start teaching any behavior in a calm, conversational tone, with confidence, sincerity, and the minimum amount of extra body language possible. This approach will set a behavioral foundation that will increase the chances you can avoid needing histrionics or excess emotion to get your dog to perform when he is under stress.

Say what you mean, mean what you say

Inconsistent use of cues is another reason your dog might not behave the way you expect him to behave. Dogs don't understand human language the same way we do. Consider the phrase "Sit down." If I told you to sit down, you would probably understand I want you to assume a seated position. But if your dog already understands the behaviors you want when you say "Sit" and "Down" separately, he might respond very differently if you cue him to "Sit down." He *should* understand your phrase "Sit down" as a two-link behavior chain: first a sit, followed immediately by a down. Therefore, one way your dog may respond would be to sit, then lie down. If you actually wanted him to sit when you said "Sit down," you might think your dog didn't do what you told him to do because he ended up lying down. But in reality, your dog did *exactly* what you told him to do.

Another possible response from your dog when you say "Sit down" is to simply sit. You probably wouldn't think of this as an incorrect response to your cue "Sit down," because you know you actually *intended* for him to sit. But you actually *told* him to sit and then lie down. When your dog doesn't lie down, it means that either your dog doesn't actually understand the "down" cue yet or, for some reason, he didn't perform the down behavior. Either way, if you don't help your dog lie down, you are teaching him he doesn't need to lie down each and every time you cue him to "Down." A third possible response from your dog may be that he lies down without sitting; this is also incorrect, based on the specific words you used to cue him.

Words have very specific meanings to your dog, so you need to be sure you use your training words carefully and consistently to help your dog perform behaviors reliably. Say exactly what you mean, and mean exactly what you say. If you want him to sit, tell him "Sit." If you follow that rule, your dog will have an easier time doing what you want him to do. Pick a unique, distinct cue for each behavior you teach him, and then use those cues consistently. For example, don't use the cue "Down" to mean lie down in some situations, and to get off the sofa in other situations. The specific words you use don't really matter; you can teach your dog to come to you when he hears the word "Jeep" and to sit when he hears the word "Mustang" if you want. As long as you teach your dog the exact behavior you expect when you say a particular word, and consistently use that word to initiate that one behavior only, your dog will understand what you expect him to do. The same rule applies to physical cues; use one discrete motion for each discrete behavior you want him to perform. If you point your finger to the floor to cue your dog to sit, use a different physical cue to tell him to lie down. Be as consistent as possible with your cue to help your dog distinguish the cue from all the other motions you do throughout the day.

Protect your cues by using them only when you can help your dog complete the desired behavior if he doesn't do it on his own; if you can't help him, don't give him the cue in the first place. In this way, your words and signals will retain their meaning to your dog and he will be more likely to respond to them reliably. Your power dog will thank you for eliminating this source of confusion for him!

The stress of stress

There are many similarities between how people and dogs learn, including how stress affects the process. Have you ever "drawn a blank" during an interview or exam, or "choked" when asked to perform some type of behavior in front of an audience (e.g., playing music, reciting a poem from memory, or playing in a golf tournament)? If so, you know firsthand how stress can directly impact performance. The biochemicals that are associated with stress cause your brain to go into "survival mode" at these times. Your ability to recall and act upon learned behaviors is drastically diminished and your behavior (or lack of behavior) reflects that. Stress can occur in anticipation of something really wonderful or something really awful; your brain doesn't know the difference between the two or that the danger signals it is receiving aren't always real threats to your wellbeing. Your brain and body simply respond to the biochemicals that start pumping into your system, and your instincts start to take over. Your brain and body get geared up to either fight the imaginary threat or flee from it. Your power dog's brain reacts in this same basic manner. It shouldn't be a surprise that when your dog starts to get excited, whether he is anticipating something positive or something negative, his ability to respond appropriately to learned cues often seems to fade away. Arousal can also lead to aggressive responses in any dog. Arousing a dog with an ancestry based in fighting or guarding and protecting can be far more dangerous than arousing a dog with an ancestry based in other types of work. Always keep your training sessions as calm as possible to help your dog learn; if you can't keep your cool, don't train your dog.

Never start any game with a young power dog, or allow him to start any game or behavior with another animal, that wouldn't be appropriate for him to do when he is an adult. Avoid any activity that arouses him to the point that he stops listening to you. For example, playful wrestling that arouses your puppy and encourages him to behave aggressively and bite you can create a problem when he is an adult; that playful behavior and puppy nipping can quickly escalate into full-blown aggression and serious bites from a much larger, stronger adult dog whom you can no longer physically control. Arousal and stress need to be constantly monitored to keep your power dog in the right frame of mind to listen to you and respond to your cues.

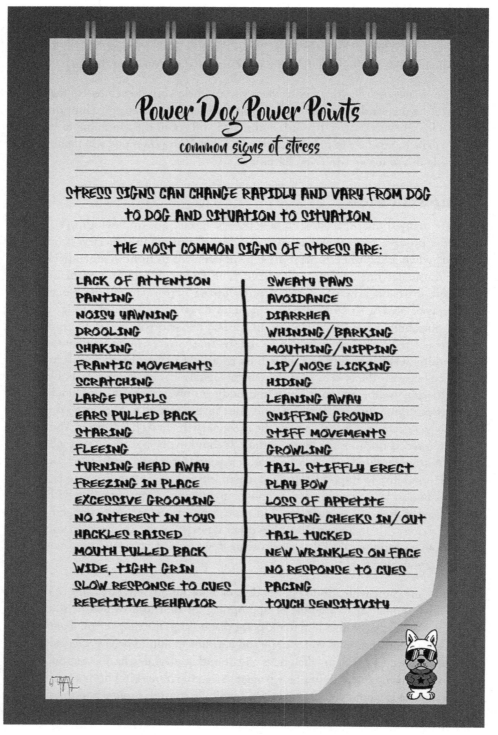

Power Dog Power Points
common signs of stress

STRESS SIGNS CAN CHANGE RAPIDLY AND VARY FROM DOG TO DOG AND SITUATION TO SITUATION.

THE MOST COMMON SIGNS OF STRESS ARE:

LACK OF ATTENTION	SWEATY PAWS
PANTING	AVOIDANCE
NOISY YAWNING	DIARRHEA
DROOLING	WHINING/BARKING
SHAKING	MOUTHING/NIPPING
FRANTIC MOVEMENTS	LIP/NOSE LICKING
SCRATCHING	HIDING
LARGE PUPILS	LEANING AWAY
EARS PULLED BACK	SNIFFING GROUND
STARING	STIFF MOVEMENTS
FLEEING	GROWLING
TURNING HEAD AWAY	TAIL STIFFLY ERECT
FREEZING IN PLACE	PLAY BOW
EXCESSIVE GROOMING	LOSS OF APPETITE
NO INTEREST IN TOYS	PUFFING CHEEKS IN/OUT
HACKLES RAISED	TAIL TUCKED
MOUTH PULLED BACK	NEW WRINKLES ON FACE
WIDE, TIGHT GRIN	NO RESPONSE TO CUES
SLOW RESPONSE TO CUES	PACING
REPETITIVE BEHAVIOR	TOUCH SENSITIVITY

Understanding common stress signs will help you manage your dog's state of mind and ability to learn.

The Humane Hierarchy

Dr. Susan Friedman, in her article "What's Wrong with This Picture? Effectiveness Is Not Enough," proposed a hierarchy for dealing with animal behavior that has since been accepted as the preferred way to approach dog training and behavioral modification by several professional organizations, including the Certification Council for Professional Dog Trainers and the Canadian Veterinary Medical Association. Usually referred to as the Humane Hierarchy, this approach attempts to change established behaviors using the most humane methods possible to effect the change, and is also useful to follow when teaching new behaviors. The goal is to go only as far up the hierarchy as absolutely necessary to obtain the desired behavioral result.

There are six levels in Friedman's Humane Hierarchy. The hierarchy starts with making sure the dog's physical needs have been met. A sick, underfed, or under-exercised dog isn't going to learn as quickly or easily as one who is healthy and physically active; in some cases, poor health is the cause of certain types of undesirable behaviors. The next level involves managing the dog's environment to encourage or prevent certain behaviors from occurring. Again, management doesn't actually teach the dog how to behave, but it makes it very difficult for the dog to act in an undesirable way, or removes the environmental triggers that cause a dog to behave inappropriately in the first place. The final four levels of the hierarchy progress through actual training approaches, starting with positive reinforcement techniques that focus on rewarding behaviors the dog does that you want him to repeat in the future, and ending with positive punishment techniques that punish the dog for behaviors you don't want him to do so he won't repeat them in the future. The closer you get to the positive punishment strategies, the more force and physical discomfort is involved. The goal of using this hierarchy is to go only as far up the levels as is necessary to achieve the desired behavioral changes or teach new behaviors. The information in this book follows this hierarchy. In the remaining chapters, we will look at the health of your power dog and general exercise suggestions, followed by management techniques for some of the most common problems power dog owners encounter with their dogs and training exercises designed to make life with your power dog more enjoyable for both of you.

6

The Magic of Motivation

The dog's agenda is simple, fathomable, overt: I want. "I want to go out, come in, eat something, lie here, play with that, kiss you." There are no ulterior motives with a dog, no mind games, no second-guessing, no complicated negotiations or bargains, and no guilt trip or grudges if a request is denied.

Caroline Knapp, author, Pack of Two: The Intricate Bond Between People and Dogs

Knowing how to properly motivate your dog in order to bring out the best in him is critical to training success. It is unrealistic to expect your dog to do what you ask him to do simply because you ask him to do it. Even though it is a rather romantic fiction that a dog should work simply to please his owner, the truth is, no dog will work just because he is told to do so, not even a devoted power dog. He needs to gain something from working for you that he wants or needs. What he gains may be your attention, a treat, the opportunity to do something else he likes to do, or the ability to avoid something he doesn't like, but he needs to gain something when he does what you ask him to do, or he won't do it in the first place. Like human learners, your dog needs to be interested in some aspect of what you are teaching him in order for him to learn. Motivating your dog is all about figuring out what rewards he is willing to work for and then using those things to enhance your dog's learning and performance, another key component of empowerment training.

Every time you work with your dog, you are competing against everything else in his environment for his attention. You will rarely be the most exciting thing around; there will almost always be things that your dog finds more exciting than you, particularly when you are outside. You will never move the same way as a squirrel or another dog would move, no matter how crazy you act. You will never sound like a squeaky toy or another dog barking, even if you scream nutty baby talk at the top of your lungs. You will never be chewy like a tennis ball. And 99.999% of the time, you will never smell as inviting as a dead, rotting animal carcass. So to expect to be the most interesting or exciting thing in your dog's life all of the time is not realistic. Squirrels, strangers, toys, other dogs, balls, and dead, stinking animals are all potentially far more exciting and interesting to your power dog than you will ever be. But fortunately, you don't have to be more exciting than other things competing for his attention and effort to effectively train him; you simply need to be more *valuable* to him than the other things competing for his attention. You can become more valuable than everything else by controlling his access to the other interesting, exciting things he wants. Becoming the gatekeeper for access to whatever your dog is willing to work for makes you more valuable than any of those other things and helps you motivate your dog to do whatever you ask, in exchange for the access he wants to those other exciting things. Building this value requires careful attention to reward selection, consistent and fair use of his rewards, and patience. You must prove to your dog that when he looks to you for direction and does what you tell him to do, you will give him access to something that is worth the effort he made for you.

Now that you understand the basics of how dogs learn and how to use rewards and corrections effectively in training, you should spend some time figuring out what types of rewards your power dog is willing to work for, so you can start building up a collection of effective motivational tools to use for training.

Who chooses the reward?

If you want to become more valuable than anything else in the world in your power dog's eyes, you have to identify rewards that will motivate him to work with you. Who chooses what these rewards are? Your dog, of course! It doesn't matter how interesting you think a toy is or how well a certain type of treat has worked as a reward for someone else's dog. If *your* dog isn't motivated enough to work for that particular treat or toy, it won't be an effective reward. Similarly, your dog also determines what constitutes a correction. If you frown at your dog and he rolls on his back and submissively urinates, you know that your body language is a powerful correction from his point of view, even if you didn't *intend* to correct him with your unhappy appearance. Or you may verbally correct your dog in your harshest voice, yet he completely ignores you. In this case, your "mean voice" doesn't work as a correction for your dog, so it is pointless to continue raising your voice. Training your dog will go much more quickly and successfully if you remember your dog is the one in charge of identifying potential rewards and corrections.

What can be used as a reward?

Nearly everything your dog wants in his life can be used as a reward! Most dog owners think of praise or treats when they think of rewards, but this is only the very tip of the reward iceberg. Think like your power dog and suddenly the world becomes one gigantic cookie jar filled with countless rewards for you to use! Watch what your dog chooses to pay attention to when he is left alone to do whatever he wants. Dogs don't lie about what interests them, so why waste time guessing at what your dog might be willing to work for, when he is showing you these things all the time? As long as: (1) it is safe for both you and your dog to interact with, (2) your dog's access to it can be controlled during training, (3) it can promptly be delivered after a correct performance (or withheld after an incorrect performance), and (4) it is practical to use, almost anything that interests your dog can be used as a reward. With careful observation, you can begin to build an extensive collection of non-food rewards to use when training. You can even include "naughty" behaviors in your reward list, too—digging holes, sniffing, and barking can all be used as rewards, as long as *you* can start and end the behavior on *your* terms and your dog is allowed to engage in the behavior *after* he has performed a behavior you asked him to do. The opportunity to interact with distractions in a safe, appropriate manner can be a powerful motivator for your power dog. Make a list of these potential distracting rewards and rate them according to just how distracting they are to your dog so you can refer to the list as you train. If you try to prevent your dog from ever engaging in "naughty" behaviors (i.e., those that are safe for him to do but that you find unacceptable), you will not decrease his desire to do them; instead, the longer he is denied any opportunity to engage in the behaviors, the stronger his desire may become to engage in them. Most of these behaviors are simply normal dog behaviors that are unacceptable to most dog owners. Giving your dog the chance to just be a dog is a powerful way to motivate him to do what you ask.

Food as rewards

Most of us are familiar with using dog treats to train dogs. Food is a powerful intrinsic motivator; you don't typically have to encourage a healthy dog to eat. Every dog alive today is food-motivated to some extent, since he is obviously motivated to eat enough food to survive. With a little creativity and perseverance, you can find some type of food to use during training with even the most finicky eater. Treats are often the first type of reward you use when teaching your dog a new behavior because they can be given quickly and are relatively easy to use during training sessions.

Be creative when considering treats to use for training. For power dogs who aren't picky about what they eat, you have a whole range of treat options available. Experiment with a selection of treats to see which ones really interest your dog. Instead of prepackaged dog treats, try treats like skinless chicken, string cheese, homemade dog treats, dried apples, sweet potato chips, raw carrot slices, dehydrated beef heart, blueberry bagels, green tripe, dried squid, or anything else you can think of that is safe for him to eat. Never give your dog food containing chocolate, cocoa, raisins, onions, xylitol (an artificial sweetener commonly found in chewing gum and some types of peanut butter), or high amounts of fat or salt. For dogs with severe food allergies, you can try to get their regular diet in an alternative form for use when training. For example, if you feed a special kibble diet, see if that same diet is available in a canned version, which you can let the dog lick off of a spoon as a training reward; alternatively, there are dog treat recipes available online that use ground kibble instead of flour that can be adapted to make special-dietary-needs training treats. If you truly have a finicky eater who is not interested even in cooked chicken or beef with excess fat removed, low-fat cheese cubes, or water-packed tuna, you can use the dog's regular kibble as a reward. Since your dog eats enough to stay alive, his regular food should work as a last-ditch food reward. Remember, no matter how tasty *you* might think a particular treat is or should be, it is your *dog* who is in charge of deciding which treats will work best as food rewards, and particularly which treats will work in stressful situations. Because stress tends to reduce a dog's desire to eat, the ordinary dry treats that work well at home for training may not do the trick under the stress of training classes; having some real meat or cheese options in your goodie bag will usually overcome the normal amounts of stress your dog may feel in class and allow you to use treats effectively there.

In addition to taking your dog's food preferences into account when selecting treats, it is also important to keep in mind how easy the treats will be to prepare, carry around for training, break into appropriately-sized tiny training tidbits without leaving behind messy crumbs, actually give to the dog, and how many you can give during a training session without upsetting your dog's stomach or making him thirsty. Create a mix of several different treats your dog likes and you will have considerable flexibility when training. No matter what type of treats you use, spend a few moments before training to break up your treats into tiny pieces, toss them in a plastic baggie to keep your training bag or pocket clean, and you will be ready to train!

Less is more when using food as a training reward. A treat should simply be a *taste* of something special, not an entire meal in every bite. The portion size of most prepackaged dog treats is far larger than necessary for use as a training reward. Even for larger power dogs, a treat reward should only be about the size of the tip of your little finger or a green pea. Your dog should be able to eat it in a second or two, with little, if any, chewing required. By keeping the treat size small, you will be able to train longer before your dog gets bored with the treat or actually gets physically full. You can also use richer, more calorie-dense treats without making your dog fat or upsetting his stomach, because you are only giving very tiny portions of these treats during a training session. If you use raw foods as treats, be sure to handle them carefully to avoid spreading foodborne illnesses. Freeze tiny training session portions so you can thaw and use up the entire portion in one session to minimize potential spoilage problems. If you are using cheese sticks, cut the sticks into several sections and only take one section out of the refrigerator at a time. And, regardless of the treats you are using, be sure to remove any leftovers from your pockets after training to protect your clothes from dog teeth and your washing machine from a gooey mess!

This one prepackaged treat can easily be broken into two dozen training-sized treats.

Toys as rewards

Toys are also potentially powerful rewards for power dogs if they are used correctly. Think outside the traditional toy box when identifying power dog toys; toys can be anything you and your dog can safely interact with together. Just because you wouldn't think of an item as a toy doesn't mean your dog won't see it as the greatest thing in the world to play with! Pay attention to the objects your dog chooses to play with on his own. Not all of them will be well-suited to use for training, but you might find a few options. Your dog is in charge of toy selection—your job is to be sure the toy can be used safely and that the toy is only used under your supervision.

Many power dogs are interested in toys that move. Balls, tug toys, and other toys that can be moved around in an erratic manner and can withstand the wear and tear inflicted by a powerful dog are all potentially good toy choices for most power dogs. Hard toys (Nylabones®️ and other hard plastic toys) aren't appropriate for training rewards because if you "toss" the toy toward your dog to deliver it to him and he catches it, his teeth might get damaged. And if he doesn't actually catch it, he might get hit in the face and get hurt or scared. Give your dog hard toys to chew on between training sessions, and use soft plastic, fabric, fleece, or rubber toys for training.

When making your training toy selection, keep in mind how easy it will be to carry and conceal the toy from your dog during training, whether you will be able to hold on to the toy while your dog plays with it, and how messy it will be after your dog covers it in drool. And expect that your dog will destroy a few toys over his lifetime. Toys are meant to be enjoyed, so buy some inexpensive ones with little or no stuffing and don't worry if they get worn out or destroyed during training.

No dog enjoys having a toy shoved in his face repeatedly, particularly if it isn't even a toy he likes. That's not playing with your dog—that's assaulting him! An easy way to invite your power dog to play with any toy is to ask yourself "What would a bunny or squirrel do?" and then move his toy around accordingly. Mimic the motion of wildlife slowly moving away from your dog in a controlled manner, standing ground and not moving at all as your dog approaches, and erratically bolting away when approached too closely. Your dog is hard-wired to be aroused by these types of movements, so the more you can make a toy act like an animal, the more likely your power dog will be interested in it. This type of play requires you to be actively involved in the game, too. Playing with your dog will help your relationship tremendously. You will have the opportunity to work on any bite inhibition issues that may exist, teach your dog self-control, and reinforce the idea that *you* provide all the fantastic stuff in your dog's life, like his toys. Besides that, it's just plain fun to have a good game with your dog!

Verbal and physical interaction as rewards

Most of the rewards your power dog receives for performing the behaviors you ask of him can originate from you. Because you will always have your hands and your voice with you when you are interacting with your dog, it is certainly worth the time and effort it takes to identify ways to talk to and touch your dog to motivate and reward him for correct behavior.

Verbal interaction with your dog can be a powerful reinforcer, if you take the time to build value into your voice. Humans are verbal creatures, and we often verbally interact with our dogs as if they are also human. Because you use your voice so much, your dog may learn to tune you out. He hears you all the time, so your everyday voice isn't all that special. Verbal rewards are only effective if you change the pitch, tone, or presentation of your voice so it stands out against the daily verbal barrage your dog experiences. Higher-pitched, "squeaky" sounds delivered in a quiet manner often catch a power dog's ear, presumably because these sounds are similar to prey sounds. Verbally praising your dog in a higher-pitched voice than normal will help the praise stand out against the background noise. This doesn't mean you have to "baby talk" or be dramatic, but just raise the pitch a little to make it different from your everyday voice when you praise, while keeping it calm and sincere. Predators also tune in to the quiet sounds of prey moving in the environment; many times quiet praise gets more attention than loud praise. You can reward any behavior any time with praise because you always have your voice with you, so it is definitely worth learning how to talk to your dog in a way that is truly rewarding to him.

You can also influence your dog's emotional state by the way you talk to him. For example, if you say "Good dog!!" in a high-pitched, upbeat manner, your dog will probably act excited by the praise. But if you say "G-o-o-o-d dog" in a low-pitched, slow, drawn-out manner, your dog may very well start to relax. The speed and pitch of your praise need to reflect the emotional response you want from your dog. Creating emotional associations with particular phrases and styles of praise can be very useful when you are training. Happy and excited praise can be used for active behaviors, such as coming when called, and soothing praise can be used for static behaviors, such as staying in one spot. The old adage "It's not *what* you say, but *how* you say it" is very true in dog training, so experiment with your voice to find styles that work best for various types of behaviors you want from your dog. Just remember not to be overly emotional or crazy with your cues; you don't want to have to resort to begging and carrying on to get your dog to respond to your cues when he is under stress.

Developing truly pleasurable forms of physical contact and play with power dogs can be a little trickier than developing rewarding verbal skills. You need to balance motivating your dog against overexciting him. Although there are always individual exceptions, many power dogs don't really seem to enjoy prolonged, stroking-type physical contact. But there are many different ways to actually pet your dog. Watch him while you pet him. Does he really seem to enjoy the contact, or is he merely tolerating being petted? Lip licking, pinning his ears back, ducking slightly to avoid contact, and vigorous shaking after you get done petting him are all subtle signs of stress that suggest your dog might not really be enjoying the type of physical contact you are giving him. Experiment with various ways to pet your power dog and watch his behavior closely to find out exactly how *he* enjoys being touched. You may find he enjoys being scratched at the base of the tail or behind the ears, but doesn't really enjoy being patted on the head or stroked down his back. You may also find that certain types of physical contact get him too excited to maintain self-control. Physical contact with your dog is a handy reward because as long as you have a hand free, you have way to reward your dog without making him lose control.

Environmental rewards

Treats, toys, praise, and pats are familiar rewards, but when you expand the definition of a reward to include *anything* your dog is willing to work for, your reward list becomes nearly limitless! The easiest way to develop a list of possible **environmental rewards** to use when training is to simply pay attention to what your dog likes to do when he's just hanging out, "being a dog." Being allowed to go outside, sniffing "pee-mail" at the corner fire hydrant, digging a hole at the beach, sleeping on the sofa, and a myriad of other interactions with the environment can all potentially be used as rewards when you are training your power dog. For example, if you cue your dog to give you eye contact when you are out for a walk and he does, you can immediately release him with a cue to go read his pee-mail on the fire hydrant for a few moments as his reward for giving you attention. Allowing your dog time to simply be a dog and do what he chooses to do (as long as you make sure it is safe) is very motivating and can be a powerful reward. It also provides a mental health boost for your dog. No matter how well-trained he is, your dog is still a dog and needs a chance to just be a dog sometimes. As long as you can control your dog's access to what he wants so he only gets it after he's performed a correct behavior, and the item or activity is safe for both you and your dog, you can theoretically use it as a reward.

You can use other trained behaviors as rewards, too. If your power dog loves to retrieve tennis balls, you can cue him to sit and, as soon as he does, release him to retrieve a ball. Soon he will be as excited to sit as he is to retrieve, because he will associate the sit with the reward of being allowed to retrieve. This type of reward is particularly useful if you are training your power dog for a competitive dog sport; you can string multiple sports-related behaviors together, using ones your power dog really enjoys as rewards for ones he doesn't enjoy as much.

To help you communicate clearly and consistently to your dog that he is allowed to have a particular environmental reward, come up with a cue for interacting with each one. For example, in the hydrant-sniffing example above, you have identified the hydrant as a potential effective reward because you know he really likes to sniff it. You can use this as an environmental reward because you can control his access to it as you walk past it, it is safe for him to interact with, and you have a way to "give" the hydrant to him as a reward for correct behavior, simply by allowing him to go over to it. When you are walking past the hydrant and you aren't using it as a reward, simply keep walking and don't allow your dog to go over to it. Hold the leash short and, if necessary, move farther away from the hydrant as you pass it so your dog doesn't get to sniff it. But when you want to use the hydrant as a reward, cue your dog for a behavior and, immediately after he performs it correctly, tell him "Good dog! Now go read your pee-mail!" and release him to sniff the hydrant. He might be confused at first, especially if you usually don't allow him to sniff the hydrant. Go over to the hydrant with him and encourage him to sniff it. If you are consistent in saying nothing about the hydrant when you don't want him to sniff it and telling him to read his pee-mail when you want him to sniff, he will eventually understand the hydrant is only available to him when you give him permission to interact with it. You will be able to use the hydrant as a reward instead of worrying that your dog will pull your arm off trying to get to it every time you walk past. And, as an added bonus, if you actually let him sniff the hydrant once in a while, it won't be quite so interesting to him anymore. Forbidden objects are always more intriguing than ones that are more readily accessible. By using distractions as rewards, you can actually decrease the power some distractions hold over your dog.

When should the reward be given?

Timing is critical to effective dog training, so you need to be on your toes when you work with your dog. One of the easiest ways to improve your timing is simply to get organized *before* you start your training session. Have your rewards readily accessible before you start asking for behaviors. If you are using treats as rewards and can't get your hand in your pocket easily, keep them in a treat bag or put them in a bowl on a nearby table so you can grab them quickly. Have them cut into small pieces and ready to go. If you are using a toy as a reward, have it in your pocket, your waistband, or your armpit, ready to be tossed out. If you are going to let your dog outside as his reward, make sure you are training by the door so you can immediately let him out. If you can't get to the rewards quickly or something happens spontaneously that you want to reward, you can always immediately reward your dog with praise and physical interaction for a job well done. Some types of rewards, such as treats, may need to be prepared before training starts; the more quickly you reward a correct behavior, the faster your dog will associate his behavior with earning his reward. Ideally, the reward should be given the split second the correct behavior is performed, and withheld immediately if the correct behavior is not performed. Realistically, delivering or withholding the reward within a few seconds of the behavior is still more than quick enough for most dogs to associate the consequence with the behavior they just performed.

Where should the reward be given?

Dogs associate rewards and corrections most strongly with what they are performing at the very moment they receive the reward or correction, so it is important to pay attention to where you deliver the reward so you don't introduce extra behaviors or confusion into your training session. For example, if you are working on teaching your power dog to sit and are using a treat as the reward for a correct performance, you should deliver the treat in a way that allows him to get it without standing up. If you hold the treat away from your dog and he has to get up and walk a few steps to get the treat, you are rewarding the walking behavior more strongly than the sitting behavior, because he is actively walking at the precise moment he gets his treat. If you put the treat right down in front of his mouth so he can eat it while he is still sitting, you are more strongly rewarding the sit position, because he is still sitting at the moment he gets his treat. If your dog is working at a distance from you, toss a reward to him while he is still at a distance from you, instead of calling him back to you to get his reward. If you don't have a tossable reward to use, praise him while he is still at a distance, and then go to him if you want to deliver another type of reward. Pay attention to where you dog is when he gets his reward; the position should enhance what you are actually trying to teach him. Be sure your dog is still performing the correct behavior before you release him to go to his environmental reward.

How should the reward be delivered?

How you deliver rewards is also important. When you deliver any reward besides physical contact, touch your power dog before and during the delivery if at all possible. This contact helps build up the idea in his mind that you are quite literally connected with every reward in the universe, no matter what form that reward comes in. For example, give your dog a light pat or a quick scratch behind the ears while you feed him his treat if he is near enough for you to do so. If you release him to get an environmental reward, praise him as he goes to it.

Match the duration of the reward to the effort your dog puts forth to perform the behavior. The longer your dog has to concentrate on performing a behavior, or the more difficult the behavior is for him to perform, the longer the reward delivery should last. Combining different types of rewards is an easy way to increase the length of time your dog is rewarded for his behavior; combine a small treat with lots of verbal praise and physical contact to prolong the reward. Make a treat reward last longer by breaking it into even smaller pieces and feeding them one at a time to him. Aim to mark very special efforts with a full 30 seconds of continuous reward to maximize the impact on your dog's learning. This type of special reward session is often called a **jackpot**; think of it as the canine equivalent of being given a bonus for working extra hard on a special project at work. Jackpots should be used sparingly, just for those special moments when your dog has had a training breakthrough or performs a behavior phenomenally well. Since most people aren't good at guessing how long 30 seconds really is, sing the Final Jeopardy song from the TV game show *Jeopardy* to yourself while you reward your dog (or sing it out loud if that makes you and your dog happier!).

Training rewards should never be freely accessible to your dog when he isn't actually working with you to earn them. For example, many dogs have free access to toys at home. If your dog can play with his favorite toys any time he chooses simply by going to the toy box and picking one out, the value of those toys as training rewards is diminished. Why should he work for you to earn a toy that he can just as easily go get any time he wants it, without doing anything at all for you? Any toy you've identified as a possible training reward should be put away so your dog no longer has free access to it. He can still play with it, but only after he has done something for you to earn that toy. For example, if you are working on teaching your dog to sit on cue, cue your dog to sit; then, when he sits, give him his favorite toy to play with as his reward. Since absence makes the heart grow fonder, your dog will be quite willing to work for his toy because he still wants it, but no longer has free access to it. You can give your dog free access to hard chew toys, like Kong toys, sterilized bones, etc., because these are not safe to use as training rewards. Likewise, if you give your power dog a tasty treat every time you pass by the treat jar "just because," regardless of what he is doing at the time you give him the treat, his motivation to do something you want him to do just to earn that same treat will rapidly fade. But if you give him a treat only after he has done something you cue him to do, he will be much more motivated to work for you to earn his treat. Environmental rewards that your dog can't access when he is alone in your yard are the most useful. Keeping rewards scarce preserves their value as training tools.

Unpredictable rewards

The type of training reward your dog will earn from you shouldn't be predictable. He should only be able to predict that he will get something he wants from you after he performs a correct behavior. If you use treats to reward your dog after every successful performance when he is in the first stage of learning, you should begin to introduce other types of rewards, including just praise, as he starts to gain fluency with the behavior. If you continue to give him a treat every single time he performs the behavior once he understands what you expect of him, he may gradually begin to quit performing if he doesn't see that treat in your hand or smell it in your pocket, because he has associated the presence of a treat as part of the initial cue for that behavior. If you cue him to perform the behavior without the treat and he doesn't perform it, it may be because you have unintentionally changed your cue (from your dog's point of view). He is genuinely confused about what you expect him to do. It isn't because he will only perform for treats, but rather he has strongly linked the presence of the treat with the cue itself and he doesn't know what the cue means when you take the treat away. But if you start to vary the types of rewards you give him for a correct performance as soon as he has learned the behavior, he won't think of treats as part of the actual cue. This unpredictability will keep him interested and working hard to obtain his rewards, since he never knows if he is going to earn a super-duper environmental reward, a tasty treat, a nice-feeling butt scratch, or simply sincere praise for his efforts. Only two things will be predictable for your dog: (1) you will always reward acceptable behavior, even if that reward is simply praise or the opportunity to continue to perform, and (2) you will be unpredictable in the type of reward he receives for a job well done.

Why go through all this work to identify rewards?

Power dogs are excellent at calculating whether or not doing what you cue them to do is worth their time and effort. In general, a dog will engage in behaviors that get him something he wants or needs and will not engage in behaviors that don't get him something he wants or needs. Learning a behavior that results in a reward empowers the dog. Having a variety of motivators at your disposal will let you mix and match behaviors and rewards to achieve the best training results possible. The harder the behavior is for your dog to perform, the more desirable the reward should be for a correct performance. Keep your dog guessing what he will earn for his efforts by varying the rewards you use. This will keep learned behaviors strong. Take the time to figure out what your power dog wants most in life. This effort will ultimately save you time in your training program and keep your dog interested in working with you long after formal training classes end.

7

Exercise for Body and Brain

A dog in his kennel barks at his fleas; a dog hunting doesn't notice them.

Chinese proverb

[Author's note: Consult your physician and your veterinarian before starting any exercise program for you and your power dog.]

The third key to empowering your power dog is providing him the physical and mental exercise he needs to stay healthy. Exercise alone won't teach your dog how to behave, but it can help put him in the proper frame of mind to learn, and keep the excess pounds off him.

Physical exercise

Dogs who lack daily physical and mental exercise can become bored, frustrated, and more prone to inappropriate behavioral outbursts than those who get regular exercise. Most healthy dogs don't get nearly the amount of exercise that their ancestors used to get, yet their bodies (with the possible exception of some of the radically altered dogs like the modern English Bulldog) are still capable of doing very physical work. All dogs need some regular physical activity appropriate to their age and physical build; putting a dog out in the back yard alone or casually strolling around the block with him isn't really providing him exercise.

In addition to keeping your dog physically healthy, exercise can also have a positive influence on certain types of behaviors. Lore Haug, DVM, cites research that indicates 30 minutes of significant aerobic activity causes the body to produce enough of the various exercise-induced biochemicals to positively impact behavior. Boredom-related problem behaviors in particular can be positively influenced through exercise, combined with consistent management and effective training.

Exercise considerations

Before heading out the door to give your power dog some exercise, there are several things you need to consider so you can select the proper type of exercise for your dog.

How old is your dog?

Your power dog's age should play a role in the type of exercise you give him. If your dog is under 18 months old, you should avoid activities that involve repetitive jarring of the leg bones and joints. Growth plates in the long bones of the legs (the spots that lengthen as your dog gets taller) don't fuse shut until your puppy is finished growing "up," which can be between 15 and 18 months for the medium- to large-sized power breeds, and even later for some giant breeds. If those plates are injured while the puppy is still growing, the damage can affect the way his leg bones develop. Ligaments, tendons, and joints are also particularly vulnerable to injury in young puppies. You shouldn't jog with your puppy or let him jump over or off of things higher than his elbow joint, just to be safe. Ask your vet for advice about if and when it is safe to start jogging with your dog if that is something you want to do with him.

For geriatric dogs, slow the exercise down and shorten your sessions. Be sure your vet gives the green light to any activity you want to do with your older dog; just like people, old dogs can develop aches and pains that may make certain activities uncomfortable or unsafe. Sight and hearing might also become impaired, so some activities might become dangerous for your dog as he ages.

Physical traits

If your dog is **brachycephalic**, with a short, somewhat flattened muzzle like a Bulldog or Pug, his ability to breathe during strenuous physical activity may be impaired by his shortened muzzle and upturned nose. This is important to keep in mind during any strenuous activities you do with him. His ability to dissipate body heat by panting may also be decreased. Always be cautious and keep a close eye on your dog for signs of heat stress, heat exhaustion, and heat stroke. Carry cool (not cold) water with you when you exercise to keep your dog adequately hydrated and to cool him off if he starts to overheat.

If you own a giant power dog, like a Great Dane or Mastiff, you need to be particularly respectful of his joints since they carry a lot of weight around. Percussive exercise can damage joints at any age, so activities that don't require jumping or running might be better choices for a giant dog. They can also easily overheat due to their large size, so keep a close eye on them when it's warm out.

Weight

It's important that you keep your power dog at a healthy weight throughout his life, whether that is 30 pounds or 130 pounds; keeping extra weight off him is one way to maintain his quality of life for as long as possible. While a roly-poly puppy is certainly cute, that excess weight puts added stress on joints, tendons, and ligaments throughout the growing puppy's body. Talk with your veterinarian and your puppy's breeder to find out what the best weight is for your puppy and how many small meals to feed him each day. (Hint: The amount of food many of the dog food companies list on the back of their food bags might not be the appropriate amount for *your* puppy!) The temptation to put pounds on your power dog just to make him look even more impressive may be there, but resist it. A fat power dog just looks fat, not impressive. It may seem like an extra pound or two won't matter, but you have to remember that an extra five pounds of fat on a dog who should weigh 50 pounds represents an additional 10% of his body weight; that's quite a bit of extra weight to carry around. You should be able to see a slight waist (even in the giant breeds) when you look at your dog from the side or from above. You should also be able to feel his ribs without pushing too hard on his sides, and see at least a hint of muscle definition, even in the small power dogs.

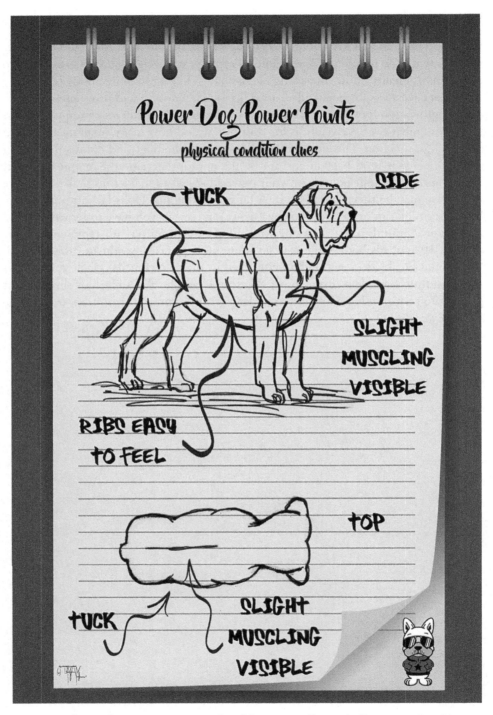

Even if your dog is a giant power dog, like a Mastiff, or a bulky power dog, like a Bulldog, you should be able to see or feel some muscle definition, his ribs should be relatively easy to feel, and at least a slight waist tuck should be apparent when looking at your dog both from the side and from the top.

Muzzles

If your dog has to wear a muzzle, harness, or other equipment when he is out in public, that may influence the type of exercise you can safely give him. If a muzzle is not correctly fitted, it can prevent him from panting, and he can overheat quickly on warm days or during prolonged activity. This type of equipment can also pose a hazard during activities where the muzzle can get caught on objects. If your dog wears this equipment because of breed-specific ordinances, you also need to check to see if these laws place any restrictions on places you can take your dog for exercise (e.g., the dog park).

Individual traits

Is your power dog reactive toward strangers or other dogs? Is he afraid of cars, trucks, or motorcycles? Has he been trained to walk politely or is he untrained? All of these factors can influence the type of exercise you do with your dog. Exercise should be a positive activity for both of you. If you own a power dog who likes to pull when walking on his leash, or barks at other dogs, or tries to greet every person he meets, you might be tempted to give up on taking him out for exercise altogether. It's hard to keep a solid mass of canine muscle under control when he hasn't been taught to behave appropriately in public. And, with some of the power breeds, it can also become socially uncomfortable when your dog acts out in public, whether he is being truly aggressive or overly friendly. Remember—most people you meet on your walks won't know how to tell the difference between a dog who is whining out of eagerness to meet a new human friend and one who is vocalizing out of aggression or fear. If your dog can't walk calmly with you and pass by other dogs and people without much more than a casual glance and acknowledgement, you need to manage where you take your dog for exercise. This might be inconvenient for you, but if your neighborhood is full of distractions your dog can't handle yet, you must be proactive and go somewhere less problematic to exercise your dog until he has learned the skills he needs to calmly handle these types of situations. Try walking in different neighborhoods, at different times of the day in your own neighborhood, or explore an out-of-the-way park with your dog. Eliminating the inconvenience of the extra time and effort this will take each day will be your motivation to train your dog to behave in public! You need to keep your dog from practicing the same unwanted behaviors over and over, while at the same time teaching him more acceptable behaviors, if you want to create permanent changes in his behavior. This applies to inappropriate behavior during exercise, too!

Your health and activity preferences

Your health and activity preferences are also an important part of creating an exercise plan for your power dog. If you don't enjoy jogging, you aren't going to enjoy jogging with your dog either, so jogging probably isn't a good choice of exercise for either of you. If you aren't healthy enough to go jogging, then it doesn't matter how much you would enjoy doing that with your dog; jogging still isn't an option to exercise him. Think about the types of exercise activities you enjoy and are physically able to do, and see if you can incorporate your dog into them in a way that will make it a workout for both of you. If you are thinking about which type of power dog to welcome into your family, your exercise preferences might influence that choice. If you want a power dog to take along as a jogging or hiking buddy every day, you should consider a breed that can handle extended aerobic activity; if you want a buddy to just casually stroll along the beach or around the neighborhood with, a power dog who doesn't require as much strenuous exercise would fit the job description. If you aren't physically able to exercise at all, you may need to hire a dog walker or dog exerciser to help keep your power dog healthy and happy.

Thinking outside the exercise box

The last thing to consider is all the different exercise activities available to you and your power dog besides the usual walking, jogging, cycling, and swimming most people think of when they think of canine exercise. Power breeds excel in a wide variety of dog sports and outdoor activities. Canine parkour (urban dog agility) is a relatively new activity that incorporates agility skills with everyday obstacles you can find when you are out with your dog. Parkour teaches a dog to jump over, crawl under, weave around, and balance on all types of objects that are readily available to anyone. There are several organizations that provide canine parkour training information to guide you. These organizations also host video competitions so you can show off your dog's amazing parkour skills right in your own neighborhood!

Another fun activity that combines mental and physical exercise is nose work, also sometimes called scent work. Your dog is taught to identify and find specific scents, similar to how law enforcement dogs are taught to find explosives and drugs. There are several organizations that sanction scent work competitions. Even if you never intend to compete, or your dog has behavioral issues that would prevent you from attending a trial, you can still train him to use his nose so you have a fun exercise game to play with him. Brachycephalic dogs can also do nose work, and the concentration and prolonged scenting behaviors required can wear your dog out quickly!

Carting can be done by any size power dog (carts are proportionate to the size of the dog) but is particularly fun to do with larger dogs. Many people over the centuries used dogs to pull carts to move people and goods around. Carting is a great way to give your dog exercise, as well as a useful job. Your dog can haul a few bags of yard waste to the curb for you, help the kids pick up toys in the yard, or pull your farmer's market veggies home. You can build your own cart or order one online.

Weight pulling is one activity that is closely associated with power breeds; they dominate and excel in this sport. There are several organizations that hold weight pulls, where dogs pull a wheeled cart on a hard surface, or a cart on runners through snow, a set distance in a set amount of time. The weight is increased after each successful round, until the dog can't complete his pull. Competition classes separate dogs by body weight. The dog who pulls the most weight relative to his body weight in each class wins. The dogs are completely in charge of how much weight they pull, because owners are not allowed to touch or force them in any way to get them to pull. Dogs are surprising powerful; a 9-pound Jack Russell Terrier, in proper physical condition and who enjoys the sport, can easily pull 200 pounds or more—over 22 times his body weight! The larger power breeds can pull absolutely incredible amounts of weight by comparison.

Canine carts have been used for centuries as a form of transportation in many parts of the world. Jack, a Rottweiler power dog mix, gets exercise pulling Jill, a Pug, and some fall yard decorations around in a cart.

There are many other nontraditional activities you and your power dog can do together to provide you both with physical exercise. Canicross, rollerblading, scootering, canine freestyle, hiking, competitive agility and obedience, horseback riding, and tracking are just some of the many things you two can enjoy together, so pick out an activity and get to it!

Stanley, a Boston Terrier, gets plenty of physical exercise while training for obedience competitions.

Even couch potatoes need exercise

It may be tempting to skip any type of regular exercise with the giant power breeds simply because they aren't known to voluntarily engage in extended periods of intense physical activity on their own very often. But that doesn't mean they don't need exercise, too! Mastiffs, Tosas, and similarly built power dogs are the sumo wrestlers of the canine world; they are built for short, powerful bursts of activity that require tremendous strength to do their traditional work. Once they make contact with their opponents, they use their sheer physical bulk and incredible power to win the contest, which rarely takes very long to do. Other power dogs, like Dobermans, Am Staffs, and even Boston Terriers, are more like canine mixed martial arts fighters. Their success depends on a combination of power, agility, and stamina to accomplish their traditional work. They may find themselves engaged in prolonged battles of strength and tenacity with their opponents. Although these are two very different athletic styles, both require physical conditioning to accomplish. No matter what breed of power dog you own, exercise is mandatory for a healthy dog.

Although heavy power dogs still need exercise, the type of exercise you choose should not involve repetitive, abrupt force on joints and bones. Walking on dirt or on a treadmill at a brisk walking speed for short distances is a good activity, as is walking through shallow water or slowly walking up and down stairs or hills. Giant puppies in particular shouldn't be forced to jog or allowed to do a lot of jumping when they are still growing; instead, use activities like scent work and casual exploration walks for daily exercise. Rather than thinking in terms of sustained aerobic activity for your giant power dog, think about ways to increase resistance during short periods of exercise so you can build muscle without overtaxing bones and joints.

And now a word about dog parks…

Dog parks and dog daycare facilities have become increasingly popular with urban dog owners. At first glance, they seem like the perfect solution to exercising and socializing dogs. Most dogs come home exhausted after spending time in either place. But before deciding to use a dog park or dog daycare to exercise your power dog, it is important to understand the risks associated with taking your dog to either place and to know how to decide if your dog is truly playing or if there are more dangerous pack behaviors going on. Remember, proper canine socialization can only be accomplished if your dog is interacting with other dogs who already possess proper social skills. Is your power dog really learning how to behave appropriately around people and dogs when he is at the dog park or daycare running around with other dogs of unknown social skills?

Dog owners often have a hard time accepting that most adult dogs don't need or want to "play" with other dogs in the same way that most puppies do. Puppies play to practice the skills they would need to survive if they were in the wild. They stalk, chase, grab, and nip at each other to perfect crucial pieces of the predatory behavior chain. They also learn how to "speak dog" and interact appropriately with other dogs. Puppies undoubtedly enjoy rough-and-tumble play with each other, but the primary purpose behind play is to perfect predatory and social skills. As puppies mature, the need for this type of interaction with other dogs naturally diminishes. Dogs who are from breeds originally developed to fight other dogs may lose the desire to play with other dogs far sooner than those dogs who have been bred to work more closely with other dogs (like retrievers) do. When socially appropriate adult dogs who know each other get together, they are more likely to engage in casual environmental exploration and just "hanging out" together than in wrestling, chasing, and chewing on each other like puppies do. This is perfectly normal; no amount of exposure to other dogs is going to change that.

Because dogs are pack animals, any time two or more dogs are put together, a pack dynamic is created. This dynamic can become very dangerous very quickly. When you take your power dog to the dog park or put him in daycare, you have little or no control over the other dogs he will interact with. Play should always involve give and take between all the participants; a dog being chased should also have the chance to chase others. But many times, when unacquainted adult dogs are put together to "play," one or two dogs end up being singled out and chased mercilessly by the rest of the impromptu pack that forms. This is more of a hunting activity than a play activity for all involved. All the dogs certainly go home tired, but for different reasons. The dogs who were being chased are just as exhausted from the mental stress of not being able to escape as they are from the physical exercise; the dogs who were chasing are exhausted from the physical exercise and the arousal that chasing causes. But none of the dogs were actually "playing" and they have all learned undesirable social lessons. The dogs who couldn't escape are learning to fear other dogs, and the dogs who were chasing are learning to be canine bullies. Putting a power dog in this type of "play" situation can be catastrophic.

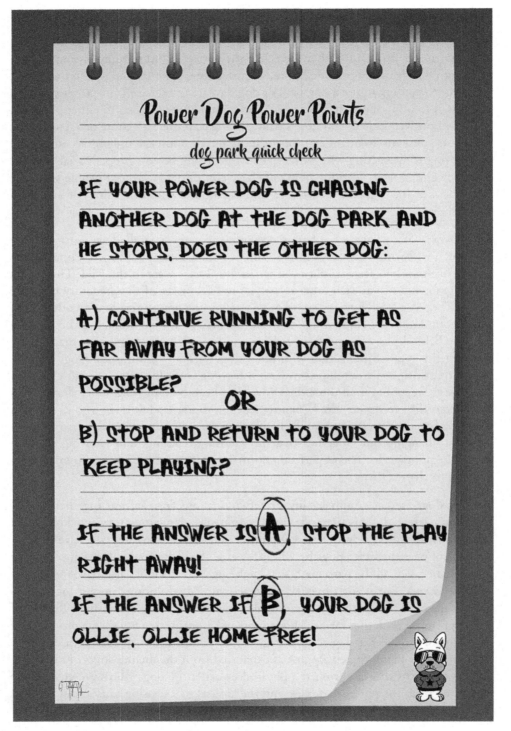

Knowing the difference between hunting and play is important any time a group of dogs gets together.

In these types of situations, even a well-socialized power dog can get into trouble quickly. There is a very fine line between play and actual predation, as we will look at more closely in the next chapter. But there are other reasons to think twice about the dog park. In some locations, your dog may be outright prohibited from the dog park in the first place because of breed-specific ordinances. If a power dog is being chased, he may quickly decide to turn and try to defend himself from the other dogs, just as his ancestors defended themselves from the quarry they were hunting or the opponents they were set against in the fight pit. This action can immediately trigger a cascade of conflict within the entire pack of dogs and a large, dangerous dog fight can quickly erupt. If the power dog is one of the dogs engaging in the chase, he may become so aroused that he will attack the dog being chased if he can catch it, just like his ancestors would attack any animal they were chasing. Or he might attack another chasing dog because he is too aroused and the instinctual urge to grab takes over. It is risky to put a power dog in a situation where his instincts might kick in; once he gets aroused and his adrenaline starts flowing, it will become increasingly difficult for him to control his instinctual behaviors.

Even if your dog is playing well with a group of dogs at the dog park, you have no control over other dogs who arrive later and try to insert themselves into the play. This might or might not go well. Your dog is completely at the mercy of other dog owners and their judgments about whether *their* dogs are appropriate to be at the dog park. They might have poor judgment, and your power dog might be the one to pay the price.

If your power dog exhibits strong fighting or hunting instincts away from the dog park, he isn't a good candidate for dog park play at all. Exposing your reactive power dog to other dogs at the dog park will not decrease his instinctual, potentially dangerous behaviors; in fact, it will likely make those behaviors even more pronounced. It is dangerous to roll the dice with other people's dogs in a misguided attempt to address your own dog's problems. You will need to work on those behaviors elsewhere and eliminate the dog park as an exercise option for your dog.

Another aspect of dog parks that affects primarily power dog owners is the impact breed stereotypes and even actual fear have on other owners you meet there. You have absolutely no control over other people's reactions to your dog when you go to the dog park; most or all the people you meet there will be strangers who have never met your dog before and have no knowledge of who he is as an individual. Stereotypes, gossip, and/or previous personal experiences may result in a less-than-welcoming attitude from other dog owners. Add in the fact that most people don't know how to correctly interpret canine play and social cues, and a potentially tense human situation can easily develop, even if all the dogs are playing quite nicely together. Unless your dog's breed is banned from being at dog parks, you have the same legal right to be there as any other dog owner, but it is still up to you whether you choose to be there or not. Remember the backfire effect we looked at in Chapter 1? You need to remember that other people will hold their core beliefs as tightly as you hold yours. You aren't going to change someone's beliefs via logical discussions or emotional screaming matches if *they* aren't open to challenging and possibly changing their beliefs. There are some people you will simply never reach because they don't want to be reached. Thinking through how you will handle being confronted by someone like this at the dog park *before* you go will allow you to take your dog out and have a pleasant time, no matter how much someone else may try to spoil it.

While it is true that many people take their power dogs to dog parks and daycares every day without any problems (from other canines or humans), there are so many variables you can never control and circumstances you can never foresee every time you take your dog there, that it is actually a fairly risky activity for any dog. With all the other options to exercise and socialize your power dog available to you, are you willing to take those risks?

Mental exercise

A casual stroll around the neighborhood to "stretch your legs" is just that, rather than actual significant aerobic exercise for you or your power dog. But that doesn't mean your dog doesn't get benefit from your walk around the block twice a day. Slow walks are great, but for a different reason: Your neighborhood strolls provide your dog with *mental* exercise, rather than meaningful *physical* exercise. And mental exercise is critical to your dog's well-being, too! If you can't get your dog out for this type of activity, you need to mentally exercise your dog at home. Obedience training, teaching tricks, and other activities that require your dog to pay attention to you, problem solve, and follow your lead are great ways to provide that mental stimulation. The internet is a rich source of trick-training videos.

If you have absolutely no other way to interact with your dog every single day, or you need to leave your dog alone for extended periods of time, interactive toys are a good temporary fix. Providing your dog a portion of his meal in an interactive toy will not only build his patience, it will also encourage your dog to problem solve and interact with his environment in an acceptable way. If you put the food in a chewing-type toy, like a Kong®, you will also be encouraging him to chew, which is a self-soothing behavior; just be sure the toys you select can withstand your dog's powerful chewing! Soak his dry kibble in water until it turns into a mush, pack a Kong or a hollow beef shin bone with the mush, and then freeze the toy before giving it to your dog. This will provide cooling comfort in warm weather and will make the food more difficult to extract so the treat lasts longer. You also won't be adding extra calories to your dog's daily intake if you use a portion of his regular meal to stuff the toy. Dr. Haug, in her article "Canine Aggression Toward Unfamiliar People and Dogs," recommends switching up toys: "Rotating toys, feeding from food-dispensing devices, and engaging the dog in activities requiring problem solving (e.g., training and discrimination tasks) all should be part of the dog's normal routine. Training even simple tricks is excellent mental stimulation and helps strengthen the dog-owner bond as well as increasing the dog's skill set." Just keep in mind that if you rely too heavily on chew toys to entertain your dog instead of giving him activities to do with you, you are actually teaching him to work alone to get what he wants, instead of working in partnership with you.

Exercising your power dog's body and brain is an often-overlooked key to setting him up for success in your home. Find a safe, fun activity (or two, or three, or ten!) to do together for exercise, and you will be setting the stage for better behavior for him, as well as better health for both of you!

8

Socialization—It's All About the Experiences

These dogs are no playthings for the rich, no status symbols, but complicated living creatures.

Carl Fleig, author, *Fighting Dog Breeds*

The fourth key to empowering your power dog is providing him with adequate and appropriate socialization experiences. Unless he is very well-socialized, he will struggle to behave appropriately in his human-controlled world his entire life. Proper socialization is vital to effectively dealing with the power dog traits of dog aggression, stranger wariness, and independence; it also lays a strong foundation for trust and a respectful working relationship between you and your dog.

What is socialization?

Socialization is how a dog learns to interact with his environment. First, and most importantly, a dog needs to learn how to interact with the people he lives with, and the people he meets on a regular basis. He needs to learn how to behave appropriately around strangers, as well as other dogs. (Play is a very important part of canine socialization, particularly for puppies, but it is only one type of experience your dog needs in order to become comfortable around other dogs.) He must learn how to interact with, and maneuver through, his environment. And he needs to figure out what is safe, and what isn't, in the human world. How well you socialize your power dog has a tremendous impact on his behavior.

So much of everyday life that we take for granted isn't "natural" from a dog's perspective. For example, a dog is born with instincts that guide him in his interactions with other dogs. He may need practice to perfect his social skills, but he is hard-wired with a certain set of behavioral tendencies that help him communicate with other members of his species. He isn't, however, born with instincts to guide him in his interactions with cars. From a dog's perspective, there is nothing inherently safe or "natural" about a big metal box zooming along smoothly, making any number of loud, unusual noises, unresponsive to any type of social signal a puppy may try to give it as it passes by. And there is definitely nothing natural about being expected to willingly jump inside one! But with proper socialization experiences, a puppy can learn to ignore these weird metal animals as things that simply exist in the environment and aren't worth paying attention to as they whiz by, and he can learn to get into one and ride around calmly. If a puppy is kept isolated away from cars when he is young, he will never learn that lesson. His instincts will tell him to either attack or run away from that metal animal. Bicycles, holiday decorations, hair dryers, and vacuum sweepers are just a few other examples of man-made items that often frighten and confuse dogs. Your puppy needs to be exposed to all sorts of "unnatural" objects so he can learn to be confident and calm wherever you take him.

When it comes to socialization, quality is far more important than quantity, if you have to choose between the two. Always aim to provide your dog a positive learning experience, even if it is a very brief one. Dogs are always learning, and forcing your dog to remain in a situation he isn't comfortable with for long periods will, more often than not, backfire and teach your dog a lesson or two that you really don't want him to learn. At the very least, he will learn that he can't trust you to keep him safe. With a power dog, this will increase the odds that he will then feel the need to step up and protect himself without your help, since that is what his instincts are likely to encourage him to do in the first place.

Why does socialization matter so much with the power breeds?

Although they can be wonderful family companions, it doesn't take much effort (or lack of effort) to potentially bring out the instincts to guard and protect in most power dogs. If you decided to bring a power dog into your home for companionship, you undoubtedly would like to include your dog in various family activities. If you bought one for protection, you still need to be able to keep the dog with you and live with him in your home. Regardless of the reason you brought a power dog into your family, proper socialization is the key to minimizing displays of aggression and living successfully with these dogs.

The "A" word: Aggression

Dogs are social animals. They have a large repertoire of behaviors designed to minimize conflict within the social group, facilitate resource acquisition and defense, and maximize reproductive potential and individual survival. There are canine social rules about life in the pack that all dogs are expected to follow. These rules are enforced by various types of behaviors, including aggression. Aggression is a normal part of dog behavior; it is used to obtain resources, protect members of the pack, establish and keep territory, and eliminate threats. Dogs may act aggressively when they are in pain, frustrated, anxious, or afraid. And dogs may act aggressively because they have been encouraged to act that way by their owners, either through neglect, abuse, or intentional training. When we bring dogs into our human pack, all these normal canine behaviors, including aggression, tag along. Dogs are born only knowing how to behave as dogs, and they will apply natural canine behaviors to their human pack, sometimes with disastrous consequences. Without plenty of socialization and consistent, persistent guidance, a dog will interact with people as if he is interacting with other dogs. And this is where things often go horribly wrong.

As Dr. Haug explains in her article on canine aggression: "All forms of aggression are modified by learning. Aggression is about local control of the environment. If an animal learns that aggression will alter the environment in a desirable way, reinforcement occurs, and the animal will show that behavior pattern in a similar circumstance in the future. The power of reinforcement emphasizes the importance of avoiding trigger situations during management and treatment." For most dogs, the aggression they exhibit toward people or other dogs is learned because their owners either ignored socialization, management, and training altogether, or didn't utilize those tools effectively. When a dog acts aggressively, it isn't enough to merely withhold treats or praise if the goal is to teach him not to aggress. There are other things going on during that event that are also potential rewards that must be taken into consideration. If the dog is barking because he wants a stranger to go away, and the stranger does move off, the dog is reinforced for his behavior because he achieved his goal of scaring away the "threat." The fact that he didn't receive any treats or praise during this time is immaterial; he has still been reinforced for his aggressive behavior by the stranger's actions. Management techniques are necessary to eliminate unintentional reinforcers in the environment. Owners who don't use management together with training are allowing their dogs to learn bad behaviors, even though they are truly trying to teach good ones.

And then there are those owners who intentionally encourage aggressive behavior. If a person is intentionally irresponsible, he can end up with a power dog who is aggressive and difficult to control; raising a dog like that is relatively easy. Responsible dog owners will put in the time and effort to control and discourage inappropriate aggressive displays through socialization, management, and training so they end up with safe, enjoyable canine companions.

Because aggression is a normal part of all animal behavior, it is unrealistic to expect a dog to never show aggressive behavior, particularly if he is from one of the breeds originally created specifically to show aggression in certain situations. There are bound to be times when your dog may act out or show his heritage; it is your job to train him to the best of your ability to be a well-behaved companion and to manage him the rest of the time to prevent him from having the opportunity to behave aggressively. Remember, regardless of the reason your dog displays aggression, any bite he inflicts will be just as painful for the recipient and just as devastating for you, emotionally, financially, and legally, so do your best to protect your power dog from situations where his instincts may end up getting the better of his behavior. Your power dog is just that. A *dog*. Never expect him to reason or react like a person.

Various studies indicate that the most important factor that influences the development of aggression in healthy dogs is the lack of socialization, although none of these studies indicate exactly how much socialization is enough to minimize the chances a dog will become aggressive. One such study conducted by Roll and Unshelm found that nearly half of all dog-aggressive dogs they analyzed had little to no socialization with other dogs from the time they left their littermates to around 5 months old. This coincides with the most important socialization period in a dog's life. In Dr. Haug's article on canine aggression, she explains:

> *Socialization deficits are arguably the most prominent factor in the development of aggression in physiologically normal dogs. Unfortunately, the amount of socialization required for optimal development of any individual is unknown. … Deficits in social interaction may become more problematic as the animal matures…* ***Mere exposure to other people and dogs is not sufficient to guarantee adequate social skills. Interactions must be monitored to ensure that the puppy has a positive and enriching experience.*** *… Fear-motivated aggression is the most common diagnosis in dogs aggressive toward unfamiliar stimuli, even when elements of territoriality are present. Offensive posturing by the dog does not rule out anxiety or fear as an underlying cause. … The distance to the stimulus and previous learning affect the dog's behavioral presentation. Many dogs show highly offensive posturing when behind a barrier or when the trigger stimulus is far away. As the stimulus approaches or the barrier is removed, the dog's behavior may become more ambiguous and finally reflect outright fear. It is common for dogs to be highly reactive or aggressive toward other dogs while on leash but then to interact appropriately while off leash… Predatory reactions are more likely to be directed toward small dogs and fast-moving objects such as joggers and cyclists.* (Emphasis added.)

Proper socialization can definitely help build a dog's confidence and reduce the chances he will react out of fear toward new things in his environment. A Japanese study by Arai and Ohta found that puppies who had socialization experience with children were more comfortable as adults in the presence of unknown children, and calmed down faster in the presence of an unknown child, than did those dogs who weren't socialized with children when they were puppies. It is reasonable to think that the same general finding would apply to any new thing a dog encounters in his environment; if he had the chance to explore and figure out if that thing was safe when he was a puppy, he will remember that general lesson as an adult and have a much easier time interacting appropriately with it the rest of his life.

In lay terms, what does all this scientific talk mean? That your power dog who is aggressing toward a person, other animal, or object may be doing so for a number of reasons, ranging from his genetic instincts as a predator, to his individual and breed-specific tendencies, to his fear of the new and unknown. It can be difficult to tell which root cause is at play, because the aggressive display may change as the conditions change during an encounter. While it is important to understand what may be the ultimate cause of your power dog's aggressive behavior, the most important things to do are socialize, manage, and train your dog so he rarely, if ever, needs to resort to it when he interacts with anyone or anything in his environment.

Stress, hormones, and other important stuff

Your puppy's physical and mental development also influence socialization. The types of experiences, the intensity of those experiences, and the responses you can expect from your power dog are affected, in part, by your dog's age. There will be changes in your puppy's behavior as he matures that have little to do with his environmental experiences, and more to do with his physical growth stage, his hormones, and other strictly biological factors beyond your control. These types of behavioral phases typically don't last long if you provide your puppy consistent, appropriate guidance and socialization. If you keep them in mind, it can help you tailor your puppy's experiences so that he receives quality, effective socialization as he matures.

Power Dog Power Points

canine developmental stages

NEONATAL	0-12 DAYS	WARMTH, TOUCH, SMELL ONLY SENSES
TRANSITION	13-20 DAYS	LIMITED SIGHT & HEARING
AWARENESS	21-28 DAYS	SIGHT & HEARING FULLY FUNCTIONAL
CANINE SOCIALIZATION	21-49 DAYS	START TO LEARN HOW TO ACT LIKE A DOG
HUMAN SOCIALIZATION	7-12 WEEKS	BONDING WITH PEOPLE STARTS; GREATEST IMPACT ON SOCIAL BEHAVIOR TOWARD PEOPLE
FEAR IMPACT	8-11 WEEKS	DISCOVER WORLD CAN BE DANGEROUS; ANY TRAUMA AT THIS AGE CAN HAVE LIFELONG IMPACT
SENIORITY CLASSIFICATION	13-16 WEEKS	BEGIN EXPERIMENTING WITH INDEPENDENT BEHAVIOR
FLIGHT INSTINCT	4-8 MONTHS	INDEPENDENT ADULT BEHAVIORS MORE PRONOUNCED
2ND FEAR IMPRINT	6-14 MONTHS	RISE IN REACTIVITY, PROTECTIVENESS, TERRITORIALITY
MATURITY	1-4 YEARS	INSTINCTUAL BEHAVIORS MATURE

Normal biological development can affect your power dog's behavior.

Appropriate socialization ideally starts for your power puppy while he is with his dam and littermates. Your puppy's breeder has hopefully provided him with a wide range of experiences before he came into your family. Your responsibility to socialize your dog starts as soon as you get him and extends well into adulthood, particularly for power breeds. If you stop letting your dog learn about his environment and how to interact appropriately with it after the prime socialization window ends when he's around 4 months old, you may find that when your well-socialized puppy turns about 9 months old, he becomes fearful of the world all over again, and might even start to act aggressively toward things he ignored or even liked as a much younger puppy. Dr. Patricia McConnell, in *The Other End of the Leash*, describes this as "juvenile-onset shyness," which begins when your power puppy starts to go through puberty and his breed-related instincts are starting to assume a more important role in his behavior. Hormones are kicking into high gear (even if your puppy has already been spayed or neutered), and his instincts to be less tolerant of strangers, guard property, and fight with other animals start to show up. If you view socialization as an activity that you need to do with your power dog for his entire life, and continue to take him out in the world, his puberty won't be nearly so difficult for both of you to survive. Providing routine socialization opportunities (many can be provided on your exercise walks together), along with consistent management and training, will keep your adult dog interacting appropriately with his environment for his entire life.

Bringing a rescue power dog into your home presents its own unique set of socialization challenges. Many rescues are older puppies or adults when they are placed in new homes, and many were not properly socialized during the first critical months of their lives. There is no agreement between researchers and behavioral experts whether adult dogs who haven't been previously socialized can be adequately socialized starting when they are older and, if they can, if they will be as successful in learning how to interact with their environment appropriately as puppies who received similar experiences during the early socialization phase. Puppies who were raised in impoverished environments certainly benefit from additional enrichment and exposure to the world. Adults must be approached as if they were puppies and carefully exposed to the environment one step at a time to identify any problem areas that require more focused socialization, management, and training experiences. It is critical when you are socializing a rescue power dog to *always* be prepared for unexpected or unusual responses from him to anything in his environment, particularly when you first bring him home. Rescues of any breed have black holes in their histories; you can never have a complete picture of their past, because you weren't a part of it. Use common sense and pay attention to your rescue as you socialize him, to keep everyone safe and the experiences positive for him.

Tips, tricks, and training for effective socialization

Socialization provides your dog with the appropriate skills to interact with *all* aspects of his environment, animate and inanimate. Dogs need to learn what is safe and what isn't in their own unique worlds to be enjoyable companions. Breeds developed to protect people and property or fight other animals need a lot of exposure to the world to learn that not everyone and everything they encounter is a threat that they must engage.

There is one ground rule that applies to *every* socialization situation you put your dog in, regardless of the circumstances: Always, always, *always* leave a back door open for your dog to escape when he is socializing (we'll examine why that is so important in a moment). That back door could simply be a long leash that allows him to retreat, an actual door to another room in the house where he won't be followed, or his crate, where he will be left alone. If you take him out in public, you must be willing to leave the situation immediately if your dog needs to leave; if you aren't willing to leave your child's peewee ballgame if your power puppy starts barking and trying to get away from strangers approaching you in the bleachers, then leave your puppy at home with a tasty chew bone while you go and enjoy the game with your child. Your puppy has no way to understand your child is next up to bat and you don't want to miss that; he will only know he's scared, he wants to run away, and he can't. You will do far more harm in these situations than good if you force your puppy to stay. It is important that your power dog has a way to retreat from any situation he is concerned about, particularly when he is young and learning how to behave appropriately. This helps him understand there are alternatives to biting always available to him.

Also, pay attention to how many times your dog uses his escape route, in order to gauge whether he is ready for the situation you've put him in. If he retreats but then comes back to check out the situation again, he's probably alright and just needs time to figure the situation out. Quietly and calmly praise him when he chooses to investigate—he's being brave! But if he keeps retreating and refusing to come back on his own (i.e., without any pressure or encouragement from you), then you've presented him a challenge he isn't ready for yet. Take a break and try him again in a similar, but simpler, situation later. For example, if you are trying to socialize your dog to people riding bikes and he is too afraid to be near fast-moving bikes, set up a situation to see if he will approach a bike leaning against a tree; if successful, then you can try a bike being pushed by a person, a slow-moving bike, and then eventually another fast-moving bike. Set your dog up for success in every situation, and if you misjudge what your dog is ready for, be prepared to make things easier. Slow-but-steady progress is important for effective socialization.

Socializing with people

In many ways, it is nothing short of a miracle that humans and dogs are able to live peacefully together the vast majority of the time. We are opposites in so many ways when it comes to communication styles. Humans are stiff and direct, and our socially acceptable behaviors and language are in constant flux. We often use verbal communication to radically alter the interpretation of our body language signals by others. We are told to sit up straight, hold our shoulders back, walk confidently forward to meet a stranger, greet the stranger with direct eye contact and a firm handshake, and explain ourselves verbally if we think our thoughts and intentions are not being properly interpreted by others. Well-socialized dogs, on the other hand, approach strange dogs with soft bodies and no direct eye contact, approaching in an arc, sniffing from the rear and then moving forward, and only rarely enhance their body language with vocalizations. When dogs approach one another head on, with direct eye contact and erect, stiff bodies, a fight is waiting to happen! We are both rather ritualistic creatures, but our rituals and communication styles are often in direct conflict with one another. Always keep this in mind when strangers approach your puppy. Try to set the meeting up in a canine-like manner to help your puppy feel more comfortable. Ask people to approach your puppy from the side, be calm and quiet, and avoid staring at him. If he shies away, don't allow them to continue to try to approach your puppy. Don't allow parents to try to socialize their dog-fearing children using your puppy, either! A fearful child and a fearful puppy forced together can lead to a bad experience for both of them. Always stand your ground and protect your puppy.

Who thought this picture was a good idea?

Socialization should never involve forcing your dog to interact with anything (or anyone) he initially finds scary or threatening. If your power puppy or dog is already afraid of strangers, forcing him to interact with every person he meets might cause him to be even more afraid of strangers and distrustful of you, too.

The spider and the truffle

Because properly socializing any power dog to people is so important, let's look at this process in a bit more detail. Imagine you have a real fear of spiders. The mere sight of one makes your heart race, your palms sweat, and your feet start moving to get you as far away from it as quickly as possible. Now imagine you have a friend who doesn't speak the same language as you; he is older, taller, and stronger than you, but you are very comfortable around this person and you two enjoy going out for walks every day, taking in the neighborhood sights together. Even though you've been walking together for several weeks, your friend has absolutely no idea you have arachnophobia.

One day while you are walking together, you look down and notice a big, hairy, scary spider. Your friend bends down to admire the spider, while you immediately start to panic and run away. You want to get as far from that spider as fast as you possibly can! But just as you start to turn away, your friend grabs you around your neck and starts to pull you closer to that big, hairy, ugly spider, all the while smiling and talking at you nonstop in a foreign language. He's trying to tell you that this spider won't hurt you, but you don't speak the same language, and you are already panicked. You have absolutely no idea what he's trying to say; in fact, you really *don't care* what he has to say because you just want to run away. So now you start struggling to get away from the spider *and* your friend, screaming that you don't want to go anywhere near the spider, and shocked that your friend is physically preventing you from running away. You never saw any of this coming based on your previous walks together. You start gasping for air; although your friend doesn't seem to be intentionally strangling you, as you struggle to get away you are putting so much pressure on your neck that it is becoming difficult to breathe. But your friend doesn't understand what you are saying, doesn't notice that you are choking yourself, and just keeps holding on to you, preventing you from moving any farther away from that terrifying, man-eating spider you are certain is just waiting to kill you. In fact, your friend is tall enough and strong enough that he is able to slowly drag you closer to the spider. The closer you get to the Arachnid from Hell, the more you struggle and try to get away. This is the stuff your spider-fearing nightmares are made of!

When you are forced within inches of "It," you glance down and realize the evil arachnid is holding up a huge, mouth-watering, absolutely exquisite chocolate truffle. You love chocolate truffles as much as you hate spiders. The arachnid is holding up the truffle, handing it to you with his creepy little spidery feet, all the while staring at you with his cluster of creepy little spidery eyes. Your stomach is in knots because of your fear of spiders, but you calm down for a split second, trying to figure out how you can grab that truffle without making contact with the spider. You find your chance when your friend turns his attention briefly toward the spider and relaxes his hold

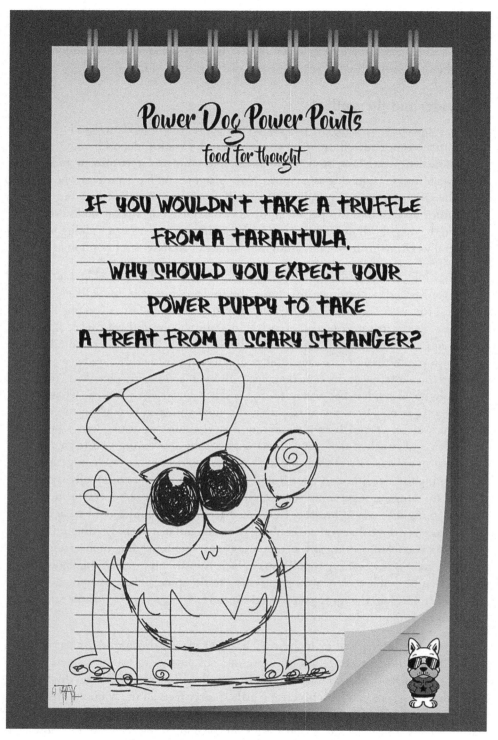

No matter how much you love chocolate, if you are really afraid of arachnids, you won't want to accept a truffle from a spider!

around your neck just a bit. You snatch the truffle (sending the spider flying head over heels) and run away. As you shove the truffle in your mouth and run, you look back over your shoulder and, sure enough, there is your friend, running after you, yelling at you. He catches up with you, grabs you by the neck again, and starts dragging you back to the spider, laughing and chatting away in his native tongue the whole time. (You figure out later—in one of many, many, many subsequent therapy sessions you need to help you deal with the trauma you suffered in this incident—that your friend was simply trying to tell you he knew this spider personally, that the spider wouldn't hurt you, and that this spider just happened to be trained by a world-famous Parisian chocolatier and only wanted to give you one of his five-star chocolate delights as a gesture of friendship.) You are *really* freaked out now—won't your "friend" ever leave you alone and let you get away? You are beginning to fear him now, too!

This time, after your "friend" physically forces you back nose-to-nose with the spider, you notice your nightmare monster isn't holding a truffle up for you. Instead, he is reaching toward you with his creepy little spider legs to give you a hug around your neck and a kiss on both cheeks! You see his pointy spider mandibles moving around, and you absolutely explode with effort to get away from him. You start hitting at your "friend," kick the spider into the next county, twist around, and escape. You run even farther and faster this time, with your "friend" in hot pursuit. You head for the hills and manage to escape; you get home, lock the door, pull down the shades, and ignore the doorbell when your friend shows up for your next outing together. The mere thought of going on another walk with him ties your stomach in knots and you come up with a long list of excuses to avoid leaving the house.

So, are you any less afraid of spiders after you were forced into these close encounters by your friend? Chances are quite good that you are *not* any more comfortable with spiders than you were to begin with. In fact, it's likely that you fear spiders even more because you had absolutely no control over the situation, were forced into close physical contact with the very thing you feared and, in the process, were physically assaulted by someone you believed was your friend. You probably don't want to go anywhere near your friend again because he forced you through that experience. If he ever reaches toward you again, you have learned that if you fight hard enough, you are able to escape him, so you will probably immediately start hitting and screaming if he moves too close to you. Your trust in him is completely shattered. And you still don't understand a word he is saying to you. All you understand are his physical actions and how they impact you. You might even develop a dislike for chocolate truffles because you now associate them with scary things you can't avoid. Your friend probably had the best of intentions trying to help you learn to like spiders, but his approach left you more afraid than ever.

Now consider a similar scenario with your power puppy and strangers. You bring your puppy home and take him out for short walks in the neighborhood to start socializing him. He doesn't really know you yet, and he doesn't understand a single word you say, but as the days go by, he starts to trust you and he definitely enjoys your walks together. One day you encounter a stranger on your walk, and your puppy plants all four feet and refuses to approach him. You have your puppy on a leash, so you physically drag him toward the person, telling him "It's okay. Don't be silly! There's nothing to be afraid of here." The pressure on his neck from struggling against his collar makes him physically uncomfortable and cuts off some of his air supply. He has no idea that it is his behavior that is causing him to choke; he may think it is you, or the stranger, who is taking his breath away, which makes him even more eager to escape. Then the stranger starts reaching out toward your puppy, trying to show him that he won't hurt him, which makes your puppy struggle even more. The leash keeps him from being able to run away, and the stranger just keeps getting closer and closer, trying to touch him. You start shoving treats in your puppy's mouth, and encourage the stranger to do the same. Your puppy can't figure out how to get the treat he wants and avoid the stranger at the same time, so he just snaps at the treat, possibly nipping the stranger's fingers in the process. The stranger yelps and moves quickly away, further panicking your pup, as well as teaching him that biting works to make scary things go away. You pull him away, scolding him for being silly and naughty, and your once pleasant walks begin to spiral out of control. You are teaching your puppy that he has no control over scary situations, that he can't flee from frightening things, and that you can't be trusted. He also indirectly learned that biting makes scary people retreat; this is a particularly dangerous lesson for a power puppy to learn, because it encourages the puppy to act on his fighting or guarding instincts. You've now left him with two options around scary strangers: to completely shut down from stress, or to start lashing out to try to keep them away. This is the complete opposite of what you were trying to accomplish by forcing the interaction between your puppy and the stranger in the first place. It probably seemed like a good idea at the time, but forcing interactions is not the way to go about building your puppy's confidence and overcoming his fears. That isn't socialization; it's terrorizing your puppy and increasing the chances his instincts will surface in very undesirable ways.

Now let's revisit and revise your spider experience. How might you feel about spiders if you and your friend are out taking a nice walk together, and he stops and points out a spider to you, saying something in his own language that you don't understand. You immediately panic and start to run, but then you realize that your friend isn't following you. He's still standing there, and he's pulled out a box of wonderful chocolate truffles and is munching on one, calmly watching the spider. Once you are far enough away to calm down, you look back and pause. You realize the spider isn't coming any closer to your friend or you, so you slowly and cautiously move back nearer to your friend. His calmness definitely gives you a little more confidence to return closer to the spider than you would have if you were alone. When you eventually get close enough, your friend holds out his box of truffles and you take a piece and eat it. You are still very nervous, and the slightest movement by the spider sends you running the other way without even thinking. But each time, you don't run as far before you calm down enough to come back to your friend's side to enjoy some more truffles. You still have absolutely no idea what he is saying to you, but you can tell by his body language and behaviors that he is obviously not scared of the spider and, in fact, even seems to enjoy looking at it. You two stand there until you are ready to leave, then you and your friend continue your walk.

A few days later, you two see a spider again. This time, although you still initially run away, you don't go quite as far, or run quite as fast, as you did the first time. Again, your friend brings out his truffles, and you two share some while looking at the spider. You might even feel brave enough to step in just a wee bit closer (as long as the spider doesn't move, of course!). You are calm enough to notice in passing that the spider's eyes are actually a very attractive shade of red. You have absolutely no desire to get right next to it or touch it. Your heart is still racing and your palms are still sweaty, but you are able to be just a little closer to it without being overcome with the need to run away. After a bit, the spider starts to move. You instinctively start to flee, but then you realize the spider is actually moving away from you, so you stand and watch it move the other direction, while eating more truffles with your friend.

Over the course of many more daily walks, you two encounter this same spider several more times, as well as many other spiders. Each time your friend spies a spider, he stops, points the spider out to you, and calmly offers you a truffle while he stands there looking at the spider. You start to pay attention to your environment a little more closely, looking for spiders, because you've learned that your friend likes to look at them and that he always likes to eat truffles while watching them. This is the only time he offers you sweets. You enjoy these times together, and before long, you actually start to seek out spiders. You still don't want to touch spiders, or be right beside one, but now you notice you are able to remain calm enough to choose to be near spiders, particularly if your friend is there with you. You are calm enough to notice the pretty patterns on different types of spiders, the amazing webs they weave, and the pests they catch in them. You still don't like spiders, but they don't really scare you anymore. You now know that if one moves toward you, you can simply step away until you feel comfortable again. You have options to keep yourself feeling safe and a supportive friend who gives you the time you need to figure things out for yourself.

Over the course of many more weeks, months, or maybe even years, you stop responding fearfully to the sight of spiders. You learn, through many repetitions, that spiders are not to be feared. Instead, they are the gateway to good things from your friend. You can calmly tolerate them, and you might even start to like them just a bit. Spiders become as insignificant to you as trees, birds, and the sidewalk when you and your friend are out walking together. Congratulations! You've been socialized to spiders and understand how to behave more appropriately around them.

Imagine the confidence your power puppy will develop if you take a similar approach to socializing him to strangers! When you encounter strangers on your walks, he is allowed to decide if he wants to interact or not. You remain calm and allow him to retreat if he wants to, and offer him a tasty treat and praise if he decides to approach the person on his own. You are completely relaxed around the stranger and seem to enjoy the person's company, but you never force your puppy to go over to him. If your puppy chooses to approach the stranger, the stranger remains calm, quiet, and respectful to the puppy. If your puppy tries to drag you over to a stranger to get petted, you calmly turn and walk away. He doesn't get to force you to interact with strangers, either! With enough

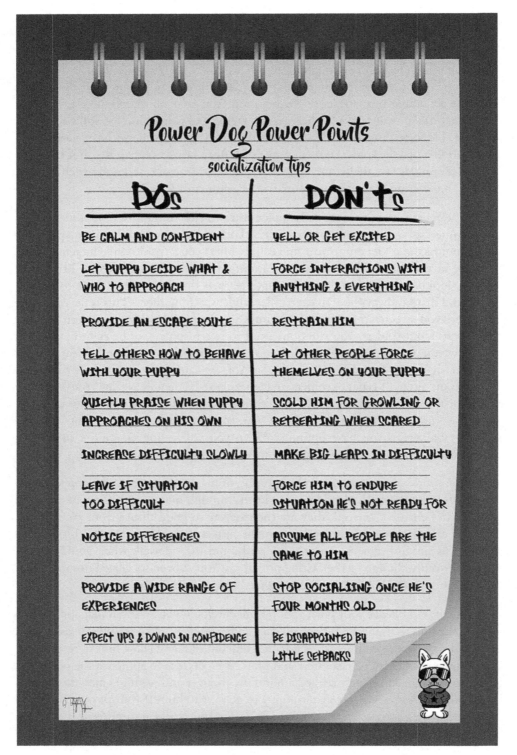

Power Dog Power Points
socialization tips

DOs	DON'ts
BE CALM AND CONFIDENT	YELL OR GET EXCITED
LET PUPPY DECIDE WHAT & WHO TO APPROACH	FORCE INTERACTIONS WITH ANYTHING & EVERYTHING
PROVIDE AN ESCAPE ROUTE	RESTRAIN HIM
TELL OTHERS HOW TO BEHAVE WITH YOUR PUPPY	LET OTHER PEOPLE FORCE THEMELVES ON YOUR PUPPY
QUIETLY PRAISE WHEN PUPPY APPROACHES ON HIS OWN	SCOLD HIM FOR GROWLING OR RETREATING WHEN SCARED
INCREASE DIFFICULTY SLOWLY	MAKE BIG LEAPS IN DIFFICULTY
LEAVE IF SITUATION TOO DIFFICULT	FORCE HIM TO ENDURE SITUATION HE'S NOT READY FOR
NOTICE DIFFERENCES	ASSUME ALL PEOPLE ARE THE SAME TO HIM
PROVIDE A WIDE RANGE OF EXPERIENCES	STOP SOCIALISING ONCE HE'S FOUR MONTHS OLD
EXPECT UPS & DOWNS IN CONFIDENCE	BE DISAPPOINTED BY LITTLE SETBACKS

Keep a few basic rules in mind to socialize your power puppy for success!

repetitions, your power puppy will start to view other people as neutral things in the environment; he can watch them, but he doesn't have to approach them or try to scare them off. And even if he isn't afraid of strangers, he will learn that he doesn't have the privilege of interacting with everyone he meets, either. You have become a trusted friend and the gateway to everything your puppy wants, whether it is to keep strangers at a distance and just watch them or to greet them with a wagging tail and sloppy kisses. Congratulations!

Quality versus quantity

For years, trainers would often tell dog owners that in order to properly socialize their new puppies, they must have their puppies see at least 100 people in the first 12 weeks of life; if an owner didn't meet that number of encounters, the puppy was doomed to a life of social incompetence and aggression. Many puppy owners would either give up on socialization altogether in the face of overwhelming expectations, or would force puppies into scary situations just to add another encounter to the tally. Yet there has never been hard evidence to prove anything magical about this number (or any other number of encounters, for that matter). It is true that your puppy needs to see a wide variety of people during the first four to five months of his life, but the experiences need to be individualized to the puppy. Quality is always more important than quantity. You should not give up or put undue stress on yourself and your puppy trying to reach some random number goal. Try to provide your puppy a broad range of experiences, hopefully every day, but don't give up and stop if you miss a day or two. Keep working on socializing; your power puppy is going to need a lot of consistent work on your part to help him learn to control his protective instincts. You also want to be careful that you don't create a dog who automatically assumes every person on the face of the planet exists solely to interact with him. If your puppy meets every person he sees, you might be inadvertently teaching him to drag you toward people. While you might be able to control this behavior when he weighs 10 pounds, when he physically matures at 100-plus pounds, you might have a social butterfly nightmare on your hands, who you have no way to physically control!

Approaching a dog head on, jutting out a hand to pet him (often on top of the head), and refusing to give the dog space when the dog asks for it (particularly if the person involved is a stranger), is a situation just waiting to explode. Even if people approach your puppy in a more appropriate manner, never allow them to force themselves on your puppy. Always be your dog's advocate. Stop people before they can interact with your puppy if he is afraid. You have your puppy in a vulnerable position by having him on a leash, so be prepared to step between the person and your puppy, walk away, or do whatever else you must do to keep the situation from scaring your puppy or reinforcing any bad habits he already has, such as jumping up on people for attention. This same rule also applies to family interactions with your puppy. Don't allow children to hit, tease, or ride on your dog at any age. Just because your dog might tolerate this type of behavior doesn't mean it is safe, kind, or appropriate to allow that type of interaction to happen. You need to be thoughtful in your approach to socialization to make positive progress with your dog and build up his trust in you, one interaction at a time.

Nice to meet you

Allow your puppy to learn about strangers one person at a time, if possible. Start with the stranger at a distance. Have the person ignore your puppy completely: no eye contact, no talking, no interaction of any type. Give your puppy room to approach the stranger, but don't force him to approach. Offer him small treats for remaining calm at whatever distance the puppy wants to maintain from the stranger and provide him a quick and easy escape route if he wants to move farther away. Even if your puppy approaches the person, if his body language suggests he is ready at a moment's notice to flee the other direction, have the person continue to ignore him. The neutral person should be just that—*neutral*, which means no sudden motions toward the puppy or direct eye contact. You want your puppy to explore and figure out about people, but he doesn't need to see them as treat dispensers, either. It is your job to be the gateway for anything your puppy wants, not theirs. For the most part, people and other dogs in the environment should be neutral—neither a good thing nor a bad thing. Your dog should look to you for exceptionally good things in his environment. When you pass by people and other dogs on your walk, offer your puppy small tasty treats as you continue to move past the distraction. If you decide to let the person interact with your puppy, wait until your pup is focused on you before giving him permission to visit (if he wants to visit in the first place). Remember, don't let your puppy pull you over to a person or dog he wants to see; if he learns to do that when he's young, he will continue when he grows too large and powerful for you to stop him.

Arrange for different people to come to your home as often as possible during the first four to five months of your puppy's life, and periodically throughout his adolescence, to help him maintain a positive attitude toward strangers you invite into your home. They don't need to come into your house for extended visits; simply have them come to the door, invite them in briefly while you keep your puppy calm (put him on leash so he doesn't learn to be a pest at the door), chat with them, shake their hands, pat them on the back, or hug them to let your puppy know you aren't afraid of them, then say goodbye. Have the majority of your guests ignore your puppy; although you want your dog to be comfortable around company, you don't want him to expect (or demand) everyone who walks through the door should pay attention to him. He may become more wary of new people coming into his house as he matures because of his breed instincts, but you can help him tolerate people whom *you* accept a little more readily, and also give him experiences that will help him remain calm and listen to you in the presence of strangers. Be sure to include children in this process if you have children living at home who may invite their friends over to visit, or if you have young relatives (e.g., grandchildren, nieces, nephews) who visit you. According to Karen Delise in *The Pit Bull Placebo*:

> *One of the most frequent scenarios for dog attacks is children visiting relatives…*
> *this is one area where seemingly innocent mistakes or slight errors in judgment*

have resulted in tragic consequences. The factors which appear to be at work here: Adults, being familiar (or having a bond) with a relative's dog, assume the dog will be equally accepting of their young children, believing their bond with the dog will automatically extend to them [the children]. Adults visiting with children fail to take into account the territorial issues found with many dogs.... Very often these parents made only minor errors in judgment. Also, many of these parents did have lifestyles in which they provided safe environments for their children. An added awareness of the danger some dogs may present to young visiting children may help these parents avoid attacks on their own children by a relative's dog.

Socializing your power dog to people in your home is just as important as socializing him to people you encounter when you go out in public.

Some people bring power dogs into their lives specifically for their protective instincts. If this is the main reason you chose a power dog, you may be tempted to skip socializing your dog with strangers, particularly those who approach or enter your home. But even these dogs need to be able to tolerate people you welcome into your home; it is *your* decision who belongs and who doesn't belong in your home, not his. If you don't teach your dog that most people in the world aren't any type of threat to you, you are placing all responsibility on your *dog* to decide who belongs in your home and who doesn't. It is unfair and unsafe to leave a dog to make that decision. This is when horrible things can happen. Your power dog needs to be socialized to prevent him from assuming every person outside the family is a credible threat that he needs to address. At the very least, socialize your dog to people he sees every day (like the mail carrier and the neighbors), friends and family who routinely come into your home, and people you may take him to see (like your veterinarian), and then be willing to closely and consistently manage your dog around all strangers for the rest of his life, no exceptions. This is a difficult lifestyle for both you and your dog to live, but it is mandatory if you don't socialize him well. Even if you do socialize him, management and common sense will still need to be part of your lifestyle with any power dog selected primarily for his guarding and protective instincts.

Welcome to the family!

If you adopt an older puppy or adult dog, the very first people this dog needs to be socialized with are the people he will spend the rest of his life with—you and your family! You might think that your dog should automatically bond to you; after all, you just saved him from being in a shelter and possibly losing his life. But when you first bring a rescue dog home, you are no different from all the other people who have been in and out of his life since he came into rescue or the shelter. It takes time and effort to help him understand and accept his new environment and his new family. One of the most serious mistakes you can make with any rescue or adult dog who is brought home is to take that dog out for extended public outings before he has any bond with you and before you have any idea what behaviors to expect from him. As we discussed in Chapter 3, just because a dog behaved well while in rescue doesn't mean you will see the same type of behavior when he is out with you after you bring him home;

everything is different for the dog, so he may react differently. Many dog-bite fatalities involve newly adopted dogs. The owner doesn't know the dog, and the dog doesn't know the owner. Throw in a small child, another dog, or some other trigger, and the dog will simply lash out in whatever way he believes is required for his own safety. Many severe dog bites and fatalities could have been prevented if the owners hadn't placed unrealistic expectations on the dogs long before they knew anything about their dogs' real temperaments, and before the dogs knew who to trust and listen to.

When you first bring an adult dog or rescue dog home, you might need to be prepared to ignore inappropriate social behaviors that aren't dangerous. For example, you may find that once you get your new dog home, he tries to stuff himself behind the couch every time he sees your spouse. You have no idea why the dog is responding that way; your spouse is very loving and appropriate around dogs and has done absolutely nothing to create this response. Something in your newly adopted dog's history triggered it. If you respond to this behavior by trying to drag the dog out from behind the sofa or, even worse, have your spouse try to physically drag him out, you are setting up a perfect dog bite situation. Remember the spiders and the strangers earlier in this chapter? The same rule applies here: let your dog interact with your spouse on his terms, not yours.

Set him up for success and approach your socialization with him just like you would with a puppy. If he shows any fear responses, let him work through them without physical force. Chances are, once he settles into his new home, if everyone is consistent with him, he will soon figure out that your spouse isn't a stranger to be feared or, even worse, chased away. As long as your dog isn't actively trying to harm your spouse, just ignore the behavior. Keep an eye on your children as well; they may be eager to hug, love on, and play with their new pet, but until that dog settles in and you know more about his true personality, be particularly vigilant to avoid bad experiences for your kids and your dog. Don't let impatience or feelings of "rejection" interfere with you doing the right thing for your dog and your family. A dog who is fearful is not rejecting anyone; that behavior is simply information from your dog about his past and what he needs from you for a better present and a more confident future. When your dog is more comfortable with "his people," then you can start socializing him to others, starting with those he will see most often and working your way as far toward strangers as he is comfortable going with you. If your rescue behaves aggressively toward anyone in your family, immediately seek professional help.

Socializing with other dogs

Current canine behavioral research shows that humans can't actually teach canine social skills to dogs. For example, you can't teach a dog the fine art of butt sniff greetings; how long to sniff, who sniffs first, what to do after sniffing, and how to interpret the scents that are sniffed are all behaviors that must be learned and developed through experiential learning with other dogs. You can't teach a dog how to sort out safe versus dangerous people, animals, objects, or sounds, either. The dog must ultimately work through that categorization process on his own. But what you can (and must) do to effectively help your dog develop appropriate social skills is facilitate his experimentation with the world in a supervised, appropriate, safe manner, and provide him with opportunities to cultivate his innate social behaviors. This is particularly important when it comes to socializing a power dog to other dogs. Breed instincts and sheer physical strength can make an under-socialized power dog a difficult, and potentially dangerous, dog to own. Power dogs with fighting ancestries in particular need early, frequent socialization experiences with other socially appropriate dogs to help them learn to control their fighting instincts.

It is important to protect your puppy from traumatic experiences while you provide him with positive ones; an intense fear period coincides with the optimal socialization period. Throwing your power puppy into a mob scene with a pack of strange dogs at the dog park to socialize him is never a good idea, even less so when he is less than a year old, and definitely not before he's at least 6 months old! Chances are good that your puppy will be scared by such an experience, and this can greatly impair his social skills development. He might think that any time he meets a strange dog, he is going to be hurt. His instincts to fearlessly face any opponent are likely to kick in and, before long, you will have a power puppy who acts aggressively toward strange dogs. It is far safer to have your young puppy interact with puppies and older dogs of known temperament or with a few well-socialized dogs under the supervision of a trainer in a controlled environment, such as a training class, than to toss him out to fend for himself in the dog park. Although this requires more effort on your part, remember that you are creating a behavioral foundation that will last your dog's entire life.

Rocky, a young Rottweiler, is learning to relax around other dogs in the safety of a supervised puppy class.

Predatory drift

Predatory drift is a behavioral phenomenon that correlates with arousal. It is a concept that all power dog owners need to understand as it relates to socialization and proactive management when your dog meets another dog. Two dogs may be playing quite well together, then, a split second later, the play changes over into predatory behavior due to predatory drift, and a fight erupts; one of the dogs may end up injured or even killed when this happens. Many times, the dog who attacks seems perfectly happy and "normal" shortly after the incident is over. As Jean Donaldson points out in *Fight!*, "While it is quite true that many [social] interactions are completely benign, predatory drift is common enough that most dog people have either witnessed it or know someone who has." This change in behavior is triggered by one of the dogs (usually a smaller dog) acting in a prey-like manner during play. This trigger behavior could involve the dog making prey-like sounds (squealing, yelping, etc.) or behaving erratically (struggling to physically escape the play, running in panic, etc.). At that point, the (usually) larger dog will stop responding to the other dog as a playmate and start responding to him as a prey animal. His instincts to catch and kill take over, and the other dog is severely harmed or even killed. This can happen with dogs of any size, but the greater the size difference between the two dogs, the more likely it is to happen if the larger dog gets overly aroused. Predatory drift can also happen in situations involving other types of animals, children, running adults, or even inanimate objects.

Although it may be difficult to imagine your goofy Boxer hunting for his meals in the wild, all dogs are predators. You see examples of his predatory instincts every time he shakes and rips up a stuffed toy, scans his yard for something to chase, or mouths another dog around the neck while playing. These are all watered-down examples of predatory behaviors. To obtain food in the wild, a dog is hard-wired to follow this basic predatory sequence: scan – chase – grab – shake – kill – eat. Dogs need to eat to survive, and they need to kill prey to eat. So predatory biting tends to be quite severe. Some dogs are known to be predatory (i.e., the dogs have a history of chasing and harming or killing dogs or other animals), while others have no history of predation prior to a predatory drift event and might not ever display the behavior again. Obviously, those dogs who are known to chase and harm other animals need to be managed very carefully; they don't require much stimulation to switch into "predator mode." But all dogs have the potential to act predatorily when a particular set of circumstances happens, and dogs from breeds that have been bred to hold or kill other animals, like most of the power dogs, need to be closely monitored for predatory drift.

Canine playmates for power dogs need to be selected carefully. To minimize the risk of predatory drift, your power dog shouldn't play with considerably smaller, frail, old, or fearful dogs. A small dog can easily be smashed by a larger dog during play, and his vocalizations will be high-pitched, like an injured prey animal. A frail, old, or fearful dog may move more erratically than a healthy or young dog, acting like a prey animal trying to evade capture. These behaviors can trigger a predatory response from the larger dog, causing an attack. The smaller dog, even if he tries to fight back, will be physically outmatched by the bigger one and likely to be hurt, or even possibly killed.

Another situation where predatory drift can happen is when there is more than one dog ganging up on another one. This can easily happen at the dog park. Two or more dogs are playing with a third dog; something happens, one of the dogs yips or struggles to escape the play, and the other two dogs flip over into predatory behavior, acting as a pack to take down a prey animal. The results for the target animal are often quite horrific, because instead of one dog attacking, there are now two or more. This can happen even when all the dogs have a long history of completely normal play behavior. If you own two or more power dogs, dropping another dog into the play mix can also be tempting fate. Your dogs will already consider themselves a pack unit because they live together; if a trigger happens, they will either spring into action as a unit, focusing on the outsider, or they will redirect toward one another out of frustration, leaving you with a squabble brewing between dogs who live together. If you have two or more dogs who play well together already, you don't really need to bring in other dogs to spice things up. If you want your dogs to play with other dogs, take your dogs, one at a time, on playdates with other appropriate dogs somewhere away from home.

Predatory drift can happen with babies or young children as well. Human children behave like prey—they squeal, move erratically, and are not able to communicate that they are not prey. Many, many reports of dog attacks against babies and young children, particularly those situations involving power breeds, often include a quote from the owner that the dog never, ever showed any signs of aggression toward the child before, had played well with the child in the past, and seemingly attacked with absolutely no warning. Aside from the fact that many of these situations happen when dogs and kids are left alone unsupervised and the owner really doesn't know exactly what happened, there may well be validity to the claim that the dog showed no problematic behavior toward the child before the bite and may have been playing quite well with the child just moments before the attack. No baby or young child should *ever* be left together unsupervised with *any* dog; even "nanny dogs" and breeds that are described as loyal and docile with children are still *dogs* and may, in the right circumstances, act out toward a child with life-altering, sometimes fatal, consequences.

Thoughtful and cautious socialization with other dogs is important for your power puppy. If you aren't comfortable choosing a canine playmate for him, or you aren't sure if play interactions are appropriate, consult a behavioral specialist or an experienced trainer to help you set up a safe, effective canine socialization plan.

Socializing with valued goodies and other precious resources

Many dog bites happen when someone tries to take food or a valued possession from a dog. In particular, a power dog can become quite protective toward property and objects that, in his mind, need to be protected against all comers. If he hasn't been taught to share with people in his family, he certainly won't be willing to share with strangers who come into your home from time to time. Given the size and strength of the power breeds, **resource guarding** is a particularly dangerous behavior for your power dog to develop. A bite from any size dog hurts; a bite from a large dog can be devastating.

One way to discourage resource guarding is to create an environment where your dog doesn't experience scarcity of highly valuable resources such as food, highly attractive treats or toys, and personal space. If your puppy or dog learns there is always more of the good stuff readily available, he is less likely to attempt to guard it.

Food guarding can be the most difficult resource guarding behavior to discourage, because eating is necessary for survival. Your dog doesn't need to chew on his favorite toy or sleep on your bed to survive, but he does need to eat! Your dog has absolutely no concept of receiving a regular meal from you. Although he gets hungry at about the same times every day, he really doesn't understand that you will always provide him with food to satisfy that hunger. Feral dogs eat if and when they can obtain food; they may stuff themselves full when the chance presents itself, and then be forced to go for several days with very little to eat because not much is available. Your pet dog is hard-wired the same way and his instincts tell him to protect and consume what he can when it is available, because it may be a while before he gets the chance to eat again. If you try to teach him to share by constantly taking his food bowl away, your dog may become increasingly frantic to stop you from doing so, and you may end up with a truly dangerous dog at mealtime. Once he backs you away from his food bowl by growling, barking, or nipping, he has learned a very important lesson—his aggression worked to protect his food. Now he knows how to get you to back off, and he will continue to behave this way. This has everything to do with survival, from your dog's perspective. Other than when your dog is eating something that might be dangerous for him to ingest, when (and why) would you actually *need* to take a bowl full of food away from him anyway? Children may try simply because they haven't been taught to leave eating dogs alone or they make a poor choice to ignore what they've been taught, but why would an adult need to do that? It certainly doesn't teach your dog to "respect" you.

One way to discourage food guarding is simply to split your dog's meals between two bowls. By feeding him from two bowls, he will soon learn two very important lessons: (1) seeing an empty food bowl isn't the end of the world, and (2) if he gets scooted away from food in one bowl, he can get more food out of another bowl. It's no big deal. The bowls don't need to be far apart; just place them far enough from each other that the puppy moves a few steps from one to the other to finish his meal. Feed your dog out of two bowls throughout puppyhood and adolescence and you have presented your power puppy with nearly 1,100 experiences (18 months, two meals per day) of running out of food one place and finding it in another. This is a particularly good way to discourage food guarding if you have young children in the house who might unintentionally force your dog to move away from his food bowl. Instead of standing his ground if this happens, your dog will wander off in search of another bowl of food that experience has taught him is around somewhere.

Another way to discourage food guarding is to create a sense of gain for your dog when you are near his food bowl. Approach him while he's eating, drop a small, super-tasty treat into his food bowl, and then walk away. He will soon learn that your approach means he's going to get something even better to eat, instead of being deprived of the rest of his meal. Approach calmly and quietly so he doesn't speed up his eating as you come near (a sign he is worried that you are going to take his food away, so he is trying to get as much as possible before you do). He will simply ignore you or he might even stop eating to see what tasty thing you are getting ready to add to his meal. And *if* you still feel the need to remove the bowl, have a second one close by that your puppy can shift over to so his food supply isn't eliminated completely when you take the bowl. If the need ever truly arises for you to remove his bowl while he is eating, your dog will happily allow you to do that because he will be anticipating more food in another bowl or something super-tasty being added to his food.

With adult dogs who weren't taught this exercise or rescues of unknown history, it is best to simply leave the dog alone while he is eating until you are certain you can safely approach close enough to drop in the tasty tidbit and walk away. Children should be supervised and kept away from the dog during mealtime. If you can't supervise your child, then set up a safe space for the dog to enjoy his food that is inaccessible to the child; this could be in another room of the house with the door closed, behind a baby gate, or in a crate in a quiet area of the house. If you have accepted a power dog into your home, you've accepted the responsibility for that dog's training and management as well. Yes, it's extra work added into an already over-full day to manage your dog's mealtimes so closely, but with the size and strength of the power breeds, combined with their instincts to guard and protect, it is critical that you respect and protect both the dog and anyone coming in contact with the dog. Abused dogs are often malnourished as well, and come from an environment where deprivation is common. If your dog already shows signs of resource guarding, contact a professional trainer or behaviorist who has experience working with rescues and with power breeds in particular, to develop a plan to help your dog change his behavior and help you learn how to manage him appropriately.

Navigating the world

Another facet of socialization involves exposing your puppy to the basic environmental conditions he will live in as an adult. Your puppy needs to learn how to accept physical confinement and brief periods of isolation, how to ride in the car or on public transit, how to cope with neighborhood noises, sights, and smells, and how to deal with unique family circumstances (such as medical equipment, apartment elevators, etc.). If your power dog is affected by ordinances in your town, or if you plan on traveling with your dog to places where he might be affected by local ordinances, he needs to be introduced to a muzzle and any other equipment he is required to wear, as soon as possible (see Chapter 10 for how to do this). Every socialization experience should be short, pleasant, and puppy-appropriate. If there are any activities you might want to do with him later, include those in your puppy's socialization plan. For example, if you want to go scootering with your power puppy when he is an adult, you can expose him to the sight and movement of the scooter while he is a puppy. He can learn about the scooter, see it moving around, and see you wearing your helmet and any elbow or knee pads you might wear. By the time your dog is old enough to start scootering, he will know all about your scooter and be ready to focus on learning how to pull you on it.

Your power puppy also needs to learn how to literally navigate through the world, which can be quite a challenge for the larger puppies! A Boston Terrier will be able to maneuver through tight spaces far more easily than an APBT, who in turn will have an easier time than a Mastiff or Great Dane. You need to protect your puppy's growing bones and joints from overuse or damage, but you also need to show him how to move his entire body forward, backward, and around things in his environment. This is infinitely easier to do while he is still light enough and/or small enough for you to offer him physical assistance if he needs it, than if you wait to teach him until he is full-grown. Puppy parkour is an easy (and fun!) low-impact way to work on these skills with your dog. This simply involves physically interacting with things in the environment. Use a treat to lure your puppy under a park bench to show him he can get low to the ground and crawl; have him step over or on different types of surfaces so he doesn't fear things that feel different under his feet; have him follow a treat in circles around a light pole in both directions to give him a light stretch and encourage him to bend; have him step or jump over objects no taller than his wrist joint to teach him to move his body up; put him in the middle of a playground merry-go-round and slowly spin it. Basically, if an object is no taller than his wrist joint and you can help him stay safe, it's fair game to use it to teach him body awareness! But remember, if he acts afraid, don't force him to interact with any object. Instead, back off and let him explore the object on his own. Only if and when he starts acting comfortable should you use it for training. If he doesn't get comfortable, move on to something else. This is simply an activity to help you socialize your puppy while exercising his body and brain. Before you start parkour activities with your older dog, check with your vet for recommendations on how high the objects he can jump over should be (your dog's height, weight, and overall physical condition will determine safe heights), and remember to start slowly and give him time to build up muscle strength. Your walks never need to be boring when you introduce this type of socialization to your power dog, and he will soon be moving his body confidently through his environment, regardless of his size!

All the noise, noise, noise, noise!

Sound socialization is one type of socialization many owners forget to address, but it's an important one to do with your power puppy. Life can be quite noisy, particularly for city dogs. Thunder, fireworks, sirens, household appliances, helicopters, construction equipment, other dogs barking, garbage trucks, and children yelling are just some of the noises your power puppy needs to get used to in his environment. Loud noises in nature generally mean danger, and dogs instinctively startle when they hear them, just like people do. But if your puppy is exposed to loud noises in a positive, methodical way, you can help him cope with them more confidently.

A commercially produced CD of assorted sounds is the simplest way to help your puppy learn about loud noises; there are many different ones made specifically for puppy socialization that you can purchase online. Alternatively, you can find sounds on the internet to use, or you can record actual sounds with your phone or a voice recorder. Once you have your sounds ready, play them quietly in the background while your puppy is doing something he enjoys. Mealtime is a particularly good time to do this type of socialization; your puppy will start to associate the noises he hears with eating instead of danger. Keep the volume low enough so you don't startle him the first few times you do this, then gradually increase the volume as he learns to ignore the noise. Eventually he will be able to cope with loud noises, which will make the 4th of July, thunderstorms, and city living in general much easier for both of you!

If you are out and about with your puppy and a loud noise happens that startles him, give him a few moments to collect himself, then calmly and confidently encourage him to move on with you. Your confidence will definitely boost his confidence and help him figure out nothing bad is going to happen to him.

Socialization *is* the most important activity to do with your power dog, regardless of his age. Although it is best to start the moment your 8-week-old puppy comes into your home, it is never too late to start providing positive socialization experiences to your dog. Common sense, patience, consistency, and persistence will go a long way toward helping him interact with his world in a safe, confident manner.

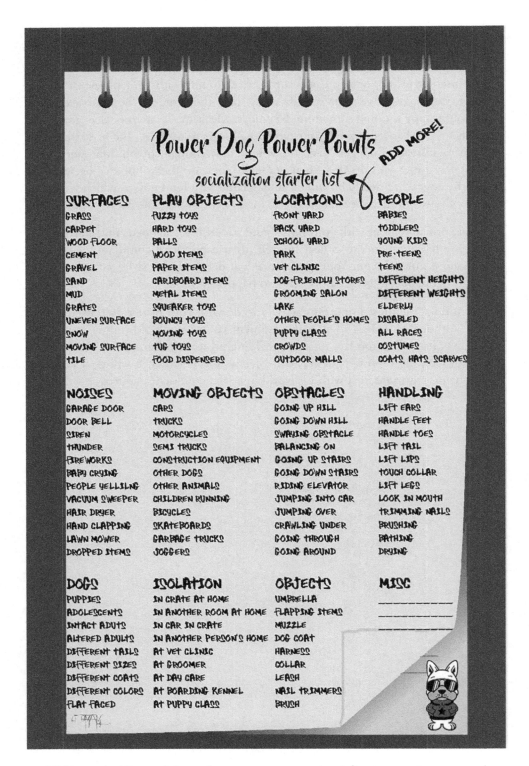

Making a checklist can help you keep your power puppy's socialization experiences on track.

9

The Power of Proactive Management

Prevention is the better cure.

Spanish proverb

The fifth key to empowering your power dog is management. By carefully managing his environment, you can maximize his chances for behavioral success. Learning doesn't happen only when you put your dog through a formal training session. Your dog is learning about you, himself, and the world around him, every second of every day. Your dog learns through observation, experimentation, and experience. The opportunities your dog's environment provides for him to act in inappropriate ways can lead to behavioral problems that are difficult to eliminate. Proper management can help reduce these opportunities to misbehave, as well as provide him opportunities to behave appropriately, all of which will increase your actual empowerment training effectiveness. Here are several simple management rules that will keep you and your power dog from ending up behind the behavioral eight ball.

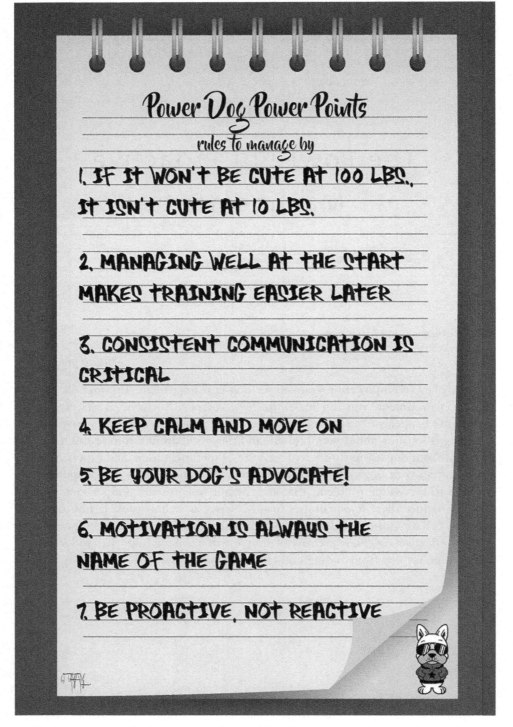

Power Dog Power Points
rules to manage by

1. IF IT WON'T BE CUTE AT 100 LBS., IT ISN'T CUTE AT 10 LBS.

2. MANAGING WELL AT THE START MAKES TRAINING EASIER LATER

3. CONSISTENT COMMUNICATION IS CRITICAL

4. KEEP CALM AND MOVE ON

5. BE YOUR DOG'S ADVOCATE!

6. MOTIVATION IS ALWAYS THE NAME OF THE GAME

7. BE PROACTIVE, NOT REACTIVE

Setting some ground rules early on will make life with your power puppy much easier later.

If it isn't cute at 100 pounds, it isn't cute at 10 pounds

It is very important to think through how you want your power dog to behave as an adult, while he is still a *puppy*. Most of the power breeds are physically large and all of them are exceptionally strong dogs. If a behavior won't be cute or safe when your dog is an adult, try to prevent your puppy from learning it in the first place; it is far easier to prevent your 15-pound puppy from getting on the couch, if you don't want him to get on it, than it is to try to teach that same dog to stay off when he's a 150-pound teenager! If you wouldn't want your adult Bullmastiff climbing into your lap for cuddles or your Boxer jumping up on you as you walk through the door after work every day, start teaching him more appropriate behaviors while he is still a young, physically smaller puppy. The sooner you start to set good habits, the more success you will have. Allowing your puppy to chase a human or bite them, even in play, should never be tolerated, regardless of age or size. Think carefully about how you want to live with your adult power dog and develop a training and management plan to help you reach your goal. Then start using that plan from the moment your new companion comes home to make life easier for everyone, regardless of how large your power puppy becomes!

Managing well in the beginning makes training easier later on

Management involves setting up your dog's environment to control his behavior. Management doesn't actually teach your dog how to behave, but it can help you prevent undesired behaviors or encourage desired ones. If you set up your puppy's environment so he can't practice behaviors you don't want him to do, you will save yourself a lot of time and training effort later. For example, if you don't want your puppy to jump up on people as they come into your house, don't allow him to jump up when he is a puppy. Put him on a leash to prevent him from jumping up on people right from the start; if you do, he won't learn that jumping up gets him attention, so he will be far less likely to jump up when he gets older. Make it difficult or impossible for your dog to act in ways you don't want him to act and it will be much easier to teach him how you do want him to act.

Keep calm and move on

At the outbreak of World War II, the British Ministry of Information created a series of three motivational posters to bolster British morale. One poster carried the simple slogan "Keep calm and carry on," to be used only in the case of extreme peril. The posters were never actually used during the war, but we can certainly make good use of this slogan today in our dog training. Sometimes you have no choice but to walk closer to another dog than your power dog may like. Sometimes your dog will see a squirrel before you do. Sometimes you will encounter something new with your dog and he will have a poor initial reaction to it. Sometimes life happens in spite of your best intentions and your power dog has an inappropriate reaction. When things like this happen and your power dog gets aroused or starts acting out, it is very important that you keep calm and carry on. It is not always easy to do, but this will minimize the trauma and drama of the situation for both you and your dog. Distance is *always* your dog's friend! By continuing to move on, you are also increasing the distance between your dog and whatever is distracting or arousing him as quickly as possible.

When something unexpected happens, keep as calm as you can, keep your feet moving, and get your dog out of the situation as quietly and quickly as possible.

An important way you can help your power dog keep his cool in the first place, and stay in the right frame of mind to listen to you and learn new behaviors, is to keep yourself as calm as possible when you are out with him. Organize yourself before getting your dog; his leash, muzzle if he wears one, poop bags, treats, keys, phone, and anything else you need to go out for your walk should be ready to go before you clip on his leash and head out the door. When you step out, talk to your dog in a calm, conversational tone. If you start yelling at him as soon as you walk out the door, he will: (1) start to get aroused by your apparent arousal, and (2) start to simply ignore you after a while, since your yelling doesn't actually deter his inappropriate behavior. If you can't get your own emotions under control, it will be difficult to get your dog's under better control. If you are simply too angry, scared, or embarrassed to successfully control your emotions, then find places to walk your dog where you aren't as likely to meet people and other dogs (or at least meet ones you know from the neighborhood), or walk at times when other people typically don't go out. If that is impossible, then skip the walks altogether until he learns better leash manners, and find other ways to exercise his body and mind at home. If you and your dog are looking for problems before you even start your walk, you will struggle to make any training progress.

Your dog is a master at body language; he can sense when you are tense. He is also marvelous at picking up on slight changes in your voice and smelling the biochemical changes that occur in your body when your adrenaline starts flowing. If you are upset, it is likely your dog will get upset as well. Although it is impossible to completely fool a dog when you are upset, you can certainly minimize the impact your emotions have on your dog's behavior by remembering to keep calm. Try to smile. Forcing a smile has been shown to elicit positive physiological changes in the body, even when you aren't emotionally happy. A soft body is harder for your dog to jerk around, so keep your knees and elbows slightly bent and use your legs more than your arms to physically control your dog if he suddenly tries to pull you toward something (your glutes and thigh muscles are typically more powerful than your arm and chest muscles). Act as if you aren't stressed out at all, and step out with confidence. Take long, slow, deep breaths. Even though undesirable behaviors will still occur, your more relaxed body language will help you maintain better control over your dog and help your dog stay a little calmer, too. One thing most people do when their dogs act out and they get really tense is hold their breath; unfortunately, this can make the entire situation even worse. When one dog is getting ready to attack another, the aggressor often freezes and holds his breath for a split second or two just prior to the attack. Your power dog can misinterpret the reason you are holding your breath and think you are getting ready to attack the other dog, or him (or both), and become even more excited. Don't yell at your dog or try to reason with him about his inappropriate behavior (do you really think he cares or even understands that the other dog is just trying to walk past him?). Keep your voice calm and quiet, take a few deep breaths, and keep your feet moving. A quiet voice is often more confident-sounding than a loud one.

Turid Rugaas has written extensively about the ways dogs use body language to calm one another, and we can use some of the same signals to try to calm our power dogs.

Yawning, licking your lips, and avoiding direct eye contact with both dogs may also help defuse a tense situation. Since many power dogs are fighters by nature, you need to use these signals before the dogs are aroused and ready to fight. And always remember, dog behavior is just that—behavior. Their actions are a very complicated mixture of instincts and environmental learning. When your power dog does something that you don't like, consider that behavior to be information. Your dog is telling you exactly what he does and doesn't know, what is distracting to him, what frightens him or arouses him, and what he would rather be doing at any particular moment. If you remain calm and pay attention to the information you are being given, you can then tailor your training plan to change the behaviors you want to alter.

Fight!

What should you do if, in spite of your best efforts, the unthinkable happens and your power dog ends up in a physical altercation with another dog? Breaking up a fight between any two dogs is dangerous, no matter their size or breed. Even a Chihuahua can inflict severe injuries; the bigger and stronger the dog, the bigger and more severe the potential injuries become. Stepping into a fight between two dogs to attempt to separate them puts very vulnerable parts of your body at risk. If you bend in to the fight to grab a collar, you expose your face and neck to bites, as well as your hands and arms. If you attempt to kick one dog off another, you risk wounds to your feet and legs. If you get tripped and fall down, your entire body is vulnerable to attack.

In a fight situation, even the most docile and sweet dog of any breed is in pure survival mode. He is no longer thinking about his moves—he is simply reacting to his opponent, looking for the opportunity to win the fight or escape. Your dog won't recognize you. He won't hear you screaming his name. Once a fight is happening, the only thing he is focused on is the other dog. If any part of your body comes between him and his opponent, he will bite it without even realizing he is biting you. This is why being proactive and protecting your dog from inappropriate contact with other dogs is so important; once a fight starts, all you can do is protect yourself and then try to minimize the damage the dogs inflict on each other.

If a fight breaks out and your dog is on leash, *drop the leash!* This may be hard to do, but it will keep you from getting knocked over and becoming very vulnerable to bites, and will also give your dog a fair chance to either escape or outmaneuver the other dog. If you do get knocked over, cover your head and neck as best you can, and quietly try to roll out from underneath the dogs. Once your dog is free and can protect himself, take a moment to assess what, if anything, you can try to safely disrupt the fight. Look for anything handy that you can throw on or over the dogs to attempt to slow them down or disengage them. Most dogs won't be deterred by loud noises, water from a hose, or a jacket thrown over them, but that type of intervention may minimize the damage they do to each other by interfering with their ability to bite and then shake. Eventually the dogs will exhaust themselves, and you can then attempt to separate them.

Physically breaking up a fight between strong or large dogs is a difficult process that few dog owners can do successfully. You must be quick and strong. You'll also need another skilled person to help you, or a way to safely secure one dog before you attempt to separate them. Even for professionals who deal with dogs on a daily basis, it is difficult to safely do without equipment such as catch poles, bite gloves, and break sticks. There are several sites on the internet that discuss the proper way to attempt to physically break up dog fights. A few of the sites are included in the Resources section at the end of this book.

Once the fight is over, you need to assess your dog's wounds and get him veterinary care. If he doesn't appear to be severely injured, get any information you can from the owner of the other dog involved and any witnesses to the situation before you leave for the vet clinic. If the person leaves without giving you information, use your cell phone or ask someone nearby to snap pictures of the person, the dog, and the car license plate if possible. This information may become very important later, depending on the injuries sustained by the dogs and any citations that the police or animal control may issue. If your dog is badly injured, use a sock, shirt, or other handy piece of cloth to make a quick muzzle for him before moving him or loading him into your car. It takes hours for adrenaline to clear a dog's system after a fight. Your dog will not be thinking clearly; he may bite you when you try to move him.

A dog fight is traumatic for everyone involved. Always be proactive to give your power dog the best chances for a bite-free, fight-free life.

Be your power dog's advocate!

Taking responsibility for your power dog's safety and well-being is an important part of being a loving dog owner. Be prepared to step in and discourage people from approaching your dog if he doesn't seem comfortable with them or he is protective of you. Even if your dog likes other people, never assume other people know how to behave appropriately around dogs! People sometimes do the craziest things around other people's dogs without even giving a second thought whether or not their behavior is appropriate. Keep interactions with strangers low key and under your control. Don't forget that your power dog may not instinctively like to interact at close quarters with strangers. Forcing him to tolerate a stranger getting near him might be more than he can ultimately handle. A well-socialized dog of any breed should be able to sit calmly at your side and tolerate a stranger's presence, but he might not want to be touched by that person. Be your dog's advocate and don't force him to interact with other people just because they ask to interact with him.

You also need to be your dog's advocate when it comes to interactions with strange dogs, and be ready to stop owners who allow their dogs to pull over toward yours uninvited. Many careless owners allow their dogs to rush up to dogs they have never met before, calling out "It's okay—he's friendly and just wants to say hi!" without giving a thought about whether it is appropriate for that interaction to occur in the first place, or if the other dog wants to be approached.

Power Dog Power Points

power dog advocacy

1. YOUR DOG = YOUR RESPONSIBILITY

2. STOP OTHER OWNERS FROM LETTING THEIR DOGS APPROACH YOURS UNINVITED

3. STOP YOUR DOG FROM APPROACHING OTHER DOGS UNINVITED

4. NEVER TRUST OTHER PEOPLE WHEN THEY SAY THEIR DOG IS FRIENDLY OR JUST WANTS TO PLAY

5. DON'T LET STRANGERS FORCE THEMSELVES ON YOUR DOG

6. DON'T BE AFRAID TO TELL OTHERS NO!

7. TELL OTHERS HOW TO BEHAVE AROUND YOUR DOG AND MAKE THEM DO IT

Your power dog relies on you to be his advocate at all times.

Remember, socially appropriate dogs approach one another in an arc, eyes diverted, body soft and calm, sniffing each other from the rear end forward. A socially inappropriate dog rushes head on to greet, starts sniffing at the head, body moving wildly, often vocalizing the entire time. It doesn't matter that this dog doesn't mean to hurt the other dog; what he is doing is offensive to any well-socialized dog. It really isn't fair or realistic to expect a power dog to take such assaults calmly and quietly. You must be your power dog's advocate and try to prevent these types of "greetings" from happening in the first place. If you don't, the odds are good your power dog will tell the other dog just how rude he is being.

To proactively deal with these types of situations, you must never assume other people will control their dogs appropriately or see anything wrong with how their dogs are behaving. When people ask if their dogs can say hi to yours, politely decline if you suspect a greeting may cause problems for your power dog; explaining that your dog is learning appropriate greeting manners should deter most owners from allowing their dog to continue to approach yours. Unfortunately, some dog owners can't talk and keep their dogs close to them at the same time, though, so be sure to keep an eye on the situation while this conversation is going on to prevent unwanted contact between the dogs from happening anyway. You may need to take control of the situation by calmly and quickly stepping away from other dogs to keep your dog safe. Never be afraid to ask others to call their dogs away from yours, particularly if the other dogs are off leash and yours is on leash. Even if an owner says "My dog's friendly!" that doesn't give that dog the right to assault your dog. The over-exuberant, "friendly" dogs are often the ones who cause the most problems in these situations. They may approach head on, choking against their collars, feet flying, and immediately throw themselves on top of the dogs they are greeting. Your dog has absolutely no way to know that the other dog is on leash and can't attack him, or that his odd body language may be the result of straining against the leash rather than trying to be rude or intimidating. The only way your dog can voice his displeasure over the rude greeting is by posturing, growling, barking, and, if none of those work, biting. It is far better for you to do the talking for him! With a power dog, all that commotion, noise, and nonsense is apt to arouse him; a completely normal response would be for him to growl, bark, and probably bite the approaching dog to get him to back off. No dog should have to tolerate that type of behavior from another dog, and power dogs generally won't. Your power dog isn't being mean or aggressive if he reacts this way when he is "attacked with friendliness"; he is just reacting to a socially inappropriate situation that never should have happened in the first place.

When your power dog is attached to a leash, the situation can become even more volatile. A leash removes your dog's ability to flee a threatening situation (assuming he wants to run away in the first place). Because he is attached to you, his only option if he wants to make an approaching dog stop is to bluff him away by growling and barking, or bite him if he gets too close. If you see someone walking a dog off leash, don't hesitate to take responsibility for your own dog's safety by politely calling out to the other owner to call the dog away from yours so the dogs don't meet inappropriately. Don't be flustered if the owner tells you the dog is friendly; ask again that the dog be called back. If all else fails, leave the area. Protecting your dog is far more important than who is "right" or "wrong" in a situation like this.

Sometimes the shoe may be on the other foot and it is *your* dog who needs to be told no and kept from approaching another dog. Most adult dogs don't have a strong desire to "play" with other dogs, especially ones they've never met before. Your dog might act "excited" to see another dog, but that behavior doesn't necessarily mean he wants to "play"; he might be straining to try to fight the other dog! Whatever the emotional reason for your dog acting in that manner, the one thing this type of behavior definitely means is that you haven't taught your dog to ignore other dogs while he is out for a walk. If you allow your dog to approach another dog while he is misbehaving, you are showing him that the way to get what he wants is to pull you around and act out. You need to accept responsibility for keeping your power dog, whatever his age, under control and out of potentially explosive encounters with dogs he doesn't know.

Kristi takes Jack, a Rottweiler power dog mix, to out-of-the-way places to canicross with him, because he doesn't like other dogs approaching him uninvited. Kristi also wears a shirt that encourages other people to give Jack the room he needs to politely pass when they are out for a run together.

Being your power dog's advocate also means being thoughtful when choosing places to take your dog. Don't bring your dog into a situation you know he isn't ready to handle yet or one you can't manage well enough to prevent him from behaving inappropriately. For example, many pet stores allow you to take leashed pets in with you to shop. The store is full of narrow aisles, limited visibility, and lots of exciting sights and smells. The floors are usually slick and difficult for dogs to walk on without slipping. Other shoppers are pushing carts that might bump into or scare your dog. Many people assume if a dog is brought into the store, he is friendly with all people and all dogs. This can be a high-stress situation for your dog; bringing him into this type of environment without first teaching him how to successfully cope with that high level of stress is asking for trouble. Leave your dog at home when you go out to buy dog food until you have taught him how to behave in highly distracting environments.

Find a quiet park where there usually aren't many dogs, or walk around the neighborhood where you are both comfortable while he is learning how to behave. As you teach your power dog behaviors to cope with more stressful environments, you will eventually be able to add more places, like the pet store, into your travels together. But if you repeatedly overface your power dog by putting him in situations he isn't able to handle, you are simply giving him more practice at the very behaviors you want to change. You're also teaching him that he can't really trust you to keep him safe. If you gradually increase the distractions your dog must deal with as he learns how to behave, before long you will end up with a dog you can take just about anywhere and one that other people would like to have!

Be proactive, not reactive!

Have you ever found yourself in a situation where your head says "Go ahead—do it!" but your gut says "This ain't gonna end well if I do!"? Your gut was probably right, wasn't it? When you own a power dog, you need to listen to your gut, no matter how tempted you are to ignore it. Let's say your power dog was attacked at some point in his life by a dog who ran up on him while you were out for a walk. He is now very defensive when he sees dogs running toward him when he is on leash. If you are walking your power dog through the park and you see several dogs running off leash near the walking path you normally use, your gut should be telling you "This ain't gonna end well if those dogs run up on my dog." But you've been working hard on teaching your dog to remain relaxed and ignore other dogs, so your head says "Hey, this is a great test of the new skills we've been working on. What's the worst that can happen? Let's go for it!" So you forge ahead, determined to walk your normal path through the park in spite of the loose dogs. And sure enough, the loose dogs see you and rush over to check your leashed power dog out. Your dog, understandably upset by the dogs rushing up on him when he has no way to escape, lashes out to protect himself. You get upset and yell, trying to shoo the other dogs away. The owner of the loose dogs is upset because your dog "attacked" his "friendly" dogs. And since he's a power dog, chances are good that no one will believe that your dog was actually the "victim" in this situation, rightfully trying to protect himself from the unwanted intrusion of the loose dogs. Congratulations! You have now made it even more difficult to teach your power dog to remain calm around other dogs in the future. Your dog is smart; he has just been told once again that: (1) you can't be trusted to keep him safe when he is on a leash, (2) barking, lunging, and carrying on pay off because the other dogs ultimately disappeared, and (3) you are just as concerned about the other dogs as he is because you yelled and carried on, too. You will never be wrong if you err on the side of caution with your power dog. If you repeatedly put him in situations that allow him to practice undesired behaviors, you are destroying all the training you've done with him, one bad interaction at a time. Don't put him in stressful situations just to see what happens!

Provide entertainment

When you have to stay in a distracting environment with your power dog, you may need to keep him busy to keep him calm. This is particularly true in group training classes where your power dog must be in close proximity to other dogs for fairly long periods of time. If you don't keep your power dog's attention, he will find something to pay attention to on his own, and the odds are pretty good it won't be you. You need to actively engage your power dog to keep him from fixating on distractions in his environment. If you attend group classes, you must focus on your dog from the moment you pull into the parking lot until the moment you leave. Keeping him close to you as you enter and leave the training building will help, but once you take your seat, you still need to pay attention to what your dog is paying attention to so you can keep him as calm as possible. A sterilized hollow bone filled with peanut butter, wet dog food, or squeeze cheese and then frozen (freezing makes the filling more difficult for the dog to get out so the treat lasts longer) is a great distractor for your dog, as long as he is calm enough to eat and doesn't guard his food. Tricks, basic obedience cues, or a game of hand targeting (if you need to teach this behavior, see Chapter 10 for more information) will also keep your power dog focused on you instead of the other dogs in the class; just be sure your dog's activities aren't too distracting for the other dogs. It is a lot of work to keep a power dog focused on you for an entire class, but if he's distracted, it will be even more work to try to teach him anything!

Giving visitors room to visit

Even though you might not mind sharing your sofa with your 130-pound Great Dane, your guests might, so teaching your dog to hang out in a defined space is one way to allow him to visit with company without being in their way or stealing their physical space. A large power dog can certainly be a trip hazard, and many people have no idea how to move a large dog who doesn't want to be moved. One way to manage this is to use food toys like the ones described above to teach your dog to stay near you. Prepare several of these and toss them in the freezer before the visit so you have them ready to go when company arrives. Put your dog on his leash before allowing guests in so he can't jump on them or try to sit on their feet or laps. Grab one of his frozen toys, and then get yourself comfortable so you can visit with your friends. Put the toy between your feet so you can keep it from rolling away, and hold the leash (or use a fixed-length *short* tether attached to a piece of nearby furniture or to your belt loop) so he can't walk away from you. Then visit! Ignore your dog, and let him focus on his toy; he will probably lie down to chew on it, and you can give him a word or two of quiet praise while he chomps. He can stand, sit, or lie down, but he can't walk away and he can't bother your guests. This is an easy way to eliminate any need to physically control a large dog, while still allowing him to be part of the social activity.

Don't pop the power dog bubble

Every power dog comes hard-wired with certain instincts that can make it difficult to take him out in public without considerable socialization and training. Whether it's protective traits or fighting ones (even if they are buried deeply within your individual dog), they are still there somewhere. This protective attitude against strangers and aggression toward other animals produced the types of dogs who were used to fight wars, protect estates, hunt big game, and fight in the pits in the past, and those same dogs were used to produce the power dogs we own today. So is it any wonder your power dog sometimes needs help behaving in public?

The easiest way to proactively prevent your power dog from getting aroused and reactive is to keep him out of situations that are apt to arouse him in the first place. You can do this by identifying your dog's personal space needs, and then doing your best to always protect that space. Personal space is simply the amount of physical space your dog needs so he is able to remain calm around a particular distraction. Power dogs can be quick to react negatively to other dogs, especially dogs who approach too fast or too close. Although some power dogs are incredibly tolerant and can handle dogs very close to them without considerable training, most can't remain calm if another dog gets too close. Perhaps the easiest way to visualize your dog's personal space needs is to imagine him moving through his environment encased in a bubble. The size of the bubble represents the amount of space your power dog needs to remain calm and listen to you in the presence of something exciting or threatening. If the bubble is intact, he can listen to you and behave accordingly. But if that bubble is popped because the thing that excites your dog gets too close, your dog gets aroused, the adrenaline starts flowing, and your dog stops responding to you, no matter how much time and effort you have put into his training. Respecting his bubble is the easiest way to reduce and, in some cases, eliminate many problem behaviors your power dog may display out in public. Of course, this doesn't teach him how to behave more appropriately (we'll look at actual training exercises to accomplish that in Chapter 10), but it quickly makes life with your power dog easier and gives you a starting point for actually teaching him more appropriate behaviors.

Bubbles can and do change size depending on past experiences, the type of distraction present, and training. A power dog who has been taught to tolerate a strange dog politely passing by him on the sidewalk has a very small bubble for that distraction. But that same dog might immediately begin to posture and lunge toward a cat walking down the opposite side of the street because he has never learned how to behave calmly around cats, so he has a very large bubble around them. Similarly, a power dog may be fine passing dogs smaller than him on the sidewalk because he has learned how to behave around small dogs and so has a small bubble around them. But, due to a negative experience with a large dog in the past, he might start barking and lunging when he sees a large dog two blocks away, so he has a much larger bubble for that type of dog. The goal of managing your dog's bubbles is to prevent outbursts in the first place; training can then be used to make all the bubbles as small as possible.

The easiest way to identify the initial size of your power dog's bubbles is to take a few information-gathering walks with him. These are not training walks per se; your goal on these walks is to determine how much distance your dog needs to remain calm in the presence of things that excite him. Pay close attention to all the things that catch your dog's attention, and note how close you are when your power dog starts focusing on them. Identify your dog's bubbles in training classes, at the veterinarian's office, and anywhere else you go with him. If he gets excited and tunes you out at home, identify his home bubbles as well. Make a quick list of these bubbles that you can refer to in the future if you need a reminder; this will also serve as a yardstick to measure the progress you make in shrinking the bubbles as you teach your power dog how to behave more appropriately.

Stephanie protects her Boxer Amira's bubble when passing by another dog on the sidewalk; by stepping off the sidewalk to give Amira enough space, Stephanie is able to keep Amira's attention on her, rather than on the other dog.

Proactive environmental scanning

Once you've identified your power dog's bubbles around various distractions, you need to start practicing proactive environmental scanning to protect those bubbles; this is particularly important if your power dog acts aggressively toward people or other dogs. When you take your dog out for a walk, the largest bubble you've identified will determine how far ahead you need to scan. If your dog reacts to approaching dogs when they are still two blocks away from you, and that is his largest bubble, you need to be proactively looking at least three blocks ahead while you are out walking together. This will give you time to see an approaching dog, decide what you need to do to protect your power dog's bubble, and then do it, all before your dog's two-block-wide bubble is burst and he starts reacting. You also need to be cautious as you approach blind corners where buildings, hedges, parked cars, or other things block your view; keep your dog close to you as you approach, or avoid the situation entirely by crossing the street where you have a better view. This is a habit that takes a while to develop, since most people don't look very far ahead when they walk, but it is similar to good defensive driving techniques. You need to walk with your head up, looking forward and scanning the environment as you walk, just as if you are driving a car. Another benefit of looking farther ahead when you walk is you will appear to walk with more confidence, which will help your power dog have more confidence in you as his leader. This can help him remain calmer. If you look at your feet instead of out ahead of you, you will appear to lack confidence and will have no way to effectively protect your dog's bubble from dogs or anything else that gets him aroused.

When Jim walks Trixie, a French Bulldog/Beagle cross, he walks briskly and confidently, keeping his attention on what is happening in front of him and his dog so he can handle any potential distractions before they distract Trixie.

Proactive scanning doesn't just apply when you are out for a walk. When you take your power dog into a training class or the vet's office, keep your dog's leash short and your eyes looking ahead. Scan the room before entering and determine where the best place is to go with your dog. Walk with confidence into the room and go immediately to the spot you picked out. You might not be able to find all the space you would like to have for your dog, but you will certainly help your dog's behavior by picking the best option available for him.

Get the heck outta Dodge

Now that you know where to look to keep your dog's bubble intact, you need to add in management techniques that will help you avoid distractions and protect the bubble. Increasing the distance between your power dog and whatever is likely to arouse him is a reliable and simple management technique you can use to protect your dog's bubble. Unfortunately, most owners are just as tenacious as their power dogs when it comes to staying on their chosen route, even in the face of a distraction that their dogs aren't ready to handle yet; they will walk their power dogs right past something exciting and risk a confrontation rather than cross the street to walk on the other side where it is safer and easier for the dogs to maintain self-control. Putting more distance between your power dog and anything that excites him will help you protect his bubble and help him remain focused on you. This might seem like an obvious thing to do, but few people instinctively take this simple step to prevent outbursts from happening. It is hard to remember to do this at first, but once you begin to appreciate how many outbursts you can prevent with this simple technique, you will become motivated to make these adjustments.

If there is a dog in the neighborhood who gets your dog excited by running along the fence as you walk, walk on the other side of the street when you pass that house or walk a different route altogether until you have taught your power dog to ignore the dog behind the fence. If your dog struggles with passing other dogs head on, you need to create as much space as you can between him and the oncoming distraction by crossing the street, walking along the street curb if it's safe to do so, or simply making an about-turn and going back in the direction you came from instead of forcing a head-on confrontation between your power dog and another dog heading your way. If rabbits hide in shrubs along a particular driveway and your power dog goes crazy trying to hunt for them as you walk past, keep your dog away from the bushes in the first place by shortening up his leash and arcing away from them so he can't physically reach either the bushes or the bunnies. As you teach your dog how to remain calmer around these distractions and his bubbles start to shrink through training, you won't need to make as many detours in your walking path. But until your power dog learns new coping skills, walk the few extra steps it takes to keep your dog out of the path of oncoming trouble.

When you alter your path, turn with confidence and authority, and step out at a brisk pace in your new direction. Talk to your dog in a pleasant, calm tone as you walk away. If your dog likes treats, offer him a few as you walk away, but only if he is going with you and not straining to turn back to the distraction. Don't nag your dog or yell at him if he keeps turning around; if he reacts to the distraction at all, it is a sign that you waited too long to try to avoid the situation and his bubble was burst. Just continue to walk away with confidence. Eventually there will be enough distance between your power dog and the distraction to allow him to regain his composure. Distance is always your friend. You will never go wrong if you calmly and promptly increase the distance between your power dog and anything that arouses him as a way to help him remain calm.

Ideally, if your timing is good and you proactively scan far enough ahead on your walk, your dog should not be distressed by the sudden change in your walking route. The key with this technique is to be confident in your body language and voice as you change your route. Remember, your dog is a master at reading body language and will pick up on any tenseness in your body or voice. This in turn will make him even more worried about the oncoming distraction, because in his mind, he might associate the distraction with your concern (which in this case would be correct!), so he might become more worried about it as well. But if you act unconcerned and nonchalant about the distraction as you change your direction, that confidence will help your power dog ignore the distraction as you move away.

Don't loiter

Many handlers freeze as soon as their power dogs start acting up or, worse, allow their dogs to pull them closer to distractions. When that happens, exactly who is walking whom? By allowing your dog to continue pulling toward a distraction, you are actually encouraging that pulling behavior to continue; from your power dog's perspective, pulling is worthwhile because it is getting him closer to what he wants to get at. The consequences of his behavior are desirable to him, so it is likely he will continue to pull toward things that arouse him. And the farther away your power dog is from you, the easier it is for him to ignore you when he is aroused. Walking at the end of a 6-foot leash is a privilege, not a right, so when you are moving past distractions that might arouse your dog, shorten up that leash and keep him close to you. Keep your feet moving and don't slow down as you move away. This will minimize the amount of time your power dog has to get aroused, ending any potential outburst that much sooner.

Being proactive and using good management techniques will make life infinitely better with your power dog. Controlling his environment so he doesn't develop new bad habits or continue to practice old ones is much easier than having to retrain him after these habits are fully formed and perfected.

10

Power Training for Power Dogs

It is a truism to say that the dog is largely what his master makes of him. He can be savage and dangerous, untrustworthy, cringing and fearful; or he can be faithful and loyal, courageous and the best of companions and allies.

Sir Ranulph Fiennes, British explorer

The sixth, and final, key to empowering your power dog is training. There are plenty of trainers and resources available to help you teach your power dog traditional skills like sit, down, and come. The training exercises in this book are designed to empower you to deal with some of the unique challenges associated with living with a power dog. This is where the fun really begins!

Consistent communication is key

Dogs, like most people, learn and perform best when they receive timely, relevant information about what they are expected to do in any given situation. One way to do this is to have a predictable, informative communication style. How you communicate with your dog will set the tone for your relationship and can impact his responses to your cues. The following communication series will help you help your power dog succeed.

Name once

Your dog's name is actually an attention cue that lets him know he is the one who should be listening to whatever you are going to say next. Say his name *once*; even if he doesn't respond by turning toward you to see what you are going to do next, it doesn't mean he didn't hear you, so don't repeat yourself. (Check out the "You talkin' to me?" exercise later in this chapter if your dog doesn't respond to his name by immediately giving you his attention.) If you keep repeating his name, eventually he will learn that he doesn't have to respond the first time you say it. Nagging isn't training, so don't get in the habit of repeating yourself. If you are consistent in doing this, he will start to understand that you aren't going to wait for him. Once you say his name, you will tell him what you want him to do, so he had better pay attention!

Cue once

Tell your dog specifically what you want him to do, but only tell him *once*. If you said his name once, he's been put on alert that you are going to tell him to do something. Now tell him what you want him to do. If you repeat yourself, you are teaching your dog that he can ignore you. One cue only, then you'll move on to the next step.

As we discussed in Chapter 5, it is important to pick a unique, distinct cue for each behavior you teach him and then use those cues consistently. For example, don't use the cue "Down" to mean lie down in some situations, and to get off of something (like the couch) in other situations. The specific words you use don't really matter; you can teach your dog to come to you when he hears the word "Rutabaga" as easily as teaching him to respond when he hears the word "Come." As long as you say exactly what you mean and mean what you say when you give cues, your dog will understand what you expect him to do and you will both be much happier!

Show the dog how to do the behavior or help him perform the behavior

If you are working on a new behavior, as soon as you say your cue word, show your dog what you expect him to do. How you do that will depend on the behavior you are trying to teach, but right from the beginning, teach him how to do the behavior on only one cue. If he's already been taught to do the behavior, but for some reason he doesn't do it with one cue, help him physically complete the behavior, but don't repeat the cue. Show him that you expect him to perform the behavior on one cue and, if he doesn't, you are going to help him do it. Once you give a cue, it is *your* job to be sure that your dog performs the associated behavior. If you can't do that, then don't give your dog the cue! Otherwise, if you say your cue but don't make sure your dog performs the behavior, you are teaching him he can ignore you and only behave when he feels like it.

Reward the behavior

Once your dog has performed the appropriate behavior, let him know he's done the right thing so he will understand it's worth his while to listen to you and do what you tell him to do, the first time, *every* time. When you are first teaching a behavior, use plenty of treats along with praise and petting to let him know he did something that you like. Keep your praise calm and low key; you don't want your dog to stop doing the correct behavior while you are praising him. If he does stop, quickly and quietly help him restart the behavior so he learns praise and treats aren't permission to stop doing what he's been asked to do. Later, when he understands the new behavior, you can eliminate the treats and rely more on praise, petting, and other things he enjoys as his reward for a job well done.

Release

Teaching your dog when to stop performing a behavior is just as important as teaching him how to perform the behavior in the first place. You are in charge of when your dog starts to perform a cued behavior, as well as when he stops performing that behavior. If you cue your dog to sit, he shouldn't get out of that sit until you tell him he's finished with that behavior. Praising and feeding aren't the same as permission to stop doing the behavior. Come up with a special word or phrase that specifically tells him he can stop doing what you asked him to do. "That'll do," "all done," "break," and "free" are examples of a release cue that you could use. This cue means your dog is now free to do whatever he wants instead of what you told him to do. You can use the same release cue for all his behaviors.

For example, cue your dog to perform a basic behavior, such as sit. When he sits, praise him calmly for sitting. If he gets up while you are praising him, quickly and quietly help him back into the sit position by gently guiding him with your hands back into a sit. Use one hand flat against his chest to keep him from moving forward and the other hand to gently tuck his back legs into a sit. (Your hands should never be anything your dog fears. They are simply things that you use to help him be successful.) Pause for a second or two while your dog continues to sit, then give him a release cue in an enthusiastic, upbeat manner and step away from your dog. He might be hesitant at first to move (after all, you just told him not to move!), so be sure to be inviting with your body as well as your voice. Move away, clap your hands, smile, and act like you truly do want your dog to come to you. If he absolutely refuses to budge, you may need to lure him a few times by tossing a treat or toy in front of him as you give him his release cue, to convince him it really is okay to move now.

Resist the urge to blurt out your release cue if you see your dog starting to break position. That isn't teaching your dog to continue performing until you tell him to stop. That is your dog teaching *you* to say your release cue whenever he decides he wants to quit behaving for you! Teaching your dog to have self-control requires you to have self-control, too.

Reward again

After you release your dog from performing the cued behavior, reward him with praise or petting again. Training should be something your dog enjoys doing with you and something you enjoy doing with him. Make it pleasant for both of you! Encourage him to come to you for this last reward. That will continue to emphasize to him that you are truly the gateway to everything he wants, and also that he must come to you (not the other way around!) to get those goodies.

Contextual cues

You may also find it very useful when you begin teaching your dog new behaviors to look for contextual cues that you can use to your advantage to help your dog's behavior become more reliable. A **contextual cue** is simply another way for you to cue your dog to perform a particular behavior in a particular environment. For example, when you are working on polite door greetings, you can teach your dog to sit when you touch the door handle. You need to touch the door handle to open the door. Your dog has observed you do this hundreds of times, and every time you touch the handle, the door opens. You can use grabbing the door knob as a contextual cue for your dog to sit as you open the door.

To turn the door knob into a sit cue, touch the door handle, then tell your dog to sit. If he sits, praise and release him; if he doesn't sit, quietly and quickly help him sit, then praise and release him. After enough repetitions of the touch/tell pairing, you will notice your dog anticipating the verbal cue to sit and he will start to sit as soon as you touch the door knob. Once that happens, you can start to fade away the verbal cue over a few sessions by literally decreasing the volume of your sit cue, moving from a conversational volume to a whisper, then dropping the verbal cue altogether. Remember, once you grab the door knob, if your dog is near the door, you need to help him sit if he doesn't do it on his own, then give him his release cue when you decide he's free to get up. You are simply substituting the door knob for your verbal cue.

Using contextual cues is also a great way to create consistency in cues between everyone in your family. Differences in pitch, inflection, volume, and the like are eliminated with contextual cues. There is really only one way to operate a door knob, so the cue to sit at the door will be more consistent between family members if you use the doorknob instead of a verbal cue. Whenever you teach your dog a new behavior, think about adding in contextual cues to help his performance; there are many choices once you start looking for them!

All of the following training exercises will benefit your dog in many different ways, but they are organized by the primary power dog traits they will help you address. Even if your power dog doesn't demonstrate one or more of these specific traits, by teaching him the following exercises, you will be encouraging him to use his intelligence and loyalty in a way that will continue to strengthen the bond between you!

Exercises for size, strength, and independence

You talkin' to me?

Exercise goal: Your power dog will look toward you when you say his name.

How many times a day do you say your dog's name for no particular reason? "Hi, Brutus!" "Who's the bestest doggie in the world? That's right! It's my Brutus!" How many times do you pair his name with some type of correction? "Brutus, no!" "Brutus, drop that!" "Bad dog, Brutus!" Because you use his name in so many different ways and so many times each day, your dog may begin to ignore his name or, worse yet, link his name with an imminent correction, and actively start to avoid you whenever he hears it. If your dog associates his name with positive things, you will always have a handy way to quickly gain his attention when you need it, simply by saying his name. Your dog's name is also the first part of the consistent communication sequence we looked at earlier.

If your dog doesn't already have a nickname, give him one. You will use his nickname when you are just chatting to him throughout the day or when you verbally correct him. (Hopefully you won't need to do that very often.) Try to use his "real" name only when you need to get his attention. It's impossible to be 100% consistent with this, but the more you protect his name by using a nickname for most interactions with him, the easier it will be to get his attention when you need it.

1. This exercise can be practiced any time, any place. Start this exercise with your dog on leash so he can't walk away from you. Say your dog's name once in a pleasant tone, and immediately give him a small treat. Repeat four to five times per session and try to do several sessions each day. It doesn't matter if he doesn't look at you when you say his name for the first few times you go through this exercise; reward him anyway, even if you need to physically reach out and put the treat in his mouth. You need to establish an association in his mind between hearing his name and getting a treat from you, so don't wait for him to look at you; just say his name and stick the treat in his mouth.

2. As your teaching progresses, you will notice your dog will start to turn toward you as soon as he hears his name, anticipating his reward. When he is looking at you immediately after hearing his name at least 80% of the time (four out five repetitions), you can begin to pair his name with another cue he knows, such as "Sit" or "Down." Instead of giving him a treat after his name, give him his reward after he performs the second cue, then release him. That reward may be a treat, praise, petting, or anything else that he finds rewarding. Keep the behavior you want quick and easy to perform. Grabbing your dog's attention by saying his name before you cue him to perform any behavior will help him focus more on the behavior he is supposed to perform.

Your dog should always associate his name with pleasant interactions with you. He should immediately give you his attention when he hears his name. Who knows what fun is going to come next?

Walk politely, please!

Exercise goal: Your power dog will walk on leash beside you without pulling.

Power dogs, by their nature, are the kinds of dogs who instinctively step out in front to take charge of any situation, unless they are taught to behave differently. Teaching your dog to walk beside you when you have him on leash is a good way to make strolls around the neighborhood more pleasant for both of you. It is also an important skill to teach your dog if you want to participate with him in competitive dog sports. This exercise also teaches your dog to walk on a loose leash, so it is well worth your time to work on this with him!

You may need to change how you exercise your power dog while you teach or reteach him polite walking manners. Remember management? Giving up your pulls around the neighborhood is the only way to keep your dog from continuing to practice his pulling behavior while you are teaching him to walk politely. You can't physically stop a strong, larger power dog from pulling; pound for pound, these dogs are significantly stronger than the average human. Avoiding situations where your dog likes to pull will be a temporary adjustment to your lifestyle while you work on his walking skills. You can use other activities to exercise him until you can start going on longer walks together again.

If possible, work through the first six steps of this exercise inside, where there will be few distractions.

1. Start close to a wall, piece of furniture, or some other significant barrier that will force your dog to walk in a straight line and stay close when he is beside you. A hallway is a particularly good area to use for your initial training sessions. Have several small tasty treats available. Attach your dog's leash and stand near the wall or barrier, facing your dog. Quietly back away from him, parallel to the barrier, encouraging him to move toward you while offering him a small treat and plenty of praise after each step he takes toward you. Your dog should come in very close to you to get his treat; if you must reach out to feed him, he is too far away and will have difficulty with the next training step. If he doesn't want to walk toward you as you back away, don't pull on the leash to get him to follow you. Instead, use a more valuable reward to motivate your dog to move with you and eliminate any distractions that are interfering with his learning. Back away eight to ten steps, then release him with your release cue. Do five repetitions of backing away per training session, three or four sessions per day.

Mowgli, an American Bulldog mix, is moving toward Stephanie as she backs away, encouraging him to move toward her and rewarding him very close to her.

2. Once your dog immediately starts following you as you back away from him, you are ready to begin the next step in teaching him to walk beside you. Before you try this with your dog, you will need to figure out the following:

a. You need to know which direction you will pivot during this exercise; the direction you pivot is determined by which side you want to walk your dog on. If you pivot 180 degrees to your right, your dog will end up walking on your left side; if you pivot 180 degrees to your left, your dog will end up walking on your right side. You need to execute this move seamlessly so your dog doesn't stop moving. You are the one who will change direction in this training step. You back up, pivot, then walk forward; your dog simply walks in a straight line forward the entire time. After you pivot, take one step forward, stop, and feed him at your side.

b. You should also figure out how close you need to be to the barrier when you pivot so you end up with your dog between you and the barrier. Your dog should have little extra room between you and the barrier; the barrier will keep your dog from swinging wide or trying to circle around you while you walk, and will build the physical habit of walking in a straight line beside you. The bigger the power dog, the more room you will need to leave for him.

c. The last thing to work through before trying this with your dog is which hand you need to hold your treats in. You should deliver treats out of the hand next to your dog when you are walking forward together. It doesn't matter if you prefer to have your dog walk on your right side or left side. Just be sure you

When you use this method to teach polite walking, you are the one who changes direction, not your dog. You back up, pivot, and walk forward; your dog simply walks forward the entire time.

feed him from the hand on the same side he is walking on to prevent him from trying to reach across your body or circling in front of you to get his treat as you deliver it. If your dog walks on your left side, deliver treats from your left hand; if he walks on your right side, deliver treats from your right hand. You want him to stay in position beside you while you deliver his treat. Slide your hand down your pant seam when you deliver it to him to help you resist the urge to reach out and reward him if he isn't right beside you. Where your dog is rewarded plays an important part in helping your dog understand the behavior you want, so be sure to only reward your dog when he is close beside you. Using your real (or imaginary) pant seam will help you be consistent with where you deliver your dog's reward and will give him a landmark to focus on when he is trying to learn where he is expected to walk. If you let him circle around in front of you before you give him his treat, you are actually teaching him to get in front of you every time you stop, which can definitely be a trip-and-fall hazard!

*Rewarding Ember, a Dalmatian, along the pant seam teaches
her to stay back whenever we stop moving forward.*

3. Once you have your mechanics down, you are ready to try this with your dog. Put your dog on leash and start backing up, feeding after every step for three or four steps, then pivot so you are facing the same direction as your dog, take one step forward, reward your dog at your pant seam before he has the chance to move out of position, and release him with your release cue. If your dog moves ahead of you before you can give him his treat, withhold his reward; just because you have a treat in your hand doesn't mean you must give it to your dog if he isn't close beside you. Instead, immediately start walking backward again until your dog catches up to you, then pivot and take a step forward and reward him along your pant seam before he has the chance to move out of position again. Don't pull on the leash or nag him to get him back into position. Use your body language, the direction of your motion, and the appropriate delivery of rewards to teach your dog exactly where you expect him to walk. Don't use a verbal cue for this walking behavior yet; your dog doesn't really understand what you want and will still make mistakes that you don't want included in the final behavior. Let your motion and where you deliver his rewards show your dog what you want right now. You can certainly praise and talk to him while you teach this behavior, but don't say "Heel" or any other cue yet. You will add a verbal cue when your dog is ready

to start training outside. Make sure you use your release cue after you reward him to let him know he is free to leave your side. After you reward and release him, set him up for another repetition. Complete five to six repetitions per training session and do three to four training sessions per day.

4. As your dog gets more comfortable walking beside you, gradually increase the number of steps you take while both of you are moving forward before rewarding and releasing him. Remember to be very consistent in only rewarding him along the seam of your pant leg so he gets his reward only when he is at your side. Use the 80% rule from Chapter 5 to decide when your dog is ready to walk a few more steps forward with you before you reward him along your pant seam and release him. Continue to back up a few steps, feeding after each step, and then pivoting to help your dog stay focused on you before you move forward together; remain close to the barrier for this step to continue to build his physical habit of walking in a straight line.

5. When your dog can walk for a dozen steps beside you without getting ahead of you, you are ready to increase the distance between your dog and the barrier. Back up a few steps, feeding after each one as you did before, but now execute your pivot about 12 inches farther away from the barrier to increase the distance between your dog and the barrier; if your dog starts to wander out of position laterally from you, adjust the distance between your dog and the barrier until he straightens out and walks close to you again. (You might need to move to a different area in your house to get enough room to do this step.) Make sure you continue to reward your dog right down the seam of your pant leg so he stays close to you. As long as your dog moves in a straight line, you can continue to slowly increase the distance between the barrier and your dog. Reward and release him with your release cue before allowing him to move out of position. Do five repetitions per training session and apply the 80% rule to help you decide when you can move even farther away from the barrier.

6. When your dog can walk in a straight line beside you for a dozen steps with the barrier at least 2 feet away, you are finally ready to add a verbal cue to this new straight-line walking behavior. Back away a few steps to get your dog's attention on you, then give your verbal cue for straight-line walking as you pivot to move forward with your dog; at that precise moment, your dog should be in perfect position at your side and should be able to maintain that position for several steps. If he isn't able to do that, wait to add the verbal cue until he can. This new cue should be distinct from the cue you previously used when you took him out for walks on leash and he pulled you all over the place. If you use your old cue, he might revert to pulling again, so pick a new cue that means "walk right beside me," such as "close," "by me," or "heel."

7. Your dog is also ready to start training outside. Start over with Step 4, using a curb, retaining wall, or similar raised barrier in place of the barrier you used inside to continue to help him understand he can, and should, walk in a reasonably straight line next to you, even when you two are outside. Pick quiet locations to start your outdoor training, and keep your training sessions very short. Don't ask him to walk beside you down the middle of the sidewalk for long distances just yet; if you need to walk

away from barriers or for long distances, use your old walking cue and be prepared for him to pull you a bit, just like he did before you started training him to walk politely. By using his old cue in situations where there isn't a barrier and he is likely to make mistakes, you are protecting his new cue and the new behavior you are working on. Only use your new walking cue when you are walking near barriers to keep his new walking skill sharp as you transition to walking outside. Eventually you will be able to use this new cue everywhere you walk, but your dog isn't fluent enough in this behavior to do that just yet.

The first few times you walk your dog around the neighborhood, be sure to take advantage of barriers such as street curbs on quiet streets to help him transition to walking politely outside.

8. When your dog can walk in a straight line beside you for a dozen steps along the outside barriers, you can start to gradually eliminate them. Start training on a sidewalk

or path that has an obvious edge your dog can see. Now the barrier is visual instead of physical; your dog can easily wander onto grass from the cement if he moves away from you, so be sure to pay attention to him while you walk. If you have slowly and methodically worked through all the previous steps, your dog has started to build a physical habit of walking in a straight line at your side, and it should be reasonably easy for him to continue to do so on the sidewalk. If he wanders off the sidewalk, or tries to get in front of you, immediately start backing away from him to get his attention back on you, then pivot and move forward again. Don't forget to give your release cue when he is allowed to move away from you to sniff, explore, or relieve himself. These environmental rewards will gradually replace his treats completely. Begin fading away the treats by replacing one treat out of five with some other type of reward the first week. The second week, replace two treats out of five with environmental rewards, and so on until you only give your dog a treat once in a while to mark extra special efforts; the rest of his rewards will come from the environment.

As you take your dog on his daily walks, start with one set of a dozen steps of polite walking per block. Use your old walking cue to fill in the gaps between sets of the new cue so you can get in the distance necessary to give your dog some exercise while he is learning to walk next to you for longer distances. This training takes time; don't expect your dog to be able to walk politely at your side for your entire walk as soon as you start walking him outdoors. As his fluency continues to improve and he starts to understand he has to walk next to you no matter where you are, gradually increase the number of dozen-step sets you do per block, until your dog is able to walk an entire block in the correct position at your side. Continue to gradually increase the distance you ask him for polite walking, one block at a time, until he is finally able to walk beside you for your entire walk, without any pulling.

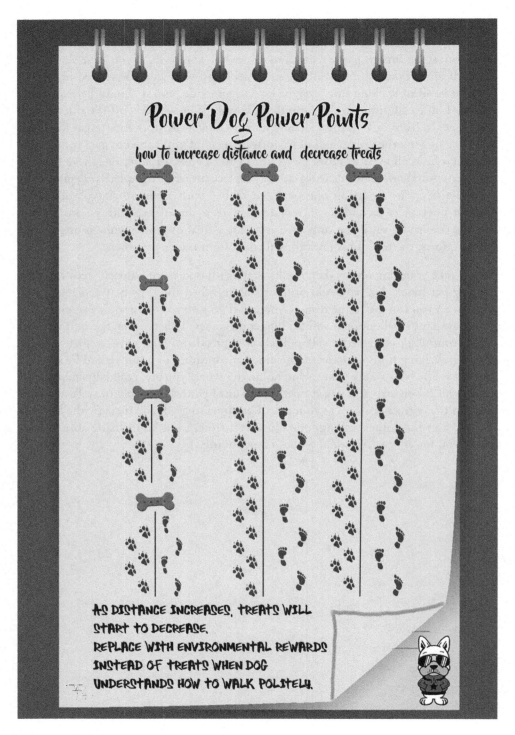

Methodically increase the distance your dog must walk politely at your side so he can be successful, right from the start. As the number of steps increase, the number of treats and other rewards you need to give him on your walk will automatically decrease, because you are only giving him treats at the end of a complete series of steps.

9. Finally, add in increasingly difficult distractions for your dog to ignore while he is walking. If you combine good management techniques with your training, and respect your dog's bubble when you are out walking, he should be able to maintain a loose leash while walking at your side, even when distractions are around. If something bursts his bubble, keep calm and move on! Over time, your dog will become more and more comfortable walking at your side, even when distractions are around.

Teaching your power dog to walk beside you takes time, effort, and patience. By giving your dog a definite position to assume while you are walking, you will help him better understand what you expect of him, and walks will become more pleasant for both of you.

Back up

Exercise goal: Your power dog will back away from you on cue.

Life with a large power dog can be uniquely challenging. Dealing with a large dog who chooses not to move out of your way, get off furniture, or change directions on cue can be both difficult and, in some cases, dangerous. Knowing how to walk backward when you step in front of him is a useful skill for your dog to master; not only will it help you physically move your dog away from potential problems without engaging in a contest of strength with him (which you *will* lose), it will teach your dog about his rear end and help keep his back and hind legs strong. This exercise will also teach your dog that your space is *your* space, not his. Powerful, large dogs often learn they can hang out wherever they please because it is difficult to physically force them to move when they don't want to, so teaching them to back up is the perfect solution. Your dog should always understand moving out of your way is a positive thing to do.

This is a good exercise to start in a hallway, between a wall and some chairs, or between two pieces of furniture, such as a sofa and coffee table. The barriers will help set your dog up in the proper position to move straight back, rather than arcing away from you as he moves backward. When you use this skill in real life, it isn't helpful if your dog arcs to one side or the other as he moves back; if he arcs, he will soon be twisted around and unable to get out of your way.

1. Have your dog on leash, but don't use the leash to guide him through the exercise. He needs to learn on his own how to maneuver his body backward. The leash is only used to keep him from walking away during the training session.

2. Have plenty of small, average-value treats in your pocket or treat bag. The treats need to be tasty enough to motivate your dog, but not so tasty that your dog will continue to move toward you trying to get the treats instead of backing away from you.

3. Start this exercise with enough space between the barriers you are using to allow you and your dog to pass through side by side without touching anything. This should be a calm, pleasant experience for your dog; you can offer him a few treats while he's walking through the chute you've made until he moves through completely relaxed.

4. After your dog can calmly pass through the wide chute, you will start to narrow the passage a few inches at a time over several training sessions until it is just wide enough for you to pass through single file, with your dog close behind you. Each session should be five to six passes; your goal is to teach your dog that he can calmly maneuver through tight spaces going forward and that he can walk calmly behind you (an added bonus and another useful skill for him to learn).

5. As your dog starts to follow you through your passage, go about halfway, then stop and do a quick 180-degree turn to face your dog. The first few times you do this, he will probably be taken by surprise and will shift away from you when you turn. As he stops his forward motion and/or shifts his weight away from you, praise him and give him a treat. The treat should be offered against his sternum (the pointy bone in the middle of his chest). By placing the treat low, you will encourage him to drop his head and continue shifting his weight away from you to get the treat. If your dog tries to sit instead of moving back, you are holding the treat too high. Repeat five to six times per session, varying how far you go into the chute before turning around each time. Once every session, walk all the way through without turning around at all. You don't want your dog to predict when you are going to turn around; if he starts to predict your actions, he won't pay as much attention to you.

Be sure to keep the treat right against your dog's sternum to get him to shift his weight away from you. Mowgli, an American Bulldog mix, shifts his weight back to get his treat, making it easier for him to walk backward away from Stephanie; we opted to forego the barrier only to make his entire body readily visible in this photo.

6. Once your dog is eagerly shifting his weight away from you when you abruptly turn to face him, you can ask him to actually start walking backward. Before you go through the chute with your dog following you, have a small treat in your hand. When you turn to face your dog, instead of stopping, drop your hand with the treat down to your dog's sternum and take a tiny step toward your dog. Be careful not to step on his toes or poke him with your knee; shuffle your foot forward along the ground and keep your knees soft as you step forward to avoid stepping on him. Your dog has already learned to shift his weight backward and bend his head down and back to get the treat you place on his chest, so the chances are very good that he will instinctively take a step or two back as you move toward him. Praise him very quietly so you don't distract him, then let him have his treat. This should be a fun game, but your dog will need to concentrate when he is first learning how to move his body backward in a straight line, particularly for the bigger dogs and puppies who aren't very coordinated yet. Repeat five to six times per session, varying how far you go into the passage before turning around, and occasionally going all the way through the chute without turning around at all. Remember, keep him guessing about when you are going to turn around and he will pay more attention to you!

7. As your dog starts to move backward, you can gradually increase the number of steps he takes before giving him his treat. This should never be a threatening move on your part. This is a slow, controlled, relaxed change of direction for you and your dog. Vary the number of steps he takes backward before he is released, and work up to about 10 steps (or as many steps as you can take in the space you have). You will be moving forward as your dog moves backward.

8. Once your dog has mastered backing up with physical barriers in place, you can start to open up the passage, a few inches at a time. Your goal at this point is to wean your dog off of any physical contact he is relying on to back up in a straight line. This may take several sessions; walking backward isn't something dogs do much in everyday life. If your dog starts to arc his rear end to one side or the other, tighten up the passage a bit and practice a few more sessions at that width before starting to widen it again. Also, be sure you are walking toward your dog in a straight line; if you veer off to one side or the other, your dog will, too.

Jeff uses furniture to create a passage to keep Ember, a Dalmatian, walking backward in a straight line.

9. You will know you are ready to put a name to the behavior and take it into the wide-open world when you have widened your passage enough that you can walk into it side by side with your dog, pivot in front of him, and walk him backward in a straight line. By waiting to put a verbal cue to the behavior until your dog has mastered backing up in a straight line, you greatly increase the likelihood that, under stress, he will still back up in a straight line for you. Some people use a beep similar to the sound a piece of construction equipment typically makes when backing up, while others simply say "Back up" or "Scootch," or use their hands as a signal to "shoo" the dog back. Whatever you choose, be sure it is something you can easily say or do while you're out walking.

10. When you first start this behavior outside, practice it on a sidewalk or along a retaining wall or fence to help your dog stay straight. Start out asking for just a few backward steps at first, remembering to keep the treat low and the praise quiet. Reward him when you stop, then pivot beside your dog so you are both facing the same direction again and start walking forward. Practice this at random times on your walks to help keep your dog's rear end strong and flexible. You can also use this to keep your dog's attention or protect his bubble by blocking his view of a distraction in front of him with your body while simultaneously backing him away from it.

11. The last step is to fade away the treats you use as a reward. As soon as your dog is able to back up without the barriers, randomly start to substitute a toy, a favorite activity, or just allowing your dog to start walking forward again as his reward for backing up.

12. This behavior should also be practiced in doorways, in the garage between the car and the wall, and any other narrow spaces in your home where you might need your dog to move backward out of your way so you can pass through. Once he has mastered moving backward without barriers, you can add in these narrow spaces to your routine.

Teaching your power dog to back up away from you is an easy way to teach him to respect your personal space without using any physical force. Backing up is also a great way to exercise your dog's hind-quarters. Once he learns how to back up on the flat, you can teach him to back up hills, stairs, and other physical challenges to keep his rear end strong and flexible.

Jeff can back Ember, a Dalmatian, away from him easily so he can walk into the house, even when his hands are full.

Move along, li'l doggie

Exercise goal: Your power dog will stand up and move on cue.

Not surprisingly, getting a giant power dog to stand up and move anywhere when he is lying down in the middle of the doorway or lounging on the sofa can be a challenge; hefting all that weight around is work! If your dog isn't motivated to move when you tell him to, no amount of pushing, pulling, or prodding will make him stand up to get out of your way. Let his natural instinct to eat do the work for you to teach him to move on cue. The best age to teach your power dog to move on cue is when he is still a relatively young puppy. If you get an adult dog, start as soon as you can with him. Standing up from a prone position is also a good way to keep back and leg muscles loose and strong, which will help your dog maintain his mobility throughout his life.

1. You can teach this behavior every time you feed your puppy a meal. (Divide your puppy's meals into two or three smaller servings if you want to get more practice in on this skill every day.) Your puppy should be lying down to start, preferably somewhere he decided to lie down on his own. Say his name once to get his attention, rattle his food in the bowl a bit so he knows it's there, then walk away a few feet with his food bowl. As you walk away, ignore your puppy and pay attention to his food; move it around in the bowl some more to make some noise, talk to it (the food, not your puppy!), do whatever it takes to capture his interest. Let him figure out on his own that he needs to get up to see what you have and find out if you are going to give any of it to him. If he is hungry, and you act very interested in the food bowl you are carrying, he will eventually get up to check it out.

2. Wait for him to get up before you set the bowl down for him. Don't repeat yourself if he doesn't come right away. Instead, crouch down where you will put his food bowl and act very, very interested in it. Curiosity will eventually get to him. Ignore him until he is very near, then calmly set the bowl down, praise him, and let him eat his meal. It's very important that the food bowl is a reward, not a bribe! If you put the bowl down first or wave it around trying to get him to come over to you, he will eventually start to wait until he sees the bowl on the floor before he starts to move. He needs to understand that getting up is what makes the food bowl accessible.

3. Once you set his food bowl down, leave him alone to enjoy his meal. You will only do one repetition of this exercise each time you put down his food bowl (which is why you may want to divide his meal into smaller portions if you want to get more repetitions in each day). Your puppy needs to understand that you aren't going to take his food away from him if he makes the effort to stand up and move. You can also unintentionally encourage food guarding if you take his food away whenever he is trying to eat. Simply set the bowl down, praise him, and let him eat. For a very young puppy, as soon as he's done eating, take him outside to relieve himself to help with housebreaking.

4. Once your dog starts to get up as soon as he sees you moving away from him with his bowl, you can add a verbal cue. Say his name once to get his attention, give him

a cue to move, such as "Get up," "Time to move," or whatever makes sense to you, and then walk away with his food. He is also ready for you to increase the distance he has to travel to get his food. Increase the distance until your puppy is walking into the next room to get his meal. This will encourage him to get up and move a distance when you give him his cue; it will also teach him to always move toward you when you tell him to get up. This will make it easier later on for you to guide him to the area you want him to go. You might want him to come over and settle next to you, or walk with you to go out into the yard or go to another room.

5. When he will come into another room for his meal, start changing up the reward he gets for coming to you. You can praise and play with him a bit, let him outside, put on his leash and go for a walk, or offer him a chew toy to enjoy while he sits beside you. Occasionally give him his food as a reward—you always want to keep him guessing!

6. If you want to add in teaching your dog to go into his crate with this exercise, simply cue him to move, and then walk away with his food toward his crate. Before he gets there, take a couple of pieces of kibble out of the bowl and then place the bowl at the back end of the crate, as far from the door as possible. As your dog comes to you, praise him and show him the pieces of kibble. Toss them into the crate while he watches, and tell him to "Kennel up," "Crate," or whatever cue you want to use, as soon as he steps inside. Praise him after all four paws are in the crate and then leave him to eat, leaving the crate door open. Your dog is free to eat and leave his crate whenever he wants.

7. When he starts to anticipate finding his bowl of food in the back of his crate and goes into it without being lured in with pieces of kibble, you can start closing the door behind him before leaving him alone to eat his food. Vary the length of time you leave the crate shut; he shouldn't be able to predict how long he will be in his crate. If he is a young puppy, don't leave him in the crate more than a few minutes after he's finished his meal. Eating may cause him to need to relieve himself, and you don't want him to make a mess in his crate.

Although it may be fairly easy to encourage your power puppy to move out of your way when he is still small, he will eventually become too strong or too massive to get him to move if he decides he doesn't want to. By turning his movement into a way to earn his meal from you, he'll learn to eagerly move for you no matter how big or strong he gets!

Exercises for tenacity and territoriality

Share the chewie

Exercise goal: Your power dog will remain relaxed when you are in close proximity to anything he values.

One way to discourage your puppy's urge to guard is to make yourself "part" of the resource. With high-value chew treats, buy long ones and only allow your puppy to chew on them while you are holding the other end. The presence of you and your hands become signals to your puppy that he is going to get something tasty to chew on, instead of a red flag that the tasty thing he is currently enjoying is about to be taken away.

This is an exercise that should only be started with a young puppy or adult who has shown no actual resource guarding behaviors (e.g., growling, barking, freezing over his items, nipping, or any other behavior that makes you nervous). Puppies may sometimes experiment with trying to dissuade anyone from taking their valuables, such as food, chew bones, or special toys. This is a natural behavior for dogs if they are fending for themselves in the wild; they have to protect resources in order to survive. Abused or neglected dogs, as well as those who figure out that they can keep things they value through intimidation or actual force, will resource guard, particularly against people they don't know. This is one of the most common reasons children get bitten. The child interferes with or tries to take away a resource a dog values, the dog doesn't understand the concept of sharing, and he responds by biting the child to get the resource back. Once a dog has been successful with this tactic, he is more likely to try it again to accomplish his goal of keeping what he values. This doesn't make the dog "bad" or "abnormal," but simply a dog who hasn't learned to behave in any way other than how his instincts tell him to behave. It does, however, make him potentially dangerous when valuable items are around. If your power dog has already learned to use intimidation or outright aggression, don't attempt this exercise. Keep all potentially valuable items away from him and seek professional help from a veterinary behaviorist or professional trainer who uses appropriate protocols to help you work through this with your dog.

1. For this exercise, you need a chew treat, like a beef leg bone, American-made raw-hide chew, or dried meat chew that is long enough to allow you to hold it while your dog chews on it without getting too close to his mouth. Puppies aren't always careful or coordinated with their mouths, so you can avoid accidental nips by practicing this with the longest chew item your puppy is interested in. If your puppy is teething, put the chewie in the freezer to cool it down; this will help soothe your puppy's sore gums and will make edible chewies last a little longer.

2. Put your puppy on a leash and let him drag it. Grab the remote, settle in a comfy chair, and present the chew toy to your dog without any drama. Just hold on to one end and allow your puppy to chew on the other end. Hold the chewie so your puppy can enjoy it while keeping all four feet on the ground.

3. If your puppy gets bored and stops chewing, put the chewie away. If you get bored and want to do something else, step on your puppy's leash so he can't jump up after the chewie when you take it, and walk away. Be careful not to wave the chewie above his head after you take it; you don't want to tease or unintentionally encourage him to jump for it after you take it from him. Once you take it away, the training session is over. Don't repeatedly give the chewie to him and then take it away. That can backfire and actually encourage him to guard anything he values. Let him chew on it for a while, then take it away and go do something else. If he doesn't let go when you stand up to take it and put it away, don't engage in a game of tug of war with him; instead, offer him a trade of his item for a few treats tossed on the floor so he realizes that when you take one good thing away, another one often follows.

Ember, a Dalmatian, is enjoying some chewie sharing time while Jeff watches TV.

Chewing is one way dogs relieve stress and pent-up energy; chew toys are Fido fidget spinners for unfocused, energetic puppies. It is also how puppies help their adult teeth come in properly and can help remove tartar from an adult dog's teeth. It is a natural, pleasing activity for dogs to do. It is important that you provide your dog with uninterrupted chew time in addition to his sharing time to keep his mouth healthy and his head happy. Trade him a handful of special treats tossed on the floor for his chewie, then put it away until the next time he has some unsupervised chew time. You can also trade him special treats for any special toy he is playing with to help you take the toy away without any conflict. Many serious and fatal bites have happened due to resource-guarding behaviors. If children are around, special items should not be accessible to your dog unless you are there to closely supervise him.

Can I have that?

Exercise goal: Your power dog will drop items on cue.

Dogs like to explore the world with their noses and mouths. Many things that have no business being in a dog's mouth can end up there, sometimes with unhappy consequences for both the dog and the thing he is holding. Dropping items on cue is an exceptionally useful skill for your power dog to have. Not only will you be able to keep your dog safe, you won't need to play potentially dangerous chase games with him to take objects out of his mouth. This skill also gives you a safe way to take objects away from a resource-guarding dog. When you chase your dog to try to take an object from him, from his perspective, you are either playing with him, challenging him for a valuable object, or simply scaring him. He may get very excited about this fun game of chase and start running even faster to keep the game going. He may swallow whatever he has in his mouth accidently or intentionally, which can be very dangerous for him. He may turn and try to bluff you into leaving him alone by growling or nipping. He may try to hide if he is afraid when you chase him. None of these scenarios is what you want. What you want is the puppy to drop what is in his mouth, even if he doesn't bring it all the way back to you; you simply want the object out of his mouth, when you ask for it. This is a different behavior than a "Leave it" cue we will teach in the next exercise. "Can I have that?" is the cue for things that he already has in his mouth that you want to remove; "Leave it" is the cue for things that aren't in his mouth yet that you want to keep out of his mouth in the first place.

To teach your puppy to drop items, you need to start with an item that is not highly valuable to your puppy, but one that he will still want to pick up and play with. One of his toys is a good item to use.

1. Put your puppy on a leash and have several special treats available. Stand on the end of his leash so he can't run away from you with the toy, and set the toy down on the floor near him.

2. Once he is playing with his toy, ask "Can I have that?" and then drop several tasty treats on the floor near him. As he eats the treats, pick up the toy and put it out of his sight behind your back or in a pocket. Once the toy is out of sight, praise him and offer him a few more treats. Then quietly hand him his toy back and let him play with it again. Handing his toy back to him teaches him that when you take an item from him, it doesn't mean he will never get it back. If he won't drop his toy to eat the treats, use tastier treats. Repeat once or twice more, then allow him to play with his toy without any further interruptions from you.

3. When your puppy starts to anticipate getting treats and is dropping the item 80% of the time when you give him his cue, start to hold the treats you offer him in your hand instead of dropping them on the floor. If he is truly ready for this step, he will do one of two things: either bring the toy to you and drop it at your feet to get his treats, or drop the toy where he is and then come over to you for his treats. Either response is acceptable; the important behavior is dropping the toy. Reach down and pick up the toy wherever it ends up and put it out of your puppy's sight while he is eating his treats. When he is finished, give him his toy back to play with again.

4. Once your puppy is dropping the toy and coming to you 80% of the time, you can start making him follow you a few steps to get his treats. When he hears "Can I have that?" he should immediately move toward you to get his treats. As he approaches, take a few steps away from him and encourage him to follow you to get his treat. This is helpful for times when you don't have a treat handy to trade him; he will be willing

to follow you to get his treats from the cupboard or refrigerator, instead of running away with the forbidden item.

5. After your puppy follows you for a treat, you can start to substitute other rewards for dropping the forbidden item. Giving him an appropriate chew toy in exchange for the inappropriate one is a good choice most of the time.

For those times when your puppy spontaneously picks up something he shouldn't have (like a shoe or a child's toy) and he isn't on leash, the steps you need to follow are similar:

1. Keep calm and assess the situation. If your dog has an object that he isn't likely to swallow and isn't an immediate danger to him, you can use the situation to continue training the "drop it" cue. Don't turn the situation into a chase game your puppy manipulates you into playing, unless it is a true emergency and you have no other choice but to try to run your puppy down to get the object. If the item is dangerous (medications, tiny objects that can easily be swallowed, sharp objects that will cut his mouth, etc.), try to get him to come to you as quickly as possible and scoop the object out with your fingers. It's less likely he will swallow the item if he is making the choice to move toward you; if you move toward him, he may get excited or scared and swallow it to keep it away from you. Obviously, it's always best to keep anything potentially dangerous out of your puppy's reach, but that's not very realistic even in the most careful homes. If your puppy's life is in danger, do what you need to do to make him safe.

2. If your puppy isn't immediately in danger, say his name once to try to get his attention, and then immediately walk away from him toward your nearest stash of dog treats or kibble. By walking away from him, you immediately remove the possibility of a fun chase game from the situation. You aren't chasing or interacting with him at all. Stealing the pillow off the couch didn't get him any attention from you; in fact, stealing the pillow resulted in you leaving him!

3. Grab a few treats or some of his kibble to use as your barter item. The first several times you work on getting him to drop the stolen item, you need to offer him a trade up front. Your goal is to get him to drop the item without approaching him or putting your hands in his mouth.

4. Face your puppy, say "Can I have that?" "Drop it," or whatever cue you decide to use, then immediately toss several treats or kibble pieces on the floor a foot or so in front and off to one side of you. They will scatter on the floor, making it difficult for him to quickly put the item down, eat the treats, and pick it back up before you are able to pick it up yourself. As soon as he drops the item, calmly and slowly pick it up and walk away. Don't scold him for picking the item up in the first place or tell him he's bad for grabbing it; that moment is over. Instead, you want to praise him for dropping the item, even though at this point, he is dropping it simply to get the food.

5. If he leaves the food and grabs the object before you can pick it up, get some better treats and scatter them farther apart. Move slowly and quietly to pick the object up, to discourage him from rushing to grab it. Soon your dog will start to associate dropping the item he has in his mouth with the opportunity to get a better item.

6. When your dog starts to drop his item before you can scatter the treats, you can wait to scatter the treats until after he has dropped the item. The treats will become rewards rather than bribes to get the item away from him at this point. If he doesn't drop the item, stand quietly and look at the floor (but don't repeat the cue!); usually dogs will get bored and lose interest in the item if you simply ignore them long enough. As soon as he drops it, praise and reward him. Even though he was slow, he still made the correct behavioral choice to drop the item, and he has earned his reward.

7. When he drops the item at least 80% of the time on cue, and you are using treats only as a reward (i.e., the treats only come out *after* he has dropped the object), you can begin to replace the treats with praise, petting, other toys, or any other reward your puppy values more than the object he has in his mouth.

Time is your ally with this particular behavior; as your puppy learns about his environment and matures, his urge to explore the world with his mouth will significantly decrease. If you don't unintentionally make this type of behavior into a game for him, you should naturally see fewer instances of your puppy picking up inappropriate objects as he matures.

Leave it

Exercise goal: Your power dog will refrain from interacting with an object on cue.

Unless you own one of the very small power dogs (Boston Terrier, French Bulldog, etc.), you don't have any way to physically stop your power dog from moving toward and grabbing anything he is truly determined to get. Teaching a "Leave it" cue allows you to prevent your dog from taking objects you don't want him to have, no matter how large or strong he is. Remember, this is different from the previous exercise; "Can I have that?" is for objects your dog already has in his mouth, while "Leave it" is for objects your dog hasn't grabbed yet.

1. Have your power dog on a leash or securely tethered to a sturdy piece of furniture for this exercise to prevent him from walking away from you while you are training. Have something your dog likes, but isn't crazy about, available as the "forbidden object." For example, if your dog will turn himself inside out for a piece of cheese, you will want to use something far less tasty, such as a few pieces of his kibble or a small dry dog treat for this exercise. If you use a toy, don't use his favorite toy that he always carries around; pick one that he plays with only when it's the only one available to him. You'll work up to the super-good stuff later!

2. Set your dog up an arm's length away from a table or some other place where you can set your training item down. You should be able to reach over and set the item down without moving your feet.

3. Stand facing your dog, with your back toward the area where you will be placing the item. Without saying anything, place the training item behind you. Your dog will be able to see the item if he moves or looks around you.

4. The rules of this game are simple: Your dog is not to move toward you, or anything he wants, without your permission when you are with him. He can change positions (i.e., sit, down, or stand) or even back away from the item, but he can't move toward it. Once the item has been set down, stand in a relaxed stance facing your dog. If he tries to move forward, simply step into his path to block his motion. Don't say anything to him; let your body do all the talking! This is a silent exercise unless you are rewarding the dog for success with praise.

If you have selected an appropriate training item to start with, your dog either won't move toward it at all or he will stop as soon as you step into his path. If you picked an item that is too valuable to start this exercise, he will continue to try to get the item. Continue to move side to side, or even toward your dog, to block his path and prevent him from getting the item, but don't move backward toward the item. If you back up toward the item, you will be teaching your dog to use his body and his size to get what he wants and to ignore your personal space. If your dog is easily stopped from moving toward the item, pick the item up as soon as your dog stops moving toward it and give it to him, along with plenty of praise. By using the item as his reward, you are teaching him to have patience; just because you tell him to leave something alone doesn't mean he won't ever be able to have it! (If the item you are working with is one you actually don't want him to ever have, be sure to substitute another item of equal or greater value for his reward.) If he is fixated on the item and simply won't stop trying to get it, move him farther away from it until he calms down and stops trying to get it. Then use a less interesting treat or toy for his next training session. Repeat five to six times per training session, three to four training sessions per day. Vary the items you use in your sessions, but keep them very boring until your dog will watch you place the item and he makes no effort at all to get to it.

You can move toward your dog or side to side, but never back toward the object. If your dog struggles with this, move him farther away from the object and try again.

5. Once your dog can leave a boring item alone, it's time to slowly add more interesting and desirable items into your training sessions. Increase the temptation in small increments; if you started this exercise using your dog's kibble, try using a dry dog treat, then later a soft treat, and finally, when he really understands the game, a piece of cheese or chicken (or whatever makes your dog dance for joy when he eats it). Your goal is to increase the value of the item slowly enough that he can be successful during the training session, but it's alright if he makes a mistake or two at first so he can learn that the same rules always apply, no matter what item is involved. Continue to work one item at a time, increasing the value of the item to your dog only after he can successfully complete Step 4 with the item you are currently using at least 80% of the time. Your goal is to be able to place your dog's absolute most favorite treat or toy on the table behind you and have your dog remain relaxed and wait until you give it to him.

6. Now that your dog really understands this game, you can add a verbal cue to the behavior to let him know with your voice as well as your body that he can't just rush up to whatever he wants to approach when he is with you. As you place the item down, say your cue ("Leave it," "Not yours," "I got this," or whatever cue you want to use). By saying this every time just before setting the object out, your dog will start to associate the cue with ignoring the object. This cue will eventually allow you to interrupt your dog's behavior no matter where he is relative to you.

7. Once your dog is successful 80% of the time or more with valuable items, start to add distance between you and your dog. Start by placing the item on the table, cue him to leave the item alone, then take a few steps away. If your dog starts to move, step into the space between him and the item to prevent him from taking it. Use the 80% rule to determine when you can add more distance to your training session.

8. When your dog is steady with treats, toys, and other non-living objects, you can start to use this same blocking technique with strangers and animals you encounter when you are out in the neighborhood or when people come to your home. Be sure to start far enough away from them that he doesn't really respond much, and gradually work your way closer. This skill will help you when you need to control your dog, and also lets your dog know that you don't always need, or want, him to act on any instincts he may have to protect you. If you tell him to ignore a person or dog, he should leave them alone just like he leaves inanimate objects alone on cue.

Exercises for dog aggression and stranger wariness

Whaddya see?

Exercise goal: Your power dog will learn to look to you for a reward when he sees something arousing in his environment.

Environmental awareness is a survival instinct in all animals, including humans. It isn't realistic (or fair) to expect a power dog to just ignore the world around him, particularly if he is worried about what is out there or is overly excited by distractions in his environment. The longer your dog looks at something that interests him, the more aroused he may become and the more difficult it will be for you to get his attention, so it is important to teach your dog how to look away from something to help him remain calm around distractions. If you are able to get your dog to voluntarily redirect his focus back toward you *before* he gets too aroused, you can help him cope better with common environmental distractions. This training takes time to accomplish, but it will definitely help your dog live a less stressful life and cope better in new situations.

Not all distractions are created equal; some are more tempting than others for your dog. Keep a mental list of your dog's distractions and rank them from the hardest for your dog to ignore (e.g., another dog) to the easiest for your dog to ignore (e.g., someone walking by at a distance). Start with the easiest distractions first, gradually moving on to the more difficult ones as your dog starts to understand what you want him to do and can remain calm around the distractions you are currently working with.

1. Start this exercise with your power dog on leash in a quiet, calm environment. Have small, extra-special treats (cheese, cooked chicken, etc.) available for rewards. The treats must be more valuable to your power dog than the distraction you will be using during training. The more distracting the situation, the more special the treat needs to be. After all, you are asking your dog to quit looking at something he finds very interesting or is instinctively driven to pay attention to, so the payoff needs to be very valuable to him. Keep the treats in your pocket or a treat bag, out of sight so they don't act as a distraction to your dog.

2. Select an easy distraction and stand close enough to it that your dog will actually look at it, but not so close that your dog refuses to look away from it to pay attention to you. It may take some trial and error to figure out exactly how far away you need to stand; the distraction needs to be balanced right on the surface of your power dog's bubble, without bursting it, for this training to be successful.

3. Once you are set up at the correct distance and your dog is calm, look casually toward the distraction, point to it, and in a very calm voice, ask your dog "Whaddya see?" It is important that you remain calm and quiet when you ask your dog this. If you get excited, your dog will get excited as well, which defeats the purpose of this exercise. As soon as your dog looks toward the distraction, count slowly to two in your head, then take a few steps away from the distraction while offering your power dog

a tasty treat. You don't want him to stare at the distraction so long that he gets more aroused by it, but you do need to give him enough time to process what he is seeing so he can feel comfortable looking away. Two seconds works about right for most power dogs when you first start this training.

Don't say anything as you move—simply move away until your dog notices your motion and turns back toward you to see what you are doing. When he looks back at you, offer him a treat and some praise. You want your power dog to figure out on his own that: (1) looking away from something exciting pays off for him, and (2) if you move, he should follow to get his reward. In this exercise, your dog is making the choice on his own to look away from the distraction and toward you, instead of you telling him to look away from it.

4. If your power dog doesn't want to turn toward you as you step away, you set him up too close to the distraction and burst his bubble, or you allowed him to stare too long at the distraction before moving away. Increase the distance between him and the distraction and try again. At some distance, he will eventually be able to regain his composure and turn toward you. Next training session, start farther away from the distraction to get some successful repetitions completed, then try again. If he is still too excited to notice you or if he refuses his treats, stop your training session and let him calm down. Then come back to this distraction in the next training session, starting even farther away from it. Remember, an aroused dog can't learn very easily, so keeping your dog calm is critical for this training to succeed.

5. If your power dog doesn't want to look at the distraction in the first place, it may be that what you are using isn't really a distraction to him at all, or that you are well outside his bubble for that distraction. Move closer to the distraction to try to interest him in it. This is actually a good training problem to have! If he is fixated on the treats you have in your pocket instead of the distraction, try using less-tasty treats so he is more willing to look away from you.

6. As your dog begins to look at the distractions you point out to him and then turn back toward you for a reward, you can gradually make the training more difficult by either: (1) increasing the difficulty of the distraction you use, or (2) moving a little closer to the easier distraction you've been practicing with. Be sure to change only one or the other in any single training session so, if the training doesn't go well, you will know what exactly your dog is struggling with. If you change more than one aspect of the exercise in the same training session and a problem occurs, you won't know which change caused the problem. You can certainly use a more difficult distraction in one training session and move closer to an easier distraction in the next one, but don't make both changes in the same session. Use the 80% rule to help you decide when to make things more difficult.

7. When you change distractions, remember that different distractions may have different-sized bubbles associated with them. You may be able to stand quite close to a toy and get your power dog to refocus on you easily, yet need to stand a block or more

away to get your power dog to look away from another dog. Adjust your distance according to the distraction you are working with. If your power dog won't look back on his own, keep moving away from the distraction until he can look at you. If you stand still and wait for more than a few seconds for your power dog to respond, you will actually be letting him get even more aroused and make it that much more difficult for him to look at you.

8. When you start to move closer to a distraction you've been working with, take it in small steps (literally). You are now starting to shrink the bubble associated with that distraction, teaching your power dog to pay attention to you in closer proximity to it. This takes time. The more valuable the distraction is to your dog, the longer it may take to start shrinking his bubble. Certain power breeds developed to have exceptional stranger wariness, like Filas and Cane Corsi, may be very difficult to redirect in close proximity to strangers. Never expect your dog to look at people if he can't without reacting aggressively toward them.

9. Use common sense when working with living distractions, such as other dogs or people. Don't allow your power dog to look at another dog for more than a second or two before you start moving him away. A few seconds is enough time for your dog to realize he is looking at another dog without getting too aroused. Allowing your dog to stare much longer will get him aroused and might also arouse the other dog. If you are in doubt about the stability of the other dog, don't ask your dog to look at him at all. Instead, get the heck outta Dodge and find a safer dog to use as a distraction. You also need to remember that there are many people who hold on to misconceptions that all power dogs are vicious animals just waiting to attack anything that moves. If you appear to be actively encouraging your power dog to stare at someone else's dog, a bystander may jump to the conclusion that you are encouraging your dog to attack, particularly if your dog is vocalizing or straining against his leash. (If he is doing either of those things, you are too close!) Use common sense and be respectful of other dog owners when you work on this exercise using other dogs or people as distractions. You need to be aware of where the other dog is looking as well as where your own dog is looking; if the other dog is fixated on yours, find another dog to use for this exercise to avoid problems.

*Dalmatian Ember struggles to stay calm when she sees children running;
Jeff works nearly one block away from a playground during their first few
training sessions so she is able to calmly look at the children Jeff points out
and then turn her attention back to him to earn a reward.*

10. If you progress slowly and methodically with this exercise, your power dog will start to anticipate receiving a reward from you every time you point out something for him to look at. You will find that distractions that used to really grab his attention now only get a brief glance before he turns to you. Your power dog may also begin to self-interrupt and look back at you when he sees distractions, even without your prompt. Pay attention when he looks back at you seemingly out of the clear blue; he may be trying to tell you about a distraction in the environment that you didn't even notice!

11. Once your power dog becomes fluent with this behavior, start substituting other types of rewards for treats to keep the behavior strong. One of the easiest environmental rewards to offer your power dog is the very distraction he is looking away from. Of course, this isn't always safe or possible to do. You certainly wouldn't let your power dog go over to another dog or chase after a car as a reward. But if it is possible, the distraction your dog looks away from is the perfect reward to use for this behavior. For example, if you are using a toy as your training distraction, you can also use that toy as a reward. When your dog looks away from the toy, you can immediately pick it

up and give it to him. If you can't provide the distraction as the reward, think about a substitute reward of equal or greater value to the distraction to give him.

By changing the association your power dog makes with distractions in his environment, you will greatly enhance the quality of his life. Many things that used to arouse and stress him will lose their importance once he knows that looking at you instead will be rewarded. You will never extinguish his protective instincts though. There will always be things that your dog will have difficulty looking away from, no matter how much training you do. For example, you might work through this exercise so your power dog becomes comfortable passing near strangers in broad daylight, but he may still get aroused very quickly and be ready to protect you when you encounter strangers after dark. You can never train the instincts completely out of any dog, but you can certainly give him the coping skills necessary to calmly deal with typical distractions in his life.

Hand targets

Exercise goal: Your power dog will touch your hand with his nose regardless of where you put your hand.

Having your power dog focus on your hand and touch it with his nose is a very useful behavior. You can use it to keep your power dog busy and focused on you, as well as to move him into different positions quickly and easily. If your power dog learns to enjoy running to you to hit your hand with his nose, you can use that behavior to get him close to you if he fails to come when you use your recall cue. And if your dog understands this game, you can easily get him to move out of your way without any physical effort on your part, which is particularly helpful with the giant power breeds!

1. Find a ruler or measuring tape. Sit it in front of you and put your thumb on the one-inch mark and your forefinger on the two-inch mark. Without moving your fingers, lift up your hand and look at the space between your fingers. That is how big one inch is. Why is this important to do before you start teaching your dog this behavior? Because you should start this training by holding your hand no more than one inch from your dog's nose. But most owners cheat and put their hands six inches or more away from their dogs the very first training session, and then get frustrated because their dogs don't do anything. Hopefully, by visually reminding yourself exactly how big one inch is, you won't make the same mistake with your power dog and will have success with this exercise right from the start!

2. Start this training with your power dog on leash in a quiet, calm environment. Have small, tasty treats available for rewards. Keep the treats in your pocket or in a bowl nearby so your dog won't be distracted by them. Sit or step on the end of the leash, or tether your dog to something secure so he can't decide to walk away while you are training, but be sure to leave enough slack in the leash so he can sit or stand.

3. For this behavior, it doesn't matter what position your dog is in when you start the training. The way you hold your hand will become the visual cue for this behavior, so

it will need to be somewhat distinctive to your dog. Hold the index finger and middle finger of one hand out (as if you are pointing to something with those two fingers), and curl your thumb, ring finger and pinky finger in toward your palm. You will present this visual cue with the back of your hand toward your dog. Hold your hand one inch in front of your dog's nose. Stand still and be quiet while your dog figures out what you want him to do—don't wiggle your hand around or nag him. Most dogs will touch your hand out of curiosity. As soon as you feel your dog's nose touch your hand, praise and use your other hand to offer him a treat. Don't cheat and move your hand toward your dog—be sure your dog moves toward your hand to touch it.

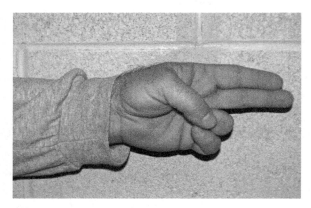

By holding your hand in a specific way, your dog will learn when he should touch your hand and when he should leave it alone.

4. If your dog doesn't show any interest in your hand within ten seconds, drop your hand to your side, move your dog a few steps away to a new spot, and try again. Make sure you are actually holding your hand only one inch from his nose. If something in the environment is distracting your dog, remove the distraction or find a less distracting place to train. If your dog still won't interact with your hand, place a very tiny piece of treat between the extended fingers of your target hand and try again. Your dog should touch your hand to try to get the treat. Repeat this three more times with a treat between your fingers, then immediately repeat without the treat between your fingers. Your dog should touch your hand in anticipation of getting the treat between your fingers, even though it isn't there. Quickly praise and give him a treat from your pocket as soon as you feel him touch your hand. If you need to jump start your power dog by using a treat between your fingers, get rid of the treat as quickly as you can. If you rely too long on the treat to get your dog to interact with your hand, he will have problems performing the behavior later when you take the treat away.

5. Practice with your hand one inch from your dog's nose until he will touch it as soon as you put it in front of him at least 80% of the time. Be sure to practice with both hands; your dog may not understand that if he performs a behavior on your right side that he can also perform it on your left side unless you help him generalize the behavior. You can also add a verbal cue to the behavior at this point, if you want one, by simply saying "Touch" as you feel him touch your hand.

6. Increase the distance your dog must reach to touch your hand by one-inch increments, using the 80% rule to help you decide when to add more distance. Once your hand is far enough away that your dog must actually take a step or two to get to it, he may seem a little confused. Up to this point, he didn't have to move his body much to perform the touch behavior. You have now essentially added another behavior he must do before he can touch your hand. Be patient and quiet while he figures out that he needs to move his entire body toward you to touch your hand. Resist the urge to move your hand toward him to "help" him. If he hasn't moved toward your hand within ten seconds, drop your hand to your side, get your dog up, and move to a different spot in the room to try again. If he still struggles, decrease the distance between your hand and his nose until he is successful, then start building distance back up from there. If you absolutely can't resist the urge to move your hand toward your dog's nose to help him with the behavior, try this exercise a few times with your eyes shut. Rely on your sense of touch to tell you when your power dog has performed the behavior correctly and earned his reward.

7. Once your dog is walking toward your hand to touch it, you can begin to present your hand in different places relative to your body. Hold it high, low, behind you, and in between your legs. Also practice showing him the target when you are both walking together. Getting him comfortable touching your hand in all different positions and in motion will turn this behavior into a handy training tool for teaching other behaviors; for example, you can use a hand target to easily move your dog into various positions. You can also start substituting toys, praise, and environmental rewards for treats at this point. For example, ask for a hand touch before you let your dog out into the yard to play. Going outside becomes his reward for performing the hand touch. This is a super easy, quick way to sneak in a little training in the course of everyday activities, and it constantly reminds your power dog that if he wants something from you, he must first do something *for* you.

8. Most dogs enjoy this behavior once they understand what you want. Sometimes they will become quite creative and start touching you even when you don't ask them to touch. If your dog starts experimenting with the behavior and touching your hand when you haven't asked for a touch, simply ignore him. Don't look at him or say anything to him. Ignore him. This spontaneous behavior will stop if it is never reinforced. He will learn that the only time he should touch your hand is when you are holding your two fingers out or you tell him to touch.

This is a particularly fun behavior for young children to do (with adult supervision), once your dog knows what to do. Hold the child's hand in yours and help him put his fingers out, then tell the dog to touch the child's hand. This will help the child learn how to interact with the dog in an appropriate manner using a fairly simple behavior, as well as reinforce to the dog that he must listen to all the members of the family, regardless of their size.

Other side

Exercise goal: Your power dog will learn how to quickly move to your other side while you are walking.

This behavior is perfect for situations when you have no choice but to pass close to something your dog finds distracting, or when it is physically difficult for your dog to walk on the side of you he normally walks on (e.g., if bushes hanging over one side of the sidewalk make it difficult to walk your dog on that side). Distance is *always* your friend when it comes to helping your dog cope with distractions, so placing him on the opposite side of you, away from the distraction, can help him remain calmer. Most dogs don't automatically understand they can walk politely on either side of you. From your dog's viewpoint, you consist of at least four different people; there is the you he sees when he is walking on your left side, the you he sees when he is walking on your right side, the you he sees when he approaches from the front, and the you he sees when he approaches from behind. He needs to learn to respond to each one of these versions of you, in addition to all the other versions that exist, depending on the position you are in (standing, sitting, etc.) and where you are relative to your dog.

If you want to see this concept in action, try a little experiment. Have your dog face you and ask him to perform a behavior he knows very well, like sit. Note how long it takes him to respond. Then try the same cue when he is on your right side, your left side, and then behind you. Chances are, he won't perform the cue as quickly on every side, because he doesn't understand that you need to be listened to, regardless of where he happens to be relative to your body. You can also try this standing, sitting, lying down, and hiding out of sight; his cue performance will vary until he learns that performing the cue is mandatory, no matter where you are or what you look like. Your position relative to your dog is an important detail you need to pay attention to when you train, because your dog certainly pays attention to it. You will need to help him generalize the concept of walking on either side of you by taking the time to show him how to do it.

1. This exercise is easiest for most people to start indoors, with the dog dragging his leash. If your dog tries to walk away from you, you can simply step on the leash to keep him from getting too far away. Start this training with your power dog standing on his "normal" walking side in a quiet environment. Hallways make particularly good training areas for this exercise, since there is limited room for your dog to move in. Be sure you are leaving enough room for him to walk on both sides of you when you work with him.

2. If your dog already understands a touch target, put your target hand behind your back (this is the hand on the opposite side of where he is standing) and cue your dog to touch. Slowly move your hand around to the other side, asking your dog to continue touching it with his nose, so your dog will follow it around behind you to the other side. Take a few steps with your dog on the "new" side, then release and reward him. If your dog doesn't understands a touch target, hold really tasty treats in your

hand opposite from your dog. In other words, if your power dog normally walks on your left side, he should be standing on your left side, and you will hold the treats in your right hand. Take a few steps forward with your dog on his normal walking side, then stop. As you stop, reach behind you as far as you can toward your dog with your treat hand, trying to keep the treat at your dog's eye level if at all possible. You may need to wiggle the treat around a little the first few times you do this so your dog realizes it is back there. For a shorter power dog, you may need to bend your knees when you stop so the treat is low enough for him to see, or use squeeze cheese (or a similar type of sticky treat) on the end of a long kitchen spoon to give you the added length you need to reach your dog's eye level. As soon as your power dog notices the treat, move it in an arc behind you to lure your dog around to your other side. Let him eat the treat, and then take a few steps with him on the "new" side before you release him. If you start with your dog standing on your left side, he will end up on your right side. If the treat is good enough, he should quickly look back for it when you stop after just a few repetitions.

3. Once your power dog is comfortable going behind you when you are standing still (either by hand targets or following food), it is time to start introducing motion into the transition. Start with your dog on his "normal" walking side. Take three or four steps forward and then slow down significantly while simultaneously luring your dog behind you with either a hand target or treats. Once he switches sides, take a few more steps and release him. As your dog gets more coordinated with slipping behind you, you can speed up your movement. Eventually, you won't need to slow up as you cue your dog to pass behind you— he will be able to switch sides at a normal walking speed.

After setting up a training chute, Jeff starts teaching Ember, a Dalmatian, to switch sides by luring her to the other side using treats.

4. When your power dog can move to the other side of you while you continue to walk at a normal speed, it's time to introduce the cue for this behavior. Be sure that the word you use for walking on this "new" side is different from the word you use for your dog's regular walking side, because these are actually two different behaviors. For example, you might use "Walk" when your dog is on your left side and "Side" when he is on your right side. It doesn't matter the exact words you use, as long as you use a different one for each side. Give your new verbal cue,

followed by your arm motion behind your back. Through paired repetitions, your dog will eventually respond to the verbal cue and you can eliminate the awkward physical cue altogether.

5. This is also the time to begin eliminating the treats in your cue hand if you are using them instead of a touch target. Signal your dog to go behind you without a treat in your hand and then give him a treat as soon as he gets all the way around you. Once he will follow your hand without the treat in it, you can begin to substitute environmental rewards for treats. For most dogs who enjoy their walks, the mere fact that you are continuing on your walk after he switches sides is enough of a reward to keep the behavior strong. But if you occasionally pair switching sides with a very special reward, such as checking out a tree for squirrels or sniffing the fire hydrant to read pee-mail, your dog will make a strong association between performing this behavior and an extra-special reward. Then if you need to use this behavior to protect your power dog's bubble, he will spend more time anticipating a great reward than worrying about the distraction you are avoiding. If you always give the reward on the side your dog switches to, you will be simultaneously teaching him to look in that direction for a reward as soon as he moves to the other side. So if you are walking with your dog on your left and you need to move him to your right side to put some distance between your dog and a distraction, he will look off to the right for his special reward and may actually miss the distraction altogether.

6. Once your power dog is moving smoothly from his "normal" side to the "new" side on cue, expand his understanding of this behavior by teaching him to go back to the "normal" side. The process is the same, but the hands you use to hold the leash and treat will be reversed. Remember that dogs don't generalize well, so moving from left to right may be very different than moving right to left from your power dog's point of view.

The ability to smoothly and calmly move your power dog from one side of your body to the other while you walk is a handy behavior to teach your dog, and it can add a little variety to your daily walks. You don't want the cue to become a predictor of exciting things, so spontaneously switch sides while you are out walking your dog even when no distractions are around. By walking your dog on both sides of you, you will also help his muscles and skeleton stay balanced over his lifetime.

Crash

Exercise goal: Your power dog will learn to go to, and stay in, a well-defined area.

This exercise will give your power dog a job to focus on even when you don't actually want him to do anything. Being able to send your dog to a particular spot in a room or have him comfortably rest on a mat in the vet clinic lobby is very useful.

A handy crash pad for your dog is a rubber-backed bath mat or rug. This type of mat will work on any surface without sliding and provides some cushioning for your dog while he is on it. It can easily be washed and is a practical size to take along when you go out with your dog to the vet clinic or training classes.

1. For this exercise, start in an area that has enough room for you to put down the mat and still have space around all four sides for your dog to walk. Have small, tasty treats ready that will be easy for your dog to see on the mat; if the mat is dark, use light-colored treats and vice versa. Treats that don't easily roll are also useful to help them stay on the mat when they're tossed. Before you bring your dog out to work, practice tossing a few treats on the mat so you don't add extra confusion to the training process through poorly aimed treat tosses.

2. Your dog's crash pad should be a place he associates with good experiences. Put his leash on and let him drag it while you are training. If he tries to leave the training area, pick up the leash and hold it until he starts working with you. To introduce him to the mat and the concept of getting good things while he is on it, start with your dog close enough that he only has to take one or two steps to get on the mat. Show your dog his treat and then toss it on the mat. Be sure your dog has to put all four feet on the mat to get his treat. As soon as your dog is on his mat and eats the treat you tossed, offer him another treat while he is still on the mat, and then quickly back away as you give him his release cue and encourage him to move off his mat. Repeat the toss four to five times per training session until your dog starts to move toward his mat as soon as he sees you move your arm to toss the treat.

3. When your dog is anticipating the treat toss (i.e., he starts to move toward his mat as he sees your arm move, but before you actually toss the treat) at least 80% of the time, take one additional step back from the mat and toss a treat. As he moves to his mat, quietly step toward the mat (if necessary) to feed him another treat when he is still on his mat, and then give him his release cue and allow him to leave his mat.

4. Continue to increase the distance between your dog and his mat one step at a time until you are no longer able to toss a treat on the mat as you tell him to go to it. If you have proceeded methodically and used the 80% rule to determine when to increase the distance, your dog should be anticipating getting a treat on his mat as soon as you move your arm toward the mat in a tossing motion, even if you don't actually toss a treat. Pretend to toss a treat to the mat using the same motion you used before. Your dog should immediately move to his mat ahead of you. Follow behind him quietly and hand him his treat as soon as he has all four feet on his mat. And don't forget to praise him, too! If he moves off his mat while you approach, lead him a few steps away and wait for him to step back on it before you reward him. After you've fed him, give him his release cue and allow him to leave his mat. Continue to increase the distance a step or two at a time until you can send him from one side of the room to the other to get on his mat. You can also add in a verbal "Go crash" cue as you move your hand now that your dog has a basic understanding of the behavior you want.

5. You are now ready to decide where you would like to permanently position your crash pad in any given room. It will be easier for your dog to go to his mat consistently if he knows exactly where to expect it to be in the room. For example, if you would like your dog to go to his mat so he isn't under your feet while you prepare dinner, select an out-of-the-way spot in the kitchen where he can see you, but not interfere

with you, and put his mat there. If you want to use mats in several rooms in your house, buy several mats and be sure to practice this exercise in each room so he learns where to look for his mat.

6. Up until this point in your training, the focus has been on just getting your dog to go to his mat. Now it's time to add in duration; in order for this to be a truly useful skill around the house, he needs to know that he may be expected to spend some time on his mat. Send your dog to his mat and follow quietly behind him. Once he is on his mat, treat him, but delay giving him his release cue for a few seconds. If you taught him his release cue, he already knows he should continue doing whatever you've cued him to do until you release him, so he should stay on the mat. If he leaves, simply direct him back on to his mat, wait briefly, and then release him before he chooses to leave again, so he has success. Use the 80% rule to gradually increase the time you wait before you release your dog to leave his mat. Be sure to stay close by him while he is learning to stay on his mat for longer periods of time. Your training will actually progress more rapidly if you increase duration a few seconds at a time so your dog has a high success rate, rather than if you try to make a huge leap from having him stay on the mat a few seconds to expecting him to stay on it a few minutes. Vary how long he stays on the mat with every repetition during a training session, so he can't predict when you are going to release him. Do a few repetitions at your goal duration for that training session, mixed in with a few repetitions that are shorter, and one or two repetitions that are slightly longer, to keep him guessing when he will be released. You may notice your dog changes position on his mat as he is expected to stay on it longer. That's okay! You did not cue him to sit or down; you cued him to go to his mat and stay on it. As long as he doesn't leave his mat, he is free to adjust himself and get comfortable any way he desires.

7. Once your dog has worked up to a minute or so staying on his mat, you need to start increasing the distance that *you* remain from him when he is on his mat. There is no point teaching your dog to go to his mat in the kitchen and stay there if you have to go over to his mat with him every time. By now, your dog knows how to travel across the room to get to his mat, but he is used to you following behind while he does this. He needs to learn how to go to his mat without you following him. Put a treat on the mat and take your dog about halfway across the room from it. Cue him to go to his mat and take one small step toward his mat as if you are going to follow him, then slowly come to a stop. Chances are good that he will continue to his mat. If he does, he will be immediately rewarded with the treat you left on the mat. If he stops moving when you stop moving, quietly step closer to his mat until he will get on it. On the next repetition, walk a little closer to the mat before stopping, so your dog will successfully go straight to his mat in one motion. Be very calm and slow with your body language if your dog struggles with moving ahead of you to go to his mat. Gradually increase the distance he has to go out in front of you to get to his mat a step or two at a time, until you can stand still and send him to his mat from across the room at least 80% of the time. Be sure to leave a treat on the mat before you take him across the room and praise him as soon as he gets on his mat. When he is on his mat,

you can wait a varying amount of time before you release him, so you are combining distance with a little bit of duration work.

8. When your dog is promptly going to his mat by himself and staying on it for a few minutes, you can introduce long-lasting rewards he can enjoy while he is on his mat. You can give him his meal, a chew toy stuffed with a tasty frozen filling, or his favorite non-food chew toy to enjoy on his mat and occupy his mind while he is waiting to be released. If he leaves his mat before you release him, pick up the reward and send him back to his mat before giving him the reward back. It is important to pay attention to your dog while he is learning he must stay on his mat with you at a distance. The faster you get him back on his mat if he tries to leave it, the easier it will be for him to understand that leaving was the behavior that you didn't want him to do; ideally, if you keep an eye on him and slowly increase the distance between you, you will be able to help him get back on his mat before all four feet have even left it. Keep the rewards you give him when he is on his mat extra valuable by only giving them to him when he is on his mat. You can also attach a tether to him once he gets on his mat to prevent him from leaving it if you can't keep your eye on him while he is learning this exercise.

Rocky, a Rottweiler, lies on his crash pad and chews on his toy while Sharon prepares dinner.

9. Distractions are the last thing to add into your mat work. The distractions you need to work around will depend on how you will use this behavior in everyday life. Now that your dog knows how to go to his mat from across the room and stay there until you tell him he can leave, you can use his crash pad as a place to hang out while you prepare dinner or as his own personal space to occupy when you go to training class. If you want to use the mat in the kitchen, you need to gradually introduce the sights, sounds, and smells of food preparation to your dog while he stays on his mat.

Feeding him his meal on his mat while you are cooking will help him have patience and remain in place. If at any time he leaves his mat without being released, you need to immediately put him back on it. If you are preparing a gourmet multi-course meal and don't have time to work with potential training issues that may pop up, either don't put your dog on his mat in the first place or tether him to keep him on it, or use alternative ways to keep him out of the kitchen and out of your way. If you want to use his mat in training class, place it next to your chair and be sure to keep an eye on him while other students are training or the instructor is talking. If he leaves his mat, put him right back on it so he understands the rules that apply to his mat behavior at home also apply in class. You may want to give him his favorite binky toy to chomp on if he is extremely nervous or frustrated with idle time in class, or if he isn't particularly food-motivated to begin with; he may get aroused to the point that he refuses food in class but will still shake, chew, or otherwise take his frustrations out on a toy while he remains on his mat.

Jeff can relax and read a book while Ember, a Dalmatian, lies on her mat near him. Ember is tethered to the foot of the sofa so she can't leave her mat while she is learning this skill and she gets to enjoy a special chew treat while she is there.

You can make his space even more relaxing by using aromatherapy in the area. Dog appeasing pheromone (DAP) and lavender have both been researched and shown to help reduce anxiety levels in dogs. You can put these on your dog's collar and his crash pad when you are away from home to help him, as well. This won't take the place of training, but it might help your dog stay calm enough to relax and stay on his mat.

Teaching your power dog to go to a mat and stay there until released has many different uses away from home, too. Visiting friends, going to the veterinarian, and traveling are just a few other times your dog's crash pad can come in very handy.

Muzzle puzzle

Exercise goal: Your power dog will put his muzzle on and wear it calmly.

In response to the fear many people have of power dogs, most breed-specific or "dangerous dog" laws require certain dogs to be muzzled at all times when out in public, regardless of the individual dog's temperament or training. (Ironically, a recent French study by Racca suggests that people who see a muzzled dog out in public consider him to be more dangerous than when they see the very same dog without a muzzle on.) Failure to muzzle a dog who falls under such an ordinance can have legal consequences that range from warnings and fines to confiscation of the dog and loss of dog ownership privileges. If a breed-specific ordinance applies to your dog where you live or where you may travel with him, teach him to wear a muzzle. If your dog has strong dog-aggressive or human-aggressive behaviors, he should also be taught to wear a muzzle, even if not required by law, to keep everyone safe while you work with a professional to modify his behaviors. Some dogs, regardless of breed, also need to be muzzled to keep everyone safe during veterinary visits if they haven't learned to tolerate handling and examination by other people or if they have a painful medical condition that needs to be treated; even the friendliest and most tolerant dog may bite if he is in shock or pain, and the larger the dog is, the more difficult it will be to restrain him when he's injured. Also, if you want to use a Gentle Leader® or similar head halter as a training tool, teach him to wear it *before* using it to train him. Wearing a muzzle or head halter can be scary for a dog who hasn't been introduced to one, so it is important to take the time to help your dog get used to it before you take him out in public.

If you own a regulated power breed, be sure when you purchase a muzzle that you check any applicable laws and buy one that is compliant; there are several types of muzzle designs, and most laws are very specific about the type you must use. Your local animal control department should be able to help you with muzzle selection if you aren't sure what type to buy. The traditional basket muzzle is made of wire, and completely encloses the dog's muzzle. These are the safest and strongest types of muzzle, and they often have an extra strap that goes over the dog's skull and attaches to his collar on the back of the dog's neck to keep the muzzle securely in place. Other muzzles are made from fabric; some are closed on the end, while others are open-ended. If you own a brachycephalic power dog, you may have to search online for a muzzle specifically designed to fit short-muzzled dogs. Most websites that sell muzzles will have instructions on selecting the correct size that will allow your dog room to pant and drink water while wearing it. If you need to buy a muzzle with a closed end, consider buying the wire basket muzzle. This type of muzzle has space for you to deliver treats through; the fabric closed-end muzzles provide you no way to offer treats to your dog while he is wearing the muzzle, and the fabric restricts his airflow. Dogs can also learn to drink water through wire muzzles, but it is extremely difficult for them to drink wearing a closed-end fabric one. (If you don't need the end closed, you can buy an open-ended fabric muzzle instead.) Your dog must be able to open his mouth to pant while wearing the muzzle, and the top of the muzzle basket should not cross his eyes or be so loose he can readily paw it off his head.

1. Experiment with some exceptionally appealing treats before starting to acclimate your dog to his muzzle or head halter. You will need to find a treat your dog will enthusiastically work to get. Every dog is food-motivated, at least to the extent that

he will eat enough to remain alive; if you have a fussy eater, you may need to resort to using his normal kibble and working with the muzzle before meals, when he is most likely to be hungry. But with creativity, it is likely you can find something other than dog food to use when you do this training. Blueberry bagels, canned tripe, roast beef, water-packed tuna, freeze-dried liver, and baby food in a jar are just some of the foods that might work for muzzle training with a finicky eater. If you need to use messy food, you can make up a treat smoothie by blending the treat items to a paste-like consistency and delivering your treat goo from a camping food tube.

2. Put your dog on leash or tether him to keep him from walking away while you introduce him to his muzzle or head halter. If you use a leash, drop it and stand on the end to free up both hands while you work through this process.

3. Hold the muzzle (or head halter) in one hand where your dog can see it, and the food tube or treat in the other. Keep your hands apart so your dog can eat the food without being scared by the muzzle. If your treats are really awesome, your dog may not even acknowledge the presence of the muzzle in your other hand. This is perfect! He might want to sniff the muzzle; that is okay, too. Let him have a tiny piece of dry treat or a lick of treat goo, then move your treat hand behind your back. After a few seconds, bring your treat hand out and offer another treat or lick. Repeat five to six times per training session, then put the muzzle and the treats away. Try to do at least three to four sessions each day, gradually moving the muzzle closer to your treat hand. If your dog tenses up, starts to eat more quickly, or moves away from the muzzle, increase the distance between the treats and the muzzle for a few sessions before moving it closer again. You want your dog to be completely relaxed and enjoying his treat in the presence of the muzzle. When you can hold the muzzle right next to the treats and your dog will happily take them, he is ready for the next step.

4. Your dog's muzzle has two parts: a collar-like strap that goes around the neck, and the muzzle part that goes over the dog's nose. Similarly, a head halter has two loops; one that goes around the neck and one that goes over the nose. With your dog on leash and your treat tube or treat pieces nearby, clip the collar strap on your dog and immediately deliver a treat or lick. If you can clip the collar on with one hand, hold the treat in the other hand to speed up the delivery; the faster you get the treat to your dog after putting on the neck strap, the faster he will associate having that part of the muzzle put on with phenomenal treats. The nose part of the muzzle or the nose loop of the head halter will be flopping on his chest for this step. Remove the collar strap and deliver another treat or lick. Any time you handle the muzzle, the dog is learning he has a chance to get a reward. Repeat five to six times per training session, and aim for three to four training sessions per day. Continue with this step until your dog remains relaxed while you put on the collar strap, and ignores the muzzle part touching his chest.

5. Before putting the basket part of the muzzle on your dog, make sure any other strap that may be on the muzzle (like the one that runs from the basket to the back of the dog's neck to attach to the dog's collar, or the one that runs around the edge of some fabric

muzzle baskets to make them fit more securely) is loosened, or make the nose loop of the head halter large enough to easily slip over his nose. (You should be able to quickly slip the muzzle or head halter over your dog's nose, but it won't be secure yet.) Again, keep your dog on a leash and step on the end of it or tether your dog securely so both hands are free. If your dog won't stay with you as you try this step, you have rushed the process; if he has learned that the sight of the muzzle and the collar portion of it are indicators that his fantastic treat will be arriving shortly, he shouldn't want to leave you. He should want to see the muzzle and have you put it around his neck. If he panics or tries to walk away when he sees his muzzle, just go back to the previous step and work on it until your dog will hang around for a treat when he sees it. Hook the collar strap on your dog and offer a treat or lick. Then calmly slide the nose portion on your dog and immediately offer another treat or lick, then attach the nose strap (if the muzzle has one) and reward

again. Alternatively, you can put treats in the muzzle, place the muzzle in a plastic container, and offer the whole setup for your dog to put his nose into; this works particularly well with muzzles that have completely open ends and no place to put the treats. Just smear the goodies on the bottom of the container, then place the muzzle in and present the setup to your dog.

Don't try to tighten the nose strap just yet; simply attach it and then feed your dog. Repeat five to six times per training session, and work for three to four training sessions per day until your dog is comfortable and relaxed with the nose piece touching his nose. If you are using a closed-end muzzle, a treat tube pressed lightly against the end will work best to get the treat to him. If you've been using dry treats, the pieces must be small enough to fit between the wires. Touching them to peanut butter will help them stick to the muzzle long enough for your dog to lick them up; dry treat pieces just

You can use a container to allow your dog to put his nose in the muzzle on his own to get a treat. This technique works particularly well with basket muzzles.

dropped in may fall completely through the wires and to the floor, removing the immediate reward for your dog. Prevent any pawing at the muzzle by offering your dog his treat or lick as soon as possible after placing the muzzle over his nose; hold the treat at your dog's eye level so he has to reach slightly up to eat it. This will place him a bit off balance and will make it harder for him to lift a paw to scratch at the muzzle. If he still insists on pawing at the muzzle, take a step back in the training progression and hold the muzzle just over the end of his nose and treat, gradually putting it farther on his nose as he shows he can leave it alone. Don't rush this step! When you can place the muzzle loosely on your dog's nose and he is only interested in getting his treat, he is ready to learn to move around with the muzzle on.

6. Although it may not seem like a big deal to you, your dog might find it difficult to listen to you, perform familiar behaviors, or even walk the first few times he has his muzzle completely on. If you are teaching your dog to wear a head halter, you should attach the leash to your dog's regular collar instead of the nose loop for this step. You don't want the loop to accidently tighten before your dog is completely used to wearing it. With your dog on leash and tasty treats or goo ready to deliver, put your dog's muzzle on. Remember to reward after clicking the neck strap on and after placing the nose piece on! Step backward and hold a treat out for your dog; you should move far enough away from your dog that he will have to take a single step to reach the tasty treats. Most dogs, if they really, really love their treats, will move without even thinking about it. As soon as the dog takes a step to get his treat, deliver it to him, and remove the muzzle, remembering to also give a treat after taking the nose piece off and the neck collar off. If the loose muzzle falls off, give him a treat or lick and put it back on with another treat or lick. Wearing a muzzle is a real treat fest for your dog! As he becomes comfortable walking, and he doesn't paw at the muzzle, add one step at a time until he can walk 10 to 12 steps following you to get his treat. Repeat the entire process five to six times per training session, and three to four sessions per day. When your dog will calmly walk 10 to 12 steps to get his treat, he is ready for the final step.

7. It's finally time to tighten the muzzle up so it fits correctly on your dog and doesn't fall off. The muzzle needs to be snug, but not so tight that it causes your dog discomfort. Tighten the nose strap on the muzzle (if the muzzle has one) ¼ inch or so and repeat Steps 5 and 6, making sure your dog is completely relaxed with the slightly tighter muzzle. Continue to tighten the strap by ¼ inch and repeat Steps 5 and 6 until you have the muzzle properly tightened. If he has been leaving the muzzle alone during the training, but starts pawing at it after you've tightened it up, chances are good that you tightened it too much. Be sure to gradually tighten the neck strap as well; all straps need to be properly tightened for the muzzle or a head halter to fit correctly.

8. As your dog becomes comfortable with his muzzle, you can ask for more challenging behaviors while he is wearing it. The treats will be phased out as you begin to take your dog out for walks with his muzzle on. You can still offer him an occasional treat while he is wearing it, but most of the rewards at that point will come from the chance to go for a walk and explore the neighborhood with you. Start with a short walk to the end of your driveway, feeding a treat every step or two to keep his mind off his muzzle. When he can easily do short walks, you can increase the distance you walk him and decrease the treats you give him. Being out in public will become his primary reward for wearing his muzzle, and for most power dogs, that will be quite a treat! Be sure you always carry water (even when it is cold outside) and watch your dog to be sure he isn't overheating as a result of wearing his muzzle. If it is properly fitted, he should still be able to pant, but keep an extra-cautious eye on him just to be sure! Also, be sure

to check the straps for proper fit every time you put his muzzle on, and examine your dog for any signs of rubbing or sores every time you take it off.

Although wearing a muzzle is an unpleasant reality for many pleasant power dogs, you can make it much easier for your dog by taking the time to properly introduce him to wearing one before taking him out in public.

Speak and quiet

Exercise goal: Your power dog will stop barking on cue.

Some dog-related ordinances include elements that address a dog "menacing" or "threatening" other animals or people. Probably the most common way that situation arises is when a dog barks, growls, or otherwise vocalizes toward person or another animal, in what appears to be an inappropriate or uncontrolled way. Remember—believe it or not, there are many, many, many people in this world who don't really understand how dogs behave, and quite a few who actually don't like dogs or are truly afraid of them. A power dog who is jumping up and down in friendly excitement and barking, or barking and pulling toward a person or dog, may very well appear (particularly to the person on the receiving end of that greeting) to be getting ready to attack, even if *you*, the dog's owner, know better. It doesn't matter how much you try to explain that your dog is actually very friendly; a Great Dane barking and pulling toward a person who is afraid of dogs or doesn't understand them can be very intimidating. Teaching your dog to be quiet on cue will help you make your dog more pleasant to be around for anyone you meet out on the street, and will help you control his barking around the house, too!

There are several management techniques that can minimize problematic barking behavior. The easiest one is making it impossible for your dog to see the things that make him bark. For example, if he barks at people walking past your house, simply remove him from the room where he can see passersby; if he isn't left unsupervised in the living room, he can't possibly bark at people he sees passing by through the living room window. Alternatively, you can put frosted glass film, stained glass film, or bottom up/top down blinds on front windows to block his vision while still allowing light into your home, or rearrange furniture to block his view. Chances are pretty good that most barking is triggered by seeing things, rather than hearing them, so anything you can do to interfere with his unobstructed view will help curb barking while you work on teaching him to be quiet on cue. If your dog fence-runs in the front yard as people or other dogs pass by on the sidewalk, put him out in the back yard or go out with him while he is in the front yard so you can disrupt his behavior. If he jumps the fence in excitement, put in a taller fence, or don't allow him outside without someone being physically outside with him. Remember, manipulating your dog's environment is vital to your training success; if you allow him to continue fence-running and barking while trying to teach him to be quiet on cue, you are making the job far more difficult and frustrating than it needs to be.

Another thing to keep in mind is that you can't interrupt problem behaviors that you don't see or hear. You can't see your dog's behavior if you aren't with him. In the emotionally charged atmosphere that surrounds power dogs, you are risking that someone with an axe to grind against your dog's breed will concoct a story that could result in confiscation of your dog, hefty fines, and possibly worse if you leave him unattended outside. It is a negative, sad situation to contemplate, but it has occurred and will continue to occur as long as all power dogs are painted with the same brush they currently are. So much better to be safe than sorry. Your power dog is counting on you to keep him safe as much as he is willing to do anything within his power to keep you safe.

Teaching your power dog to bark on cue can help you teach him to be quiet on cue. Dogs learn well by contrast, and pairing "Speak" with "Quiet" will help you teach your dog both cues more quickly.

1. This is one exercise that you will want to train in an area where you know your dog will see something that will start him barking. If he barks at passersby out of your front window, you can start this training in your house. Put your power dog on leash and have some extremely tempting treats ready to use. These treats need to be more enticing to your dog than whatever he might bark at, so you may need to use tidbits of cheese or real meat for this training.

2. Stand quietly while your dog looks around. Be sure you aren't intimidating him or discouraging him from barking in any way. As soon as your dog starts barking, quietly and calmly tell him "Speak." Allow him to bark just two or three more times. You need to keep these sessions very, very short; you don't want your dog to get so excited while he's barking that he quits listening to you.

3. After two or three barks, start backing away excitedly from the distraction, praising and feeding him his extra-special treats while you create distance between him and the distraction that triggered the barking. If you are teaching him in your home, back away from the window he is looking through to stop his barking, feeding him a treat each step you take. As soon as he quits barking, quietly and calmly tell him "Quiet," while you continue to praise and feed him. If he starts barking again as you are backing away, quietly continue to increase the distance between him and whatever he is barking at until he can remain quiet. The first few times you work on this, you may have to move quite a distance away from the distraction to get your dog to be quiet after he is allowed to bark at it, so be prepared to keep moving away until your dog quits barking. As he gets more experience with this routine, he will need less luring and distance to help him stop his barking and look to you for a reward.

4. You can also use unplanned barking moments to train "Speak" and "Quiet" at home. If your dog is looking out the window and starts barking unexpectedly, go into the room he is in, cue him to "Speak," allow a couple more barks, then pick him up or lead him by the collar away from the window. As soon as he quits barking, tell him "Quiet" and praise him profusely as you work your way toward your stash of dog

treats. As long as you continue to praise your dog as you move toward the treats, he will understand both rewards are linked to him being quiet.

5. Initially you will be saying "Speak" just after your dog starts barking. Over time, he will begin to associate hearing this cue with his barking. Once he makes this association, you can cue him to "Speak" and he will start barking, even if there is nothing exciting around. Similarly, you will start giving him the "Quiet" cue after he quits barking, but he will soon associate "Quiet" with receiving something really good from you and will stop barking and start moving toward you when he hears this cue.

As your dog becomes more fluent in "Speak" and "Quiet," you will be able to tell him "Quiet" when he is barking, thereby disrupting the behavior. Don't be stingy with your rewards for this behavior; it is very difficult for an aroused power dog to suppress his natural inclination to be protective. Remember that rewards aren't just treats. You can give praise, pet him, give him his favorite toy, or let him outside as a reward for his behavior. He should never know for sure what he is going to get as a reward for being quiet when you give him the cue, but he should be able to count on the fact that you will give him some type of meaningful reward each and every time he listens and stops barking on cue, even if it's simply a few words of sincere praise.

You can use "Speak" as a reward for other behaviors once you've taught "Quiet." It takes energy to bark and is self-soothing to your dog, so it is a great reward to allow your dog to bark a little after performing a difficult or stressful behavior. Barking helps pick up a dog's attitude as well, and can get him in the mood to work together with you. "Speak" is also one of those timeless dog tricks that is fun to teach your dog. Just be sure you don't actively encourage your dog to bark at people; this could inadvertently get you and your dog in trouble with the law!

Training new behaviors to your power dog may take time, but teaching him exactly how you want him to behave is crucial to his success as a positive canine family member. Incorporate training into your everyday interactions with your dog and before long, you two will be working together as a fantastic team!

11

Meeting the Letter and Avoiding
the Long Arm of the Law

---

*…The case of dogs was specially dealt with by a lex Pesolania. If a dog was in a
square or public road and not tied up in the day-time and did mischief, the owner
was liable: and if a dog was led by one incompetent to hold him or in a place
where he ought not to be and did mischief, the leader, not the owner, was liable…*

Henry Roby, author, Roman Private Law in the Times of Cicero and of the Antonines

[Author's note: Although I am an attorney licensed in Nevada and Nebraska, the following is not offered or intended as legal advice. Consult your attorney for legal advice
and your insurance agent for insurance advice specific to you and your dog.]

The legal concept that a person is liable for damages his dog causes to other people or
property has been recognized as early as the third century BCE. The burdens associated
with owning a power dog in today's society can be quite substantial. Social pressures, insurance requirements, and legal restrictions impact many power dog owners. It is always your
responsibility to be aware of and comply with any breed-specific ordinances that affect
your power dog, as well as all general dog-related ordinances, wherever you live and travel.

Insurance coverage conundrums

Based on risk analyses, most insurance companies have a list of dog breeds that they either will not insure at all, or require proof of training or some other proof of responsible
ownership before they will issue policy coverage. Dr. Stanley Coren reported in *Psychol-
ogy Today* on the top 14 blacklisted breeds in 2014; ten of those breeds are power breeds.
In 2017, they are still the likeliest breeds to be excluded by most insurance companies.
(Insurance companies often include crosses of these types of dogs as well.) Every insurance company maintains its own list of breeds, and these can change often based on

the company's risk assessment of owning particular types of dogs. Renter's and business insurance may also have exclusions for certain dog breeds and rental properties may have different requirements for tenants with power breeds than they do for other dog owners.

The time to find out if damage caused by your power dog is covered by your insurance policy is before anything happens. This is particularly important if you brought a power dog home after you took out your homeowner's or renter's insurance policy. Few people think to let their insurance carrier know when they get a new dog. But it is important to do that. Your power dog doesn't have to bite anyone to cause harm. He could knock someone over with his friendly greetings. He could scratch someone's arm while trying to crawl up into a lap for snuggle time. He could trip someone and cause a fall. If your insurance company isn't aware of your power dog, or your policy specifically excludes his breed, you may find yourself paying out of pocket for a situation that might have been covered by your homeowner's policy if you owned a different dog breed. There are insurance companies that provide coverage for power dogs, but you need to be prepared to shop around for the best coverage and premiums.

The long arm of the law

According to the website www.dogsbite.org, over 1,000 U.S. cities in 36 states, as well as nearly 300 military installations, have enacted some type of breed-specific legislation that affects many power dog owners as of 2017. Even though 17 states have pre-empted the creation of breed-specific legislation, the majority of states still allow these types of local ordinances to be put in place. These laws vary widely from jurisdiction to jurisdiction; some involve outright ownership bans on certain types of dogs, while others involve extra ownership responsibilities (e.g., extra-tall fencing, use of muzzles and double leashes, etc.). Some even apply to people just traveling through their jurisdiction with a banned dog. Furthermore, there are 43 countries throughout the world with breed-specific bans, many enacted on a national level. There may be far more to owning a power dog than simply training him to be a good member of society. If you aren't sure whether breed-specific ordinances are in place where you live or plan to travel, contact the local animal control or animal welfare authority or humane society to find out. Ignorance of the law is never an excuse for violating it; if you live in a jurisdiction that has such laws, you may be subject to fines, have your dog taken away by animal control authorities, or even face jail time if you violate any applicable legal requirements. Rather than protest against these breed-specific laws by ignoring them and risk losing a beloved pet, as well as time, money, and possibly personal freedom, make the case for change by complying with the laws in place, training your dog to be the very best power breed ambassador possible, and working with appropriate state and local authorities to make sensible changes to the laws.

Owning a power dog is quite a responsibility. Do yourself and your dog a favor and familiarize yourself with any laws that may apply to your dog, double check your insurance coverage, then step out and enjoy life with your well-mannered power dog!

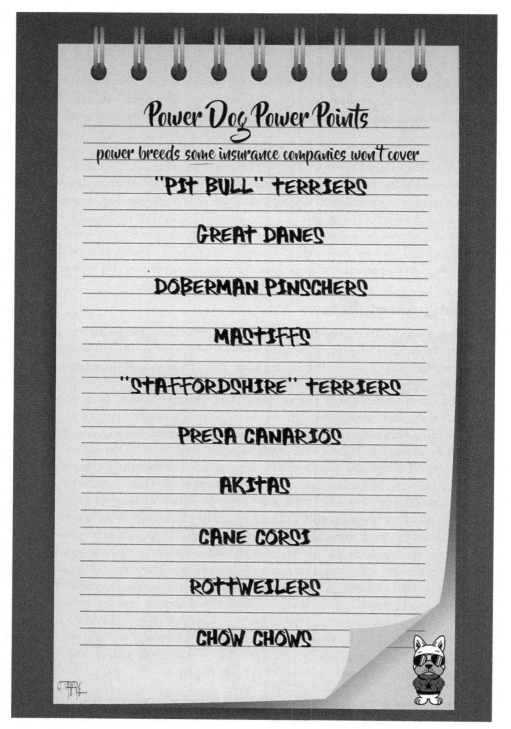

Power Dog Power Points
power breeds some insurance companies won't cover

"PIT BULL" TERRIERS

GREAT DANES

DOBERMAN PINSCHERS

MASTIFFS

"STAFFORDSHIRE" TERRIERS

PRESA CANARIOS

AKITAS

CANE CORSI

ROTTWEILERS

CHOW CHOWS

Although not every insurance company excludes these breeds, they are the most-often excluded types of power dogs in the United States as of 2017. Be sure to check your insurance coverage if you own a power dog to avoid the possibility of an unpleasant surprise.

Conclusion

'Give a dog a bad name and hang him' is an old proverb which has been, unfortunately, exemplified at the expense of the British bulldog. 'The virtues of this dog are his own, the vices those of his master.' The bulldog is, in fact, a dog—neither more nor less, and as capable as any other variety of dog of being 'the companion and friend of man.' Like children, dogs have their mental characters formed by their training and associations, and, although different individuals have different dispositions or temperaments, it is not to be imagined that they have different natures. … If, therefore, a dog is treated by man as though it were a fiend incarnate, to be ruled with the harshest measures and used in the most cruel and dangerous occupations, to have all the good feelings of its nature crushed by its master, who takes a pride in its ferocity, is it to be wondered at that the poor beast which survives the hardening process should appear to merit the bad character assigned to it by those only who fear it? If all affection is suppressed by ill-usage, and the animal is kept chained and solitary, in order to cultivate a savage disposition, it learns to look upon man as its enemy, and to be ready to resent the brutality it expects, so that if any—it matters not what breed of dog—be reared in such a manner, the result must be the same if the dog has sufficient courage to sustain its trials… But if reared and trained with the same care and kindness expended on other breeds, there is no dog that can serve the sundry uses of men so aptly or so conveniently as this sort.

Hugh Dalziel, author, British Dogs

Living with a power dog can be one of the most rewarding, as well as one of the most challenging, experiences you will ever share with a dog. These dogs have centuries-old breed histories that continue to haunt them even today, placing social pressures on power dog owners that other dog owners never experience. Power dogs are associated with everything evil by some people, and everything wonderful by others. But in spite of all this, power dogs have long been, and continue to be, some of the most popular canine companions in existence. This is testimony to their endearing, enduring qualities and the commitment most owners have to them. Empowering your power dog to be the best-mannered breed ambassador he can be is the greatest gift you can give yourself, your power dog, and generations of power dogs to come.

Appendix A
Power Breeds From Around the World

Abraxas Bulldogge

Afghan Mastiff

Afghan Tiger Dog

Akita

Aidi

Alangu

Alano Español

Alpaha Blue Blood
  Bulldog

Alpine Mastiff

Altman White English

American Bull Ridgeback

American Panja Mastiff
  Bulldog

Bully Kutta

Alunk

American Bulldog

American Pit Bull Terrier

Am. Staffordshire Terrier

Anatolian Shepherd

Arkansas Giant Bulldog

Bandog

Banter Bulldogge

Bisben

Black Russian Terrier

Boerboel

Boston Terrier

Boxer

Brazilian Bullmastiff

Broholmer

Bullmastiff

Bull Terrier

Ca de Bou

Campeiro Bulldog

Cane Corso

Canis Panther

Catahoula Leopard Dog

Caucasian Shepherd Dog

Cheju Dog

Chinese Shar-Pei

Cimmaron Uruguayo

Corso Pugliese

Cuban Mastiff

Cypro Kukur

Dalmatian

Doberman Pinscher

Dogo Argentino

Dogo Guatemalteco

Dogue de Bordeaux

Dogue Brasiliero

English Bulldog

English Mastiff

Epir Moloss

Fila Brasiliero

Fila de Terceira

French Bulldog

Great Dane

Gull Dong

Gull Terr

Haitian Bulldog

Hellenic Mastiff

Indian Sindh Mastiff

Iranian Bear Dog

Jindo

Kai Dog

Kanawar Dog

Karakachan Dog

Karelian Bear Dog

Khurasani Dog

Kintamani Dog

Kishu

Kombai

Kopaonik Watchdog

Kuvasz

Lakota Mastiff

Leonberger

Lyme Mastiff

Mastiff

Neapolitan Mastiff

Olde English Bulldogge

Patagonian Dog

Perro Cimarron

Perro de Presa Canario

Persian Sarabi Dog

Phu Quoc Dog

Pit Bullmastiff

Podolian Mastiff

Poongsan

Powinder Dog

Price Boar Beisser

Puertorican Mastiff

Pug

Pyrenean Mastiff

Rafeiro do Alentejo

Rajapalayam

Rottweiler

Sanshu Dog

Sapsaree

Sarplaninac

Serbian Defense Dog

Shakhi

Shenkottah Dog

Shikari Dog

Sicilian Branchiero

Sindh Hound

Singidunum Molossus

Skilos tou Alexandrou

Skilos tou Pyrrou

Slovensky Kopov

Spanish Mastiff

Staffordshire Bull Terrier

Swinford Bandog

Terceira Mastiff

Thai Ridgeback

Tibetan Kyi-Apso

Tibetan Mastiff

Tornjak

Tosa

Transylvanian Alps
Sheepdog

Turkish Bulldog

Turkish Kars Dog

Turkish Mastiff

Vaghari Dog

Valley Bulldog

Victorian Bulldog

Vuccirisco

Xander Bulldog

Xochaso

Yorkshire Bandogge

Zulubull African Bull
Terrier

Appendix B
National Breed-Specific Legislation

Nation	Type of national law enacted	Breeds Affected
Australia	Banned for importation	Dogo Argentino, Fila Brasiliero, Japanese Tosa, American Pit Bull Terrier, Presa Canario
Brazil	Banned for importation, breeding	Pit bulls and derivative breeds
Bermuda	Banned	Pit Bull Terrier, Staffordshire Terrier, Akita, several mastiff breeds, others
Denmark	Banned	American Bulldog, Boerboel, Dogo Argentino, Kangal, Fila Brasiliero, others
Ecuador	Banned	Pit Bull Terrier, American Staffordshire Terrier, Staffordshire Bull Terrier, Bull Terrier
Germany	Banned for importation	Pit Bull Terrier, American Staffordshire Terrier, Staffordshire Bull Terrier, Bull Terrier

Nation	Type of national law enacted	Breeds Affected
Republic of Ireland	Restricted	American Pit Bull Terrier, English Bull Terrier, Staffordshire Bull Terrier, Bull Mastiff, Doberman Pinscher, German Shepherd, Rhodesian Ridgeback, Rottweiler, Japanese Akita, Japanese Tosa, Bandog
Israel	Banned for importation	Dogo Argentino, Pit Bull Terrier, Bull Terrier, American Staffordshire Terrier, Staffordshire Bull Terrier, Rottweilers, Fila Brasiliero, Tosa Inu
Malaysia	Banned	Akita, American Bulldog, American Pit Bull Terrier, Dogo Argentino, Fila Brasiliero, Japanese Toda, Kai Ken, Presa Mallorquin, Presa Canario, Tibetan Mastiff
	Restricted	Alaskan Malamute, American Staffordshire Terrier, Belgian Shepherd, Dogue de Bordeaux, German Shepherd, Miniature Bull Terrier, Neapolitan Mastiff, Rottweiler, Staffordshire Bull Terrier
Malta	Banned for importation	American Pit Bull Terrier, Argentine Dogo, Fila Brasiliero, Japanese Tosa
New Zealand	Banned for importation	American Pit Bull Terrier, Dogo Argentino, Fila Brasiliero, Japanese Tosa
Norway	Banned	Pit Bull Terrier, American Staffordshire Terrier, Fila Brasiliero, Tosa Inu, Dogo Argentino, Czechoslovakian Wolfdog
Poland	Restricted	Pit bulls
Portugal	Restricted	Staffordshire Bull Terrier, Rottweiler, American Staffordshire Terrier, Fila Brasiliero, Dogo Argentino, Tosa Inu, pit bull

Nation	Type of national law enacted	Breeds Affected
Puerto Rico	Banned	Pit Bull Terriers, Staffordshire Bull Terriers, Argentino Dogo, American Staffordshire Terrier, American Pit Bull Terriers, crosses
Romania	Banned for importation	Boerboels, Pit bull–type dogs, Bandogs
	Restricted	Pit bull, Boerboel, Bandog, American Staffordshire Terrier, Staffordshire Bull Terrier, Tosa, Rottweiler, Dogo Argentino, Neapolitan Mastiff, Belgian Malinois, German Shepherd Dog, Doberman Pinscher, Presa Canario, Komondor, Giant Schnauzer, Kuvasz
Singapore	Banned for importation	American Pit Bull Terrier, American Staffordshire Terrier, Staffordshire Bull Terrier, American Bulldog, Neapolitan Mastiff, Tosa, Akita, Dogo Argentino, Boerboel, Fila Brasiliero, all crosses
Spain	Restricted	American Pit Bull Terrier, American Staffordshire Terrier, Argentino Dogo, Bull Terrier, Staffordshire Bull Terrier
Switzerland	Restricted	No national law, but extensive local ordinances
Turkey	Restricted	Pit bulls, Japanese Tosa
Ukraine	Restricted	Over 80 breeds, including Bull Terrier, Bulldog, Boxer, Labrador Retriever, Welsh Terrier, American Pit Bull Terrier, Presa Canario, Kangal, Dalmatian, American Bulldog, American Staffordshire Terrier, English Mastiff, Dogo Argentino, Dogue de Bordeaux
United Kingdom	Banned	Pit Bull Terrier, Japanese Tosa, Dogo Argentino, Fila Brasiliero
Venezuala	Banned	Pit bull–type dogs

In the United States, the Armed Forces have restrictions on the types of dogs allowed on military installations, but the remaining breed-specific legislation has been enacted at the local level across the country. These ordinances vary widely; some even apply to anyone traveling through the impacted area with a banned or restricted dog. It is important to know before you travel with your power dog if he is included in any ordinances wherever you are planning on going, and you must be prepared to meet the ordinances, even if you don't have restrictions at home.

* Information current as of 7/2018.

Resources

Recommended reading and viewing

Aloff, Brenda. *Aggression in Dogs: Practical Management, Prevention and Behavior Modification*. Collierville, TN, Fundcraft, Inc., 2002. Excellent information on canine aggression and behavioral modification protocols for aggressive dogs.

Aloff, Brenda. *Canine Body Language: A Photographic Guide*. Collierville, TN, Fundcraft, Inc., 2005. Comprehensive visual guide to all aspects of canine body language.

American Kennel Club, *The Complete Dog Book*. Twenty-second ed., Metuchen, NJ, Companionhouse Books, 2017. Information on all breeds recognized by the AKC.

Arai, Sato, and Mitsuaki Ohta. "The Importance of Dogs Having Contact with Children During the Canine Socialization Period." *Journal of Veterinary Behavior: Clinical Applications and Research* 4.2 (2009): 94-95. Research study on canine-human interactions.

Baxter, Elizabeth and Patricia Hoffman. *The History and Management of the Mastiff*. Second ed., Wenatchee, WA, Dogwise Publishing, 2004. Comprehensive work on the Mastiff breed throughout the world.

Casey, Rachel A., Bethany Loftus, Christine Bolster, Gemma J. Richards, and Emily J. Blackwell. "Human-directed Aggression in Domestic Dogs (*Canis familiaris*): Occurrence in Different Contexts and Risk Factors." *Applied Animal Behaviour Science* 152 (2014): 52-63. Research study on canine aggression.

Cauis, Johannes. *Of English Dogges–The Diversities, the Names, the Natures, and the Properties*. First ed., London, Richard Johnes, 1576, as reprinted by Warwickshire,

UK, Vintage Dog Books, 2005. Reprint of one of the earliest descriptions of various dog breeds in the English language.

Ciribassi, John. "Forget Dominance: Fear-based Aggression in Dogs." *Veterinary Medicine* 110.8 (2015)3. Research study examining aggression triggers.

Coppinger, Raymond and Lorna. *Dogs: A New Understanding of Canine Origin, Behavior, and Evolution.* Chicago, IL, University of Chicago Press, 2001. Outstanding presentation of issues relating to the canine-human bond.

Dalziel, Hugh. *British Dogs – Their Varieties, History, Characteristics, Breeding, Management and Exhibition.* First ed., London, UK, Alfred Bradley, 1888 as reprinted, London, UK, Ersham Press, 2007. Reprint of late 18th century book describing contemporary dog breeds.

Delise, Karen. *The Pit Bull Placebo: The Media, Myths and Politics of Canine Aggression.* Ramsey, NJ, Anubis Publishing, 2007. Examination of societal variables that lead to common perceptions about various dog breeds.

Delta Society. *Professional Standards for Dog Trainers: Effective, Humane Principles.* Renton, WA, Delta Society, 2001. Standard of professional conduct designed to provide a framework for effective, humane dog training.

Donaldson, Jean. *The Culture Clash.* Berkeley, CA, James & Kenneth Publishers, 1996. Easy-to-read exploration of why humans and canines often have communication problems with one another and how to communicate effectively with dogs.

Donaldson, Jean. *Fight! A Practical Guide to the Treatment of Dog-Dog Aggression.* San Francisco, CA, Kinship Communications, 2004. Practical information about canine aggression and how to deal with behavioral issues arising from aggression.

Duffy, Deborah L., Yuying Hsu, and James A. Serpell. "Breed Differences in Canine Aggression." *Applied Animal Behaviour Science* 114.3 (2008): 441-460. Scientific article examining role of breed selection in canine aggression.

Fleig, Dieter. *Fighting Dog Breeds.* Neptune, NJ, T.F.H. Publications, Inc., 1996. Excellent historical work on traditional fighting breeds, including extensive historical illustrations, general history, care, and health.

Fox, Richard. *The Dog Pit–Or, How to Select, Breed, Train and Manage Fighting Dogs, with Points as to Their Care in Health and Disease–1888.* First ed., Franklin Square, NY, Richard Fox, K., 1888 as reprinted, Cookhill, Warwickshire, UK, Read Country Books, 2005. Graphic examination of dog fighting and pit sports in late 19th century America.

Friedman, Susan. "What's Wrong with This Picture? Effectiveness Is Not Enough." *Journal of Applied Companion Animal Behavior* 4.1 (2010): 42-47. The Humane Hierarchy explained.

Ganley, Dee. *Changing People Changing Dogs: Positive Solutions for Difficult Dogs.* Chipping Campden, UK, Learning About Dogs Limited, 2006. Strategies and techniques for canine behavior modification utilizing positive reinforcement techniques.

Hancock, Col. David. *The Heritage of the Dog.* Alton, UK, Nimrod Press Ltd., 1990. Interesting historical images accompany breed histories of many different dog breeds.

Haug, Lore I. "Canine Aggression Toward Unfamiliar People and Dogs." *Veterinary Clinics of North America: Small Animal Practice* 38.5 (2008): 1023-1041. Research study on canine aggression.

Homan, Mike. *A Complete History of Fighting Dogs.* New York, NY, Howell Book House, 1999. Graphic explanations of the various historic dog sports and some of the breeds involved.

Hsu, Yuying, and Liching Sun. "Factors Associated with Aggressive Responses in Pet Dogs." *Applied Animal Behaviour Science* 123.3 (2010): 108-123. Research study on canine aggression.

Hunthausen, Wayne. "A Better Walk: Training Dogs Not to Lunge, Growl, and Pull on a Leash." *Veterinary Medicine* 110.1 (2015): 7. Veterinary practitioner article on teaching leash manners.

Immordino-Yang, Mary Helen. *Emotions, Learning, and the Brain: Exploring the Educational Implications of Affective Neuroscience (The Norton Series on the Social Neuroscience of Education).* W. W. Norton & Company. Kindle Edition. Information on the interplay between emotions and learning.

Kalnajs, Sarah. *Am I Safe? The Art & Science Of Canine Behavior Assessments* DVD Set. Blue Dog Training and Behavior, 2006. Excellent video on canine body language and safe handling techniques.

Lindsay, Steven. *Handbook of Applied Dog Behavior and Training: Vol. 1 Adaptation and Learning.* Ames, IA, Iowa State Press, 2000. Scholarly work on research and findings related to how canines evolved and how the canine brain works.

Lindsay, Steven. *Handbook of Applied Dog Behavior and Training: Vol. 2 Etiology and Assessment of Behavior Problems.* Ames, IA, Iowa State Press, 2000. Scholarly work on research related to the physical basis and identification of canine behavioral problems.

Lindsay, Steven. *Handbook of Applied Dog Behavior and Training: Vol. 3 Procedures and Protocols.* Ames, IA, Iowa State Press, 2000. Scholarly work on research and findings related to the theory of cynopraxis and behavioral modification.

Morris, Desmond. *Dogs: The Ultimate Dictionary of Over 1,000 Dog Breeds.* North Pomfret, VT, Trafalgar Square Publishing, 2008. Comprehensive listing of dog breeds grouped according to traditional uses, with extensive bibliography for each breed.

O'Heare, James. *Empowerment Training, 2nd Edition*. BehaveTech Publishing, 2018. An excellent overview of empowerment concepts, training for it and rehabilitating disempowerment.

Oliff, Douglas (ed.). *The Ultimate Book of Mastiff Breeds*. New York, NY, Howell Book House, 1999. Collaborative effort by mastiff authorities covering popular as well as rare mastiff breeds.

Parker, Heidi, Dayna Drager, et al. "Genomic Analyses Reveal the Influence of Geographic Origin, Migration, and Hybridization on Modern Dog Breed Development." *Cell Reports* 19 (Apr., 2017): 697-708. Fascinating genetic relationships revealed between many modern dog breeds.

Parsons, Emma. *Click to Calm: Healing the Aggressive Dog*. Waltham, MA, Sunshine Books, Inc. 2005. Detailed exercises for behavioral modification of aggressive dogs using clicker training.

Racca, Anaïs, and Claude Baudoin. "The Dog or Its Muzzle as a Signal of Danger for Humans." *Journal of Veterinary Behavior: Clinical Applications and Research* 4.2 (2009): 94. Research study showing increased fear response to sight of muzzled dog by public.

Reid, Pamela. *Excel-erated Learning: Explaining How Dogs Learn and How Best to Teach Them*. Berkeley, CA, James & Kenneth Publishers, 1996. Exploration of learning processes in dogs.

Riddle, Maxwell. *Dogs Through History*. Fairfax, VA, Denlinger's Publishers, Ltd., 1987. Canine history presented through interpretations of art and written records.

Roby, Henry. *Roman Private Law in the Times of Cicero and of the Antonines, Vol II*. Cambridge, UK, University Press, 1902. Comprehensive treatise on Roman law, including laws applicable to dogs and other animals.

Rogerson, John. *The Dog Vinci Code*. United Kingdom, John Blake Publishing, Ltd., 2010. Engaging and unique approach to common behavioral and dog training problems.

Roll, A., and J. Unshelm. "Aggressive Conflicts Amongst Dogs and Factors Affecting Them." *Applied Animal Behaviour Science* 52.3 (1997): 229-242. Research study on canine aggression.

Rugaas, Turid. *My Dog Pulls. What Do I Do?* Wenatchee, WA, Dogwise Publishing, 2005. Tips and techniques for teaching loose-leash walking skills.

Semencic, Carl. *Pitbulls & Tenacious Guard Dogs*. Neptune, NJ, T.F.H. Publications, Inc., 1991. Examination of history and characteristics of several rare breeds before they became popular in the United States.

Semencic, Carl. *The World of Fighting Dogs*. Neptune, NJ, T.F.H. Publications, Inc., 1984. Explicit exploration of various dog breeds developed for fighting.

Sternberg, Susan. *Assessing Aggression Thresholds in Dogs: Using the Assess-A-Pet Protocol to Better Understand Aggression*. Wenatchee, WA, Dogwise Publishing, 2017.

von Reinhardt, Clarissa. *Chase! Managing Your Dog's Predatory Instincts*. Wenatchee, WA, Dogwise Publishing, 2010. Explanation of predatory instincts and exercises designed to promote off-leash activity.

Wendt, Lloyd. *Dogs: A Historical Journey*. New York, NY, Howell Book House, 1996. Development of the human/canine relationship through the centuries.

White, T.H. *The Book of Beasts: Being a Translation from a Latin Bestiary of the Twelfth Century*. Mineola, NY, Dover Publications, Inc., 1984. Ancient descriptions of real and imaginary animals, including dogs.

Yamamoto, M., T. Kikusui, and M. Ohta. "Influence of Owners' Attentional Focus on the Response of Their Dogs, *Canis familiaris*." *Journal of Veterinary Behavior: Clinical Applications and Research* 4.2 (2009): 4. Research study examining impact of owner behavior on dog behavior.

Ziv, Gal. "The Effects of Using Aversive Training Methods in Dogs—A Review." *Journal of Veterinary Behavior: Clinical Applications and Research* 19 (2017): 50-60. Research review article examining consequences of certain types of training methodologies on canine behavior.

Selected internet resources

American College of Veterinary Behaviorists. http://www.dacvb.org. Professional association for veterinary behaviorists (11/2018).

American Kennel Club. http://www.akc.org. Largest all-breed dog registry in the United States, also offering various competitive activities for power dogs, including scentwork and carting (11/2018).

Association of Professional Dog Trainers. http://www.apdt.com. Organization promoting humane training methods and trainer education (11/2018).

Becker, Marty. Do You Know the Best Way to Break Up a Dogfight and Come Out Unscathed? https://healthypets.mercola.com/sites/healthypets/archive/2016/03/21/breaking-up-dogfight.aspx Suggestions for safely breaking up dog fights from a veterinarian.

Certification Council for Professional Dog Trainers. http://www.ccpdt.org Independent certification organization for dog trainers and behaviorists (11/2018).

Clothier, Suzanne. "He Just Wants to Say Hi!" http://www.suzanneclothier.com/the-articles/he-just-wants-say-hi. A must-read for all dog owners who take their dogs out in public (11/2018).

Coren, Stanley. "14 Dog Breeds Blacklisted by Insurance Companies." https://www.psychologytoday.com/blog/canine-corner/201405/14-dog-breeds-blacklisted-insurance-companies. List of dog breeds commonly excluded from insurance policy coverage (11/2018).

Dogfoodadvisor.com. https://www.dogfoodadvisor.com/dog-feeding-tips/dog-ideal-weight/. Provides information and links to canine weight and nutrition topics, including the Purina Body Condition System chart (11/2018).

Dogwise.com. https://www.dogwise.com. Premier source for dog-related publications and puppy sound socialization CDs (11/2018).

Dogworks.com. https://www.dogworks.com/carting/. Source for carts and carting harnesses (11/2018).

Dogsbite.org. http://www.dogsbite.org. Useful website to obtain statistical information on breed-specific ordinances and bite-related statistics (11/2018).

Fédération Cynologique Internationale. http://www.fci.be/en/. Largest canine registry in the world (11/2018).

Gadbois, Simon. "It is Not What You Like, But What You Want that Counts: The Neurochemistry of Behaviour and Motivation." http://www.sparcsinitiative.org/watch/it-is-not-what-you-like-but-what-you-want-that-counts-the-neurochemistry-of-behaviour-and-motivation/ Presentation on current research in canine motivation at SPARCS Initiative 2014 (11/2018).

Indestructibledog.com. https://www.indestructibledog.com/collections/dog-leashes. Source for various lengths of Vir-chew-ly indestructible leashes and other products for power dogs (11/2018).

International Dog Parkour Association. http://www.dogparkour.org/. Website of IDPA, whose mission is to promote outdoor exploration and positive reinforcement dog training (11/2018).

International Weight Pull Association. http://iwpa.net. One of several organizations sponsoring weight pull competitions (11/2018).

J & J Dog Supplies. http://www.jjdog.com. Well-established source of competitive obedience training supplies (11/2018).

Laurence, Kay. "Performance Jitters: Avoiding a Drop in Performance at Shows and Events." http://www.clickertraining.com/node/71. Explores benefits of delaying attachment of performance cue until behavior generalized (11/2018).

Leroy, Julie. Yes, There Is a Smart Way to Break Up a Dog Fight. https://www.thedodo.com/yes-there-is-a-smart-way-to-break-up-a-dog-fight-1488888838.html Suggestions for safely disrupting dog fights by a former animal control officer.

Molosserdogs.com. http://www.molosserdogs.com. Internet resource for information on breeds descending from ancient molosser lines (11/2018).

National Association of Canine Scent Work. http://www.nacsw.net/. Website of the official sanctioning and organizing body for the sport of K9 Nose Work (11/2018).

Petco. https://www.petco.com. Source for dog appeasing pheromone (DAP) (11/2018).

National Association of Dog Obedience Instructors. http://nadoi.org. One of the oldest organizations for obedience instructors (11/2018).

Premier Dog Products. http://www.premier.com/store/. Great source for high-quality dog training products and toys (11/2018).

REI Co-op. https://www.rei.com/product/696007/coghlans-squeeze-tubes-package-of-2. Reliable source for squeeze tubes to use for treat dispensing into muzzles (11/2018).

Roderiguez, Alexia. "The Cane Corso Is Not the Right Breed for Everyone…" http://www.potrerocanecorso.com/is-a-corso-right-for-you.html. Excellent article on breed considerations from a breeder; also applicable to any number of other power breeds (11/2018).

United Kennel Club. http://www.ukcdogs.com/Web.nsf/WebPages/HRC/Home. Nationwide registry started as registry for pit dogs, offering various competitive activities for all breeds, including nosework and weight pull (11/2018).

World Canine Freestyle Organization, Inc. http://www.worldcaninefreestyle.org/. One of several organizations hosting canine freestyle and canine heelwork-to-music competitions (11/2018).

Yin, Sophia. How to Break Up a Dog Fight. http://www.pethealthnetwork.com/dog-health/dog-behavior/how-break-a-dog-fight Suggestions for safely interrupting a dog fight from a veterinarian/behaviorist.

YoungLiving.com. https://youngliving.com. Source of lavender and other essential oils for dogs (11/2018).

About the Author

Since leaving the practice of law in 2006 to become a professional dog trainer, Dawn Antoniak-Mitchell, Esq., MPA, CPDT-KSA, CBCC-KA, has helped dog owners and fellow dog trainers worldwide better understand and appreciate the role instincts play in family dog behavior and how to work with those instincts to help dogs achieve their full potential as enjoyable family companions. She owns BonaFide Dog Academy LLC, an award-winning training facility in Omaha, Nebraska.

Dawn has been a Certified Professional Dog Trainer – Knowledge and Skills Assessed since 2005 and is also a Certified Behavioral Consultant Canine – Knowledge Assessed, an American Kennel Club (AKC) obedience and rally obedience judge, an AKC Canine Good Citizen evaluator, and a World Cynosport rally obedience judge. A member of the Dog Writers Association of America, her work has been published in local, national, and international publications, including *Top Tips from Top Trainers*, published by the Association of Pet Dog Trainers. She has been interviewed nationally and internationally on a variety of dog-related topics. Dawn is the author of *Teach Your Herding Breed to Be a Great Companion Dog: From Obsessive to Outstanding*, winner of the 2015 Capt. Haggerty Award for Best Training Book of the Year, as well as *Terrier-Centric Dog Training: From Tenacious to Tremendous*, and *From Bird-brained to Brilliant: Teaching the Sporting Dog to Be a Great Companion*, all published by Dogwise. Dawn is also a lecturer and advocate for the Americans with Disabilities Act and service dogs; she has been invited to medical schools and disabled veterans' conferences to speak on the ADA, the rights and responsibilities of service dog owners, and psychiatric service dog training, allowing her to combine her legal expertise and her dog training experience in a unique way to help others.

Over the years, Dawn has successfully trained and competed with dogs from the herding, non-sporting, sporting, and terrier groups in a wide range of activities, including conformation, obedience, rally obedience, agility, tracking, scent work, earthdog tests, musical freestyle, canine parkour, and weight pulling. Several of her dogs have been nationally ranked in their respective sports. Her dogs have also been regularly featured in local and national print and video projects, as well as in stage productions. She volunteers with her Jack Russell Terriers in reading therapy programs in local schools. Her power dog Dalmatian, Ember, is her current partner in many different activities.

Dawn and her Dalmatian, Ember.

Index

V

W

Also available from Dogwise Publishing

Go to dogwise.com for more books and ebooks.

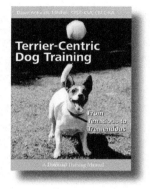

Terrier-Centric Dog Training

From Tenacious to Tremendous

Dawn Antoniak-Mitchell, CPDT-KSA, CBCC-KA

Terriers and terrier mixes are different from other breeds. Learn how to work with your terrier's instincts to get good behavior by getting inside his head and using management techniques to avoid problems at home and out in the world.

Teach Your Herding Breed to be a Great Companion

From Obsessive to Outstanding

Dawn Antoniak-Mitchell, CPDT-KSA, CBCC-KA

Herding breed dogs have incredibly strong instinctive behaviors to do the work they were bred for—controlling various kinds of livestock. Fortunately, these instincts can be redirected in a number of ways that keep these energetic dogs busy and happy as well as out of trouble.

From Birdbrained to Brilliant

Training the Sporting Dog to Be a Great Companion

Dawn Antoniak-Mitchell, CPDT-KSA, CBCC-KA

Sporting breeds are high energy and hard working. Also gregarious and loveable. Understand the unique qualities of your sporting breed to help her become a great companion and all-around good citizen. Make life better at both ends of the leash.

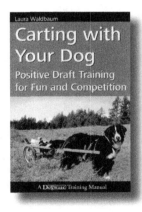

Carting with Your Dog

Positive Draft Training for Fun and Competition

Laura Waldbaum

Learn how to develop a "happy draft dog" whether for competition or carting the kids around the back yard. Step-by-step instructions on selecting equipment, conditioning and training will get you going in what may be your next dog sport!

Dogwise.com is your source for quality books, eBooks, DVDs and VOD.

We've been selling to the dog fancier for more than 30 years and we carefully screen our products for quality information. You'll find something for every level of dog enthusiast on our website Dogwise.com or drop by our store in Wenatchee, Washington.

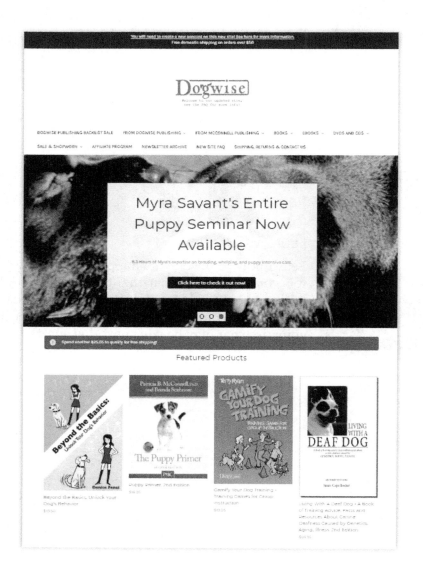